ITALIAN WOMEN POETS

ITALIAN WOMEN POETS
OF THE TWENTIETH
CENTURY

———————

Catherine O'Brien

IRISH ACADEMIC PRESS

This book was typeset
in 11 pt on 12 pt Plantin by
Carrigboy Typesetting Services, Durrus, for
IRISH ACADEMIC PRESS
Kill Lane, Blackrock, Co. Dublin, Ireland,
and in North America for
IRISH ACADEMIC PRESS
c/o ISBS, 5804 NE Hassalo Street,
Portland, OR 97213.

A catalogue record for this book
is available from the British Library.

ISBN 0–7165–2603–4 hbk
0–7165–2617–4 pbk

Printed by
ColourBooks Ltd, Dublin

For John, Eoin, Anne, Eimear, Catherine and Tom

The translation work in this book has been grant-assisted by the European Commission.

Contents

Preface

THE IDEA OF PRESENTING a study on some modern Italian women poets first came to me when, in the course of other research on contemporary Italian poetry, I realised that little had been written about them in Italy and almost nothing can be found in the English speaking world. Whereas some Italian women prose writers have made their mark both inside and outside Italy little is known about these women poets despite the significant contribution they have made to contemporary Italian poetry.

My awareness of their situation was further heightened when I translated some of the poetry of Nuala Ní Dhomhnaill into Italian. The feature which struck Italians most with Ní Dhomhnaill was, first, that she should select Irish, a minority European language, as the vehicle for her poems, and second, that she is a woman poet. I felt the time had come for me to do something to set the record straight, to show that there were many excellent women poets writing in Italy and to share some of the pleasure I have derived from the work of these Italian poets.

The poems are presented in the original Italian together with parallel translations in English. The purpose of these translations is to provide a faithful rendition of the text and spirit of the Italian original for those who are not familiar with the Italian language. The English translations should stand on their own as poems in English, reflecting the peculiar distortion of syntax and word pattern apparent in many of the poets, especially the younger ones.

A short biography has been provided for each author together with the historical context that also moulded their work. The reaction of the critics over the years is also assessed and finally an analysis is made of the place of these women in Italian poetry today.

I wish to thank Biancamaria Frabotta, Jolanda Insana, Vivian Lamarque, Biagia Marniti, Amelia Rosselli, Maria Luisa Spaziani and Patrizia Valduga for allowing me use some of their poems in this book. I also wish to express my gratitude to Lucia Pezzini Guarnaschelli for granting me the use of poems by her aunt Daria Menicanti and to Margherita Guidacci who gave me similar permission shortly before her death in 1992. My warmest thanks goes to all these poets for their generosity and cooperation at all times. I am grateful to the following publishers who have allowed me reproduce poems by individual authors:

Garzanti, Milan, for texts by Antonia Pozzi, Einaudi, Turin, and Scheiwiller, Milan, for texts by Alda Merini and Mondadori, Milan, for the texts of *La Viandanza* by Biancamaria Frabotta.

I am also indebted to Bruno De Marchi for his assistance in helping me trace poets and texts in Milan. My colleagues and friends Roberto Bertoni, Clotilde Bowe Soave, Mark Chu, Alessandro Gentili and Edoardo Saccone have given me invaluable assistance and stimulating suggestions in their reading of my various texts and translations. I gratefully acknowledge their help and any errors that remain are entirely mine. The poet Tom McCarthy offered practical and precious advice on how I could improve my English translations while his suggestions were given with enthusiasm and generosity. Without the help and generous technical assistance of Kay Doyle and Aisling O'Leary of the Italian Department, University College Cork, this work would not have been completed. Aisling O'Leary's skill and enthusiasm is apparent in the overall layout of this book while her dedication to the cause of poetry is much appreciated. Thanks are also due to Michael Adams of Irish Academic Press for having accepted this book for publication and for his continued promotion of Italian literature over the years.

That this project has reached its completion is entirely due to the support offered by my family. To Kathleen my deepest gratitude for her faithful presence during my repeated absences. Eoin, Anne, Eimear, Catherine and Tom have been encouraging and understanding at all times. John has provided more help than words can express.

CATHERINE O'BRIEN

Introduction

FOR THE LAST SIXTY years Italian poetry has reflected a profusion of literary currents and poetic fashions that have appeared and disappeared at a bewildering pace. When examining this poetry it is often difficult to establish where one trend begins and another ends just as it is almost impossible to distinguish any single line of continuity down through the years. During and immediately after the Second World War Italian poets highlighted a feeling of void and absence in their poetry while no dominant single trend emerged after hermeticism. The War, the Resistance and the fall of Fascism had a direct impact on literary life. Writers and poets opted for realism with increased emphasis being placed on their link with reality together with their feeling of civil and moral responsibility.

In the Fifties, Sixties and Seventies there were increasing debates as to what the objective of poetry might be with the consequent appearance of divergent literary schools which introduced a variety of ensuing polemics. The topic chosen by Eugenio Montale for his Nobel acceptance speech in 1975, *La poesia è ancora possibile?*, questioned the viability of poetry in the future with Montale attesting that further horizons were indeed possible in the years ahead. The last fifteen years have been a confirmation of Montale's hopes with significant collections being published by leading and long established poets together with the emergence of the work of many younger poets who have made a decisive impact.

Most studies of modern Italian poetry consider the work of male poets and, apart from brief representation in a few anthologies, the work of women poets has been largely ignored despite their constant presence and activity in this field over the last sixty or more years. It is true that male poets outnumber female poets but this should not warrant the quasi exclusion of the latter from any consideration of modern Italian poetry, particularly when that contribution merits serious attention. The result of this neglect, whether accidental or otherwise, is that the work of many of these women poets has been unavailable or largely unknown. Therefore this presentation of their writings attempts to put the record straight.

The objective has been to present a cross section of some of the most interesting women poets who, in different ways, have made an important contribution to modern and contemporary Italian poetry. Of its nature selection implies exclusion so that this study is by no

15

means final or definitive. Every effort has been made to offer a varied and balanced picture of these poets who represent north and south, east and west, city and country in Italy and whose work reflects the concerns of women over the last six decades.

The increased awareness of women writers in Italy since 1970 can be attributed to a number of factors. One of the most important has been the establishment and proliferation of women's cultural centres throughout Italy from 1977 onwards. These centres have afforded women a platform in which to voice and discuss their ideas and to present readings of their work in prose or poetry. This public exposure has made people aware of the female dimension in literature while also providing further creative stimulus to many of these poets. Many of them have been actively involved in the political, social and cultural sphere and this has given them a new self confidence, not often apparent in their predecessors. However, as many of these women poets chose not to be part of the prevailing literary fashions or trends and to pursue their own individual source of inspiration, they easily risk being relegated, like many independent male poets, to the very margins of poetry itself.

In the anthology, *Poeti italiani del Novecento*, Pier Vincenzo Mengaldo opted not to use critical categories to encapsulate poets within particular trends, as had previously applied in Italian literary criticism, but rather chose to evaluate the individual voice of each poet for what it was worth. The value of poetry is related to its ability to signify and to communicate and the crucial question then is to try and ascertain what it is these women poets contribute or have contributed to Italian poetry since the late 1930s.

The chronological panorama presented here goes, broadly speaking, from the post-war period to the present day and of the older poets presented here only one appeared in print prior to the Second World War. Antonia Pozzi's sole collection of poetry was published posthumously by her father in 1939 following her suicide the previous year. That she wrote poetry was a closely guarded secret and only a handful of people were aware of her interest in this sphere. Had she lived further it is possible to make a number of surmises on what might have happened to her poetry. It may well have been published or, conversely, it may have continued to be a secret passion shared only with those few close friends. The discovery of Pozzi's poetry after her death has much in common with the posthumous publication of Emily Dickinson's poetry and, although outside the chronology considered in this study, the substance of her poetry and its late recognition merits inclusion here.

What all these poets have in common is an enthusiasm for poetry that is seen as an expression of passion, a search for freedom and an extension of their personality. For them, poetry is that extra meaning you can give to life. Their individual viewpoint may vary but poetry is what remains constant. For Antonia Pozzi poetry has a vital confessional dimension, 'Poesia, mi confesso con te', while Maria Luisa Spaziani values its redemptive aspect, 'la poesia salva la vita'. Alda Merini considers it to be what saves the individual from evil, 'la poesia è la liberazione dal male' and Biancamaria Frabotta declares her independence as a woman poet through its medium, 'Io sono poetessa e intero non appartengo a nessuno'. Patrizia Valduga finds consolation in the formal creation of verse, 'scrivo per non ammattire' and for Jolanda Insana it is an organiser both of pain and pen, 'ordinatore di pena e di penna'.

The majority of the poets considered here have been remarkably singular and independent in their approach to poetry. For them the most important consideration has been what poetry could offer them as a means of self expression and a vehicle of literary communication with others. Few were prepared to adhere to specific ideologies and therefore chose to stay outside the many and varied schools of poetry. Amelia Rosselli is the one who came closest to belonging to a particular school of poetry as she flirted with the neo-avantgarde when trying to accommodate her triple linguistic formation and her search for suitable rhythm to express her thoughts in poetry. Apart from initial attraction with what this school had to offer Rosselli subsequently opted for absolute independence as she voiced her convictions on the agony of existence often in prose-like poems in English or in Italian.

Margherita Guidacci's voice remained isolated amid neo-hermeticism and neo-symbolism and eventually fell silent for a number of years until she found new courage and determination as a poet in the early 1970s. Maria Luisa Spaziani's early poetry borders on Hermeticism but she was only drawn to the form of the poems themselves and not the ideology behind them. Her later work also differs from that of other poets as she opts for formal, balanced and controlled verse that differs greatly from that of other poets particularly over the last thirty or more years. Pozzi's poetry reflects some influence of the crepuscular and hermetic poets but her spontaneity is found, most of all, in poems that spring independently from the heart. Daria Menicanti's style is finely tuned and often reflects the influence of the *linea lombarda* through the immediacy of the images used in her work although what she has to say is in no way exclusively determined by this influence. Vivian Lamarque's poetry is clear and direct, its purpose often therapeutic and its objective is straightforward communication of the message to hand.

Biancamaria Frabotta's poetry takes a stance on feminist issues but in a measured and balanced way that never takes from the impact of her verse. What she has to say can be stimulating, enigmatic and ironic and, of all these poets, she is the one who comes closest, particularly in translation, to the most challenging poetry now written in English. With Jolanda Insana language is taken several steps forward as she deconstructs it in an attempt to find suitable and challenging forms of expression. She pushes language to its extremes and while the result may appear fragmented the linguistic impact is both resourceful and powerfully evocative. Patrizia Valduga remains independent from her fellow poets as she has a marked passion for classical metre and poetry structures. Formalist in her poetry she is also strongly metaphysical and she presents her thoughts in a variety of poem structures that allow her work on all elements of language at her disposal. The effects she achieves are rigorous in language and striking in a phonic dimension.

Love is one of the themes that is most central to the work of all these poets though what it represents for them can vary enormously and can be bound up with other themes as well. For Margherita Guidacci it is joy and fulfilment whereas it confirms her disillusionment in personal relationships for Biagia Marniti. Daria Menicanti shows considerable scepticism which makes her wary of its fickle nature when she says that 'l'amore (non) è eterno'. Amelia Rosselli reaches the other extreme and sees nothing but loneliness all around her and so she concludes that 'tutto il mondo è vedovo'. Alda Merini experiences the exhilaration and also the desolation of love: always drawn to the former she mostly experiences the disappointment caused by the disappearance, for varied reasons, of the one she loves. Like many of these poets Vivian Lamarque also experiences the torment caused by abandonment so that for her love is almost always unattainable. In Patrizia Valduga's poetry love is essentially sensual with the poet constantly stressing its integral role in her life with particular emphasis on the stimulation of its physical dimension.

These women often share a strong sense of place with memory playing a dominant role in their poetry. Recollections of her native Sicily and of other places, particularly in southern Europe, are a dominant force in Jolanda Insana's poetry and are particularly reflected in the vocabulary entrusted with their evocation. Maria Luisa Spaziani is particularly obsessed with this theme which is at the source of all her writings. She indicates the importance of its role in the title of the collection, *Utilità della memoria*, while the objective of two other works, *Giovanna d'Arco* and *Donne in poesia*, is that of recalling to the attention of the reader the lives of women who have made their mark in the past and whose memory must not be allowed fall into oblivion.

Daria Menicanti and Biagia Marniti share a common passion for a particular place: for Menicanti it is the urban environment of Milan, her adopted city, and for Marniti it is the contrasting rural region of Apulia where she was born and which is still a live presence in her life: 'ti sento ancora nell'aria di montagna'. Though belonging to the younger generation Biancamaria Frabotta also uses memory as a theme in her poetry where it can recall places and people, journeys and new experiences. For Patrizia Valduga and Vivian Lamarque it is a source of pain as they realise that the ones they love have disappeared from their life.

For Alda Merini and Amelia Rosselli memory brings fear and terror in its wake and they try to escape from its clutches. In Rosselli's case memory is synonymous with violent death and painful personal recollections which finally proved too powerful for her with the only escape imaginable being that of self destruction through suicide. Constant in Rosselli's poetry is the conviction that life is in mortal combat with death while her own fragility is never far from the surface: 'La mia anima è/ triste come il soldato in guerra'. Equally frightening too is Alda Merini's memory of twenty years spent, voluntarily and involuntarily, in asylums both north and south in Italy. In her poetry she attempts to bridge this gap in her life, to liberate herself from the past and to come to terms with the future. Most moving of all is her confession that her lucidity of mind made her realise, while interned, that only sadness and suffering existed for her: 'Mai donna è stata più perduta/ in un mare di tristezza e di angoscia'. Although Margherita Guidacci was intrinsically more optimistic in her outlook she did traverse a period of darkness in the poems of *Neurosuite* which recall the trials of those suffering from mental disturbances while also coinciding with a period of doubt and uncertainty in her own life.

The problems that have beset society in this century are naturally reflected in the work of these poets. Although a beneficiary of exceptional educational opportunities and stimulated by the intellectual rigour of the environment in which she found herself, Antonia Pozzi was unable to reconcile the personal with the public. Convinced that society could offer her no further help her despair prevailed and she ended her life. Biagia Marniti too echoes Pozzi's insinuation regarding the aridity of life and the despair so evident in the surrounding world. By contrast, it is her firm faith in the Christian belief that helps Margherita Guidacci cope with the vicissitudes of life. There is a broader cosmic dimension to Biancamaria Frabotta's vision of life when she concentrates on the toll it takes on the animal kingdom too with particular emphasis placed on the flattened shape of the sole – it is the passage of time that has reduced this fish to its now familiar shape. Jolanda Insana sees the space of poetry as one that is constantly under threat by a culture that values things of little worth and so she takes a vigorous and strident stance in defence of poetry: 'il referente sono io/ e me ne vanto'. The dilemmas encountered in life are ones that make Patrizia Valduga look inside her and what she reveals is the abyss and the torment within: 'O gran dio, nell'inferno sono per certo'.

Life and the passage of the individual through life leads to death, so therefore, considerations of dissolution and what lies beyond is one of the concerns shared by many of these poets. For Biagia Marniti it offers an uncertain future. The closing line of the poem *Ritratto d'agosto*, which considers the impending demise of her father, is an abrupt one that reveals the poet's own apprehension and scepticism: 'Fu. Esiste. Dove andrà?' Few poets echo Margherita Guidacci's optimism and most would share Daria Menicanti's lapidary statement that emphasises the loneliness and separation from loved ones that become reality through death: 'Amore dice solitudine/ separazione strappo'. That it is seen in palliative terms by Antonia Pozzi is apparent from the note left to her parents where she asked them not to lament her passing: 'Non piangete perché ora io sono in pace'. Throughout her poetry Patrizia Valduga courts death and is inextricably drawn towards it. For her, it permeates life and she is inevitably drawn towards darkness, towards figures that speak from this abyss or towards people like her father who have crossed this divide and are now no more.

While these women poets have not created specific schools or been responsible for radical changes in Italian poetry, their sensitivity and perceptions of life are often more acute than those of their male contemporaries. Although they share an awareness of the contours of contemporary Italy and the major human emotions of love, place and death with male authors, there is no attempt at imitation. Theirs are female responses, totally idiosyncratic with touches that are quite distinct from their male counterparts. While some of these poets are conscious of being female writers, especially Spaziani, for the majority, their femininity is such a natural part of their personality, that it is only apparent in the mood which their poetry creates. It is hoped that readers of this book will share that mood and so gain a greater appreciation of the unique insights of these female poets into modern Italian life.

Antonia Pozzi

ANTONIA POZZI is one of the most curious figures in twentieth cen-
tury Italian poetry. She died at the age of twenty six and her only col-
lection of poetry was published posthumously. Her notoriety as a poet
has been the subject of much discussion while interest in her work has
fluctuated dramatically since her death in 1938. The attention given to
her work has ranged from initial enthusiasm to subsequent assignment
to the periphery of modern Italian poetry whereas the closing decades
of this century have witnessed a renewed interest in her as a person
and a re-evaluation of her as a poet.

Antonia Pozzi was born in Milan on 13 February 1912. Her back-
ground was privileged as her parents belonged to the Milanese upper
class. An only child, she was given every material comfort that her par-
ents considered necessary for the proper upbringing of a young and
wealthy society lady. Her mother was Lina Cavagna Sangiuliani and
was the great-granddaughter of the poet Tommaso Grossi.[1] She was
however, emotionally fragile and this caused her to be somewhat dis-
tant and withdrawn both as a person and as a mother. The dominant
role in the parent–child relationship was that occupied by Antonia's
father, Roberto, a wealthy lawyer with an active interest in culture
which he transmitted to his daughter.

Although reared in the sophisticated urban surrounds of Milan,
Antonia always preferred the contrast with the proximity to nature
which life in the family summer residence could offer her. In 1917 her
parents bought an eighteenth century villa in Pasturo, a small village
in the Valsassina region of north east Lombardy, that offered full access
to healthy countryside and bracing mountain air. The intention of the
family was to find respite in the cooler region of Pasturo and to enjoy
all the facilities it could offer. For them, it was an ideal place where
their daughter would have healthy living and also enjoy the many sports
facilities which it offered. The acquisition of the villa in Pasturo marked
a turning point in Antonia's life as she fully empathised with the

---

1 Tommaso Grossi (1790–1853). Poet and writer. A friend of Alessandro Manzoni
   and Carlo Porta he was a zealous supporter of Romanticism. He is best known
   for his poem *I lombardi alla prima crociata* (1826) which was the source of
   Verdi's inspiration for his opera of the same title composed in 1843. He also
   wrote a historical novel *Marco Visconti* (1834).

simplicity of the people who lived there and with the stunning mountains which form a backdrop to this village.

Antonia's parents gave her the best that a broad education could offer at that time. She was sent to choice schools, studied the piano and applied art and took an active part in sport. She was an excellent skier, swimmer and horsewoman and showed exceptional ability in all of these pursuits. In 1927 she enrolled in the Manzoni Liceo Classico in Milan where, in addition to other subjects, she increased her knowledge of French, English and German and took a passionate interest in contemporary and classical literature.

Antonia's intellectual ability was striking and her desire to learn more and more was stimulated by Antonio Maria Cervi,[2] her teacher of Greek and Latin at this school. A man of absolute intellectual and moral integrity, he encouraged her to study philosophy and ancient history and discussed these topics with her. Fascinated by his depth of knowledge and his willingness to share it with her Antonia soon grew dependent on him. She was also struck by the difficulties and tragedies he had encountered in life, the main one being the death of his brother Annunzio, a poet, in the War. Before long Antonia had fallen in love with him and he, later, with her.

Initially pleased at the intellectual interest Cervi had taken in their daughter, Antonia's parents were subsequently horrified when they discovered she had fallen in love with this man whom they considered socially unsuitable for their only daughter. Determined to put an end to her affections for and contact with this person Antonia's father had him transferred to a school in Rome in 1929. Following this enforced separation Antonia corresponded with Cervi for a number of years and met him in secret on a few occasions. Some more years were to pass before she finally bowed to her parents' and particularly her father's will and finally abandoned her intentions of marriage with Cervi. The imposition of her parents' will and her own inability to resist their decision had severe repercussions on Antonia's mental and emotional psyche from which, it is possible, she never recovered.

The following year, in 1930, she enrolled at the University of Milan where she studied modern philology. For her degree thesis she opted for Aesthetics and was supervised by Antonio Banfi, a then renowned professor of the history of Philosophy and Aesthetics at that university. Her thesis dealt with the literary formation of the French writer Gustave Flaubert and she graduated in 1935. While at university she had many

---

2 For a further account of Cervi's life and his relationship with Antonia Pozzi see A. Pozzi, *Diari*, edited by O. Dino and A. Cenni (Milan, Scheiwiller, 1988), pp.21–23.

interesting friends and colleagues, many of whom attained considerable success in their chosen spheres in later years. Among them were Luciano Anceschi,[3] Giancarlo Vigorelli,[4] Mario Monicelli,[5] Alberto Mondadori,[6] Luigi Rognoni,[7] Enzo Paci[8] and Daria Menicanti.[9] Her closest friends however were Remo Cantoni,[10] the poet Vittorio Sereni[11] and Dino Formaggio.[12]

Having completed her studies Pozzi travelled considerably throughout Italy and Europe and, in 1937, in an effort to achieve some form of economic independence, she accepted a post as teacher at the Schiaparelli Technical Institute in Milan. Her work as a teacher offered her a certain form of fulfilment and she also did some voluntary social work. Pasturo was always her refuge and it offered her contact with people who were different from those in her urban environment. She sympathised more perhaps with them and their sense of the real values in life rather than with the values that prevailed among those people cultivated by her family and which she often considered artificial.

Her health became increasingly fragile and she spent a short convalescent period in hospital in June 1938. The news of the threatened danger of imminent war in Europe coupled with the expansion of repressive and dangerous laws on race and censorship in Italy greatly disturbed her.

Increasingly isolated both emotionally and intellectually and convinced that life would never reward her with the happiness of requited love (her feelings of affection for Remo Cantoni were also unreciprocated) she resumed her teaching post in Milan in the autumn of 1938. On 2 December she taught her normal classes and later that day her unconscious and semi-frozen body was found on the deserted snow clad slopes of the city suburbs near the Abbey of Chiaravalle. She had swallowed a large quantity of tablets and contracted pneumonia through exposure to the cold. All efforts to save her were in vain and she died

3   L. Anceschi (1911–1995), literary critic, teacher of aesthetics and influential figure in twentieth century Italian poetry.
4   G. Vigorelli (1913–   ), journalist and essayist.
5   M. Monicelli (1915–   ), film producer and scriptwriter.
6   A. Mondadori (1889–1971), member of the Mondadori publishing family. It was he who decided to move the offices to Milan and was responsible for the great success of this publishing house from 1923 onwards. Mondadori published the first version of Pozzi's poems for her father in 1939.
7   L. Rognoni (1913–1986), musicologist.
8   E. Paci (1911–1976), philosopher.
9   D. Menicanti (1914–1995), teacher and poet.
10 R. Cantoni (1914–1978), philosopher.
11 V. Sereni (1913–1983), poet.
12 D. Formaggio (1914–   ), philosopher.

the following morning on 3 December. By one of those extraordinary coincidences in life, the Argentinian poet, Alfonsina Storni,[13] also chose to commit suicide on that same day in another continent. Neither knew the other but they opted out of life for similarly despairing reasons: Storni chose the sea for her death while Pozzi opted for the snow.

Pozzi's poetry came to light after her death when several copy books were found to contain over three hundred poems that she had written from 1929 to 1938. Her parents were unaware either of her interest or her skills in this sphere and only a few of her closest childhood friends, particularly Lucia Bozzi and Elvira Gandini, were party to this secret. When, in later years, efforts were made to trace all of Pozzi's poems Lucia was the person who had the largest number in her possession. Pozzi had called her poems 'Il mio diario segreto' and many were dedicated to Lucia and Elvira, Antonio Cervi, Vittorio Sereni and Remo Cantoni.

Proud of his daughter's ability as a poet, her father had ninety one poems published in a private edition in 1939[14] and distributed them to friends and relatives. The reaction was so positive and enthusiastic that the first public edition of her poems was published by Mondadori six years later in 1945.[15] The number of poems was increased to 159 in 1948 and the edition included the laudatory introduction by the poet Eugenio Montale. The fourth and final Mondadori edition was published in 1964. Interest in Pozzi waned during the Sixties, Seventies and early Eighties. However, thanks to the painstaking work of Alessandra Cenni and Onorina Dino there is now a new interest in Pozzi that has led to the publication of some previously unpublished works and provided a new and more faithful edition of her poems. Cenni and Dino produced previously unpublished poems in 1986,[16] her diaries in 1988[17] followed by her letters in 1989.[18] Even more significant was the publication in that same year of a new and more complete version of Pozzi's poems by these two scholars.[19] The problem with the earlier

13 A. Storni (Switzerland 1892–Argentina 1938).
14 This private edition of *Parole* was published by Mondadori, Milan, 1939. Reprinted in 1943 it then included 157 poems.
15 A. Pozzi, *Parole*, with an Introduction by E. Montale (Milan, Mondadori, 1945). The fourth edition, with 176 poems, dates from 1964. Both editions were published by Mondadori.
16 A. Pozzi, *La vita sognata e altre poesie inedite* (Milan, Scheiwiller, edited by A. Cenni and O. Dino, 1986).
17 A. Pozzi, *Diari* (Milan, Scheiwiller, edited by A. Cenni and O. Dino, 1988).
18 A. Pozzi, *L'età delle parole è finita, Lettere 1927–1938* (Milan, Archinto, edited by A. Cenni and O. Dino, 1989).
19 A. Pozzi, *Parole* (Milan, Garzanti, edited by A. Cenni and O. Dino, 1989).

editions of Pozzi's poetry was that her father had censored much of
her writing and so the texts were often amended to fit the image he
wanted to project of his daughter. Cenni and Dino are therefore respon-
sible for the first really faithful editions of Pozzi's poems and writings
as they are based on Pozzi's own texts and carefully avoid any of the
amendments carried out by her father after her death.

What then were Pozzi's objectives in writing poetry and what was
it that she hoped to express through her poems? Her ideas on what
poetry represented in her life are concisely expressed in a letter she
wrote to her friend Tullio Gadenz on 29 January 1933, where she says
that poetry, for her, is a life line just as blood infuses life in our veins:
'Vivo della poesia come le vene vivono del sangue'.[20] One of the bet-
ter studies of Pozzi's work is that done by Rossella Lovascio who con-
siders the following to be Pozzi's purpose in writing poetry:

> La dinamica è unica: la liberazione dall'inviluppo esterno per giungere alla
> critica nudità dell'anima, alla contemplazione dell'assoluto nella monade
> quotidiana, non angariato dalle contingenze prosaiche del reale; e questa
> dinamica [. . .] non avrà mai termine [. . .] Tutta la poesia è una lotta tra
> volontà di non annullarsi nelle prestabilite forme borghesi, e fatti concreti che
> questa volontà annullano, tra desiderio di trovare un ruolo ben preciso nella
> società [. . .] e comprensione che a tutto ciò la società oppone un chiaro e fermo
> rifiuto.[21]

> (The dynamics are singular: to free oneself from the external tangle to reach
> the critical bareness of the soul, the contemplation of what is absolute in the
> daily monad, not harried by the prosaic contingencies of what is real; and
> these dynamics [. . .] will never end [. . .] All this poetry is a struggle between
> the desire not to lose oneself in predetermined middle class forms, and concrete
> facts that wipe out this desire and the longing to find a precise role within
> society [. . .] and the understanding that society withstands all this with a
> clear and firm refusal.)

In what way then are these features represented in her poetry and
what are the characteristics that distinguish it from that of other poets?
There is nothing conventional in her poetry. Through it she is intent
on finding a form of truth that may satisfy her youthful ambitions and
aspirations and she does not shirk from revealing herself fully to the
reader:

In this chapter all quotations from Pozzi's writings are taken from the Cenni
and Dino editions of her poems, diary and letters.

20 A. Pozzi, *Lettere*, p.53.
21 R. Lovascio, *Antonia Pozzi. Il naufragio dell'essere* (Bari, Interventi Culturali,
1980, pp.15–16).

Se qualcuna delle mie povere parole
ti piace
e tu me lo dici
sia pur solo con gli occhi
io mi spalanco
in un riso beato
ma tremo
come una mamma piccola giovane
che perfino arrossisce
se un passante le dice
che il suo bambino è bello.   (*Parole*, p.113)

(If you like/ one of my words/ and tell me so/ if only with your eyes/ I burst into/ a blissful smile/ but I tremble/ like a tiny young mother/ who even blushes/ if a passer-by tells her/ that her child is handsome.)

There are many themes that Pozzi deals with in her poetry and they seem to interlock on several occasions. The topics that interest her most are those of childhood, love, death, religion, the sense of void and the suggestive beauty of nature. In her early poems the theme of childhood is linked with that of happiness and nostalgia and in the poem 'Prati', written in 1931, she confesses that happiness for her was, perhaps, a thing of the past:

Forse la vita è davvero
quale la scopri nei giorni giovani:
un soffio eterno che cerca
di cielo in cielo
chissà che altezza.   (*Parole*, p.85)

(Perhaps life is really/ as you find it in your early days:/ an eternal breeze that searches/ from sky to sky/ who knows what heights).

Pozzi has nostalgic ideas on childhood that are probably linked to the fact that her own precocious intelligence together with the intellectual stimulation provided by her father may have cut her off too early from normal childhood pursuits and interests. Frightened by what the future might hold in store, on occasion she seems unwilling to grow up. A particularly revealing diary entry tells us that

Del tempo ho paura, del tempo che fugge così in fretta. Fugge? No, non fugge, e nemmeno vola: scivola, dilegua, scompare [. . .] e non lascia sul palmo che un senso spiacevole di vuoto.   (*Diari*, p.31)

(I fear time, time which flees in such a hurry. It flees? No, it does not flee and neither does it fly: it slips away, vanishes, disappears [. . .] and only leaves an unpleasant feeling on the palm of your hand.)

Pozzi was greatly drawn to the natural beauty of mountain land-
scapes which, in her opinion, allowed life, repressed and mortified
elsewhere, call out in its own language: 'dove la vita repressa e morti-
ficata, ancora grida le sue "parole"'.[22] The freshness and candour of
such places makes her admire their untold beauty in 'Bontà inesausta':

Chi ti dice
bontà
della mia montagna? –
così bianca
sui boschi già biondi
d'autunno –

e qui nebbie leggere alitano [. . .]
sulle foglie morte –   (*Parole*, p.186)

(Who can describe you/ grace/ of my mountain? –/ so white /above the woods
now pale/in autunn–/and here light mists blow gently [. . .]/on fallen leaves –)

In the poem 'Esempi' the mountain too stands as a symbol of resis-
tance that the poet longs to resemble and it is also a metaphor for life
that always aims on high:

Anima, sii come la montagna:
che quando tutta la valle
è un grande lago di viola
e i tocchi delle campane vi affiorano
come bianche ninfee di suono,
lei sola, in alto, si tende
ad un muto colloquio col sole.   (*Parole*, p.72)

(Soul, be like the mountain:/ when the whole valley/ is one great violet lake/
and bell chimes ring out/ like white nymph sounds,/ it alone, on high, reach-
es up/ for a silent talk with the sun.)

Pozzi found comfort and solace in her contact with nature and her
enthusiasm for what nature offers is often paralleled with her love for
Cervi. In her initial enthusiasm she considers the experience to be a
reflection of what is divine as is apparent in the clear allusion to reli-
gion in these lines from 'L'allodola':

Le nostre mani
congiunte
componevano una tenace

22   G. Bernabò, 'Antonia Pozzi: poesie e lettere' in *Uomini e libri*, n.123, aprile-
     luglio 1989, p.48.

conchiglia
che custodiva
la pace.
Ed io ero piana
quasi tu fossi un santo
che placa la vana
tempesta e cammina sul lago.   (*Parole*, p.367)

(Our hands/ holding each other/ formed a stubborn/ shell/ that protected/ peace./ And I was calm/ as though you had been a saint/ who placates the futile rage/ and walks on the waters of the lake.)

But love can frighten her too as she contemplates the terror life may have in store:

Afferrami alla vita,
uomo. La cengia è stretta.
E l'abisso è un risucchio spaventoso
che ci vuole assorbire.   (*Parole*, p.40)

(Cling me to life/ man. The ledge is narrow./ And the abyss a frightening undertow/ that wants to absorb us.)

The enforced separation from the subject and object of her love revealed a gap between her dream of happiness and the severe reality of impossible fulfilment:

Tu
eri il cielo in me,
che non mi amavi per la mia persona
ma per quel seme
di bene
che dormiva in me.   (*Parole*, p.207)

(You/ were the sky in me,/ you did not love me for my person/ but for that seed/ of good/ that slept in me.)

The separation is also seen as a precursor of death in 'Saresti stato' where Pozzi alludes to the child she longed to bear for the one she loved. This child, now relegated to the idealised realm of her imagination, would, in Pozzi's opinion, have helped perpetuate the memory of Cervi's dead brother Annunzio in addition to being a symbol of new life born through love:

Annunzio
saresti stato
di quel che non fummo [. . .]

In te sarebbero
ritornati i morti
e vissuti i non nati . . . (*Parole*, p.371)

(You would have been/ an announcement/ of what we were not [. . .]/ Through
you the dead/ would have come back/ the unborn lived . . .)

Disappointed by love and religion Pozzi then opts for death which
offers release and comfort. In her later poems she frequently refers to
tombs, funerals and death that recall the lines of an earlier poem,
'Novembre', where she suggests the possibility of an early demise:

E poi – se accadrà ch'io me ne vada –
resterà qualche cosa
di me
nel mio mondo [. . .]
Qualcuno cercherà i crisantemi
per me
nel mondo
quando accadrà che senza ritorno
io me ne debba andare.   (*Parole*, p.49)

(And then – if it happens that I must leave –/ something will remain/ of me/
in my world [. . .]/ Someone will look for chrysanthemums/ for me/ in this
world/ when it happens that I must go away/ never to return.)

The poem 'Sentiero', written in 1935, reflects the mark left by love
that was either impeded or unrequited and life now appears as a path
that narrows ever increasingly:

Viali sognavi per la vita
e un esile
sentiero ti rimane.   (*Parole*, p.258)

(You dreamt of wide avenues for your life/ and a narrow path/ is what remains.)

The tragedy that Pozzi perceived in her own life is encapsulated in this
poem that opens with the optimism of the verb 'sperare' and closes
with the desolation of the noun 'solitudine'. In her letters and diary
her feeling of isolation becomes more acute and in a letter written to
Remo Cantoni in June 1935 she described her fragile existence:

Vivo come se un torrente mi attraversasse [. . .] Sempre così smisuratamente
perduta ai margini della vita reale: difficilmente la vita reale mi avrà e se mi
avrà sarà la fine di tutto quello che c'è di meno banale in me.

                                        (*Lettere*, pp.78–79)

(I live as though traversed by a deluge [. . .] Increasingly lost at the edge of real life: with difficulty real life will have me and if it has me it will be the end of all that is less ordinary in me.)

The poem 'Messaggio' was written in June 1937 and in it Pozzi addresses the night star that will record her life:

ma nel mio buio conquistato
brillerai, fuoco bianco.
parlando ai vivi della mia morte.   (*Parole*, p.339)

(But you will shine through/ my conquered darkness, white fire,/ and speak to the living of my death.)

The images of light in darkness and of a white fire are in themselves contradictory but it is possible that Pozzi envisages here that she has earned the endurance of her memory through the written word.

Before she died Pozzi left parting words to her parents. Her father, perhaps in grief, burned her note and later rewrote it from memory so its fidelity to the original could be questioned. The closing words of this reconstructed note ask her parents not to weep for her as she is at peace: 'E non piangete, perché ora io sono in pace' (*Lettere*, p.112). The door had finally closed on her life and in its place she hoped to find the coolness and silence of deep night (*Parole*, p.55).

Pozzi's father was central to her life both before and after her death. His too was the tragedy of a parent who had lavished all on his only child who then fell in love with someone almost his own age and who would have been unacceptable as a son-in-law. Having successfully impeded any further development in her romance with Antonio Cervi, Roberto Pozzi then had to suffer the humiliation and remorse of her suicide at a time when the word suicide was hardly mentioned. In fact, the official verdict on her death speaks of an 'improvviso malore' or sudden illness. What is important to remember, however, is that what we know of Pozzi today as a poet is due almost entirely to her father as it was he who was responsible for the first editions of her poetry and he actively did what he could to perpetuate her memory and also encouraged translations of her poems so that her work would be known outside Italy too.

Although the immediate reaction to her poetry was positive, part of the evaluation then expressed contained the seeds of a problem that accompanied her poetry for decades. Many of the early critics refer to her youth and suggest that her poetry displayed potential and that had she lived a normal live span she could have become a worthwhile poet. Others underline the fact that she was a young woman who wrote valid but sentimental poetry and who brought her own life to a tragic conclusion.[23]

Montale was the first person to suggest that her poetry was a *caso curioso* and that it deserved to be viewed for what it had contributed to poetry rather than always being anchored to the poet's biography: 'Ha bisogno che di lei si parli in modo diretto e non per vie traverse'[24] he says. Pozzi's poetry almost inevitably reflects some influence of the crepuscular and hermetic poets but, generally speaking, she writes poetry on her own terms and, in Montale's opinion, part of the attraction of her work is that she attempts to reduce words to the essential, to the minimum 'peso delle parole'.[25]

That Pozzi was a woman who wrote poetry also created its share of problems too. Although Ada Negri[26] had written extensively as a poet she achieved greater recognition as a prose writer than as a poet during her lifetime. Sibilla Aleramo[27] too had written some fine poetry but was better known for her prose writings and social involvement. It was as though women poets were not to be taken seriously and so, Pozzi, was seen as a young woman who had written emotional and sentimental poetry that was different from poetry written by men. The critic Glauco Cambon pointed out that her poetry was:

la storia intima di un'anima squisitamente femminile [. . .] nella misura in cui ella seppe arrivare alle radici della sua femminilità [. . .] riuscì a conseguire un'oggettività poetica.[28]

(the intimate story of a delightfully female soul [. . .] in so far as she knew how to reach the roots of her femininity [. . .] she succeeded in achieving poetic objectivity.)

Cambon also noted the difference between her earlier and later poems and her increasing maturity as a poet – a valid point – given that the first poems in *Poesie* are dated 1929 and it would be normal to expect

23 See Elisabetta Rasy, 'Antonia, silenzio e ritorno' in Panorama, 26.2.1989, pp.135–137, where she states: 'La morte improvvisa e drammatica creò un piccolo clamore e un polemico caso su questa ragazza'. (Her sudden dramatic death created some sensation and a controversial discussion around the figure of this girl.)
24 A. Pozzi, *Parole*, 1964, p.13. Montale's original introduction to Pozzi's poetry is reproduced in this edition.
25 *Parole*, (1964), p.18.
26 A. Negri (1870–1945), writer and poet.
27 S. Aleramo (1876–1960), writer, poet, social and political activist.
28 G. Cambon, 'All'insegna della felicità delle lettere' in *Saggi di umanesimo cristiano*, n.2 (Pavia, 1949), p.89.

some progression and maturity in the intervening years until her death in 1938.

Pozzi's suicide initially seems out of character though there are a number of reasons which may go some way towards finding a reason for such a drastic end to a life which seemed to offer much. When she grew to adulthood she seemed to have little in common with her parents especially her mother. Her father had provided intellectual stimulation in her youth though he later thwarted her path of love. Although only fifteen when she first fell for Antonio Cervi, Pozzi's love for him endured the test of time but her father was unprepared to accept him. Constrained perhaps by the social mores that then prevailed and anxious to obey the father she still loved, Pozzi acceded to his wishes. She later fell in love with her fellow student and philosopher Remo Cantoni, who would have been socially acceptable to her parents, but her feeling for him was unrequited. In June 1935 she wrote to her friend Vittorio Sereni saying that she felt her destiny in life would simply be to write children' stories for children that would never be hers. (*Lettere*, p.80.)

Despite her involvement with the circle centred around the figure of Antonio Banfi and her apparent intellectual emancipation, this group was largely misogynist and this made her acutely aware of the limitations of her own life. Frustrated on the emotional and intellectual level Pozzi expressed her feelings through the secret outlet of writing. But it is possible that Pozzi was far more sensitive and fragile than her poetry, letters and diary would indicate. Convinced that emotional happiness was beyond her reach, suicide then may have seemed to offer an alternative to the emotional void she saw around her.

In 1978 Biancamaria Frabotta drew attention once again to the figure of Pozzi in her mould-breaking anthology *Donne in Poesia*. Frabotta uses her as an example of a poet who speaks her mind clearly and courageously and is therefore viewed as a watershed by later poets, especially women poets.[29] Pozzi's poetry reflected the frustration experienced at her inability to control her own life, a point now appreciated by men and women alike.[30] Her poetry is important both for the independent stance she took as a woman in speaking honestly about

29 *Donne in Poesia*, edited by B. Frabotta (Rome, Savelli, 1978), p.14.
30 In his article, *Una donna sconfitta*, in 'Il nostro tempo' (30 aprile, 1989), Sergio Pautasso recognises this fact: 'Le pagine di diario e le lettere di Antonia sono una testimonianza della sua sofferenza esistenziale e della sua irrealizzazione di donna imputabile agli altri e alle convenzioni sociali di cui era vittima.' (Antonia's diary and letters bear testimony to her existential suffering and the fact that her complete realisation as a woman was impeded by other people and by the social conventions of which she was a victim.)

her feelings and also because many of her later poems demonstrate a style that shows considerable growth in expression and versification. It is pointless to try and assess what she might have achieved in poetry had she lived longer. Therefore, all judgments of her must be based on the material currently accessible. Alessandra Cenni and Onorina Dino have ensured that reliable editions of her poetry and writings are now available to the reader who can then properly assess the value of the direct dialogue which Pozzi establishes with the reader.

Novembre

E poi – se accadrà ch'io me ne vada –
resterà qualche cosa
di me
nel mio mondo –
resterà un'esile scìa di silenzio
in mezzo alle voci –
un tenue fiato di bianco
in cuore all'azzurro –

Ed una sera di novembre
una bambina gracile
all'angolo d'una strada
venderà tanti crisantemi
e ci saranno le stelle
gelide verdi remote –
Qualcuno piangerà
chissà dove – chissà dove –
Qualcuno cercherà i crisantemi
per me
nel mondo
quando accadrà che senza ritorno
io me ne debba andare.
                              Milano, 29 ottobre 1930

Nostalgia

C'è una finestra in mezzo alle nubi:
potresti affondare
nei cumuli rosa le braccia
e affacciarti
di là
nell'oro.
Chi non ti lascia?
Perché?
Di là c'è tua madre
– lo sai –
tua madre col volto proteso
che aspetta il tuo volto.   Kingston, 25 agosto 1931

November

And then – if it happens that I must leave –
something will remain
of me
in my world –
a slender trail of silence
in the midst of voices –
a rarefied breath of whiteness
in the heart of the blue –

And one evening in November
a frail young girl
will sell lots of chrysanthemums
at the corner of a street
and the stars will be
cold, green and distant –
Someone will weep
who knows where – who knows where –
Someone will look for chrysanthemums
for me
in this world
when it so happens that I must go away
never to return.

Milan, 29 October 1930

Nostalgia

There is a window in the middle of the clouds:
you could sink your arms
in the rose hued masses
and lean out
from there
into the gold beyond.
Who thwarts you?
For what reason?
Over there is your mother
– you know it –
your mother with her face outstretched
waiting for your face.

Kingston, 25 August 1931

Maternità

Pensavo di tenerlo in me, prima
che nascesse,
guardando il cielo, le erbe, i voli
delle cose leggere,
il sole –
perché tutto il sole
scendesse in lui.

Pensavo di tenerlo in me, cercando
d'essere buona –
buona –
perché ogni bontà
fatta sorriso
crescesse in lui.

Pensavo di tenerlo in me, parlando
spesso con Dio –
perché Dio lo guardasse
e noi fossimo
redenti in lui.   24 ottobre 1933

Prati

Forse non è nemmeno vero
quel che a volte ti senti urlare in cuore:
che questa vita è,
dentro il tuo essere,
un nulla
e che ciò che chiamavi la luce
è un abbaglio,
l'abbaglio supremo
dei tuoi occhi malati –
e che ciò che fingevi la meta
è un sogno,
il sogno infame
della tua debolezza.

Motherhood

I thought that I would hold him in myself
before he was born,
looking at the sky, the grass, the flight
of all things weightless,
the sun –
so that all the sunshine
would descend on him.

I thought that I would hold him in myself,
trying to be good –
good –
so that all goodness
would become a smile
and grow in him.

I thought that I would hold him in myself,
often speaking to God –
so that God might watch over him
and through him
we might be redeemed.   24 October 1933

Fields

It is not even true perhaps
that which you hear at times roaring in your heart:
that this life,
within your being,
is nothing
and what you called light
is a blunder,
the supreme blunder
of your feeble eyes –
and what you feigned as your goal
is a dream,
the infamous dream
of your weakness.

Forse la vita è davvero
quale la scopri nei giorni giovani:
un soffio eterno che cerca
di cielo in cielo
chissà che altezza.

Ma noi siamo come l'erba dei prati
che sente sopra sé passare il vento
e tutta canta nel vento
e sempre vive nel vento,
eppure non sa così crescere
da fermare quel volo supremo
né balzare su dalla terra
per annegarsi in lui.

Milano, 31 dicembre 1931

L'allodola

Dopo il bacio – dall'ombra degli olmi
sulla strada uscivamo
per ritornare:
sorridevamo al domani
come bimbi tranquilli.
Le nostre mani
congiunte
componevano una tenace
conchiglia
che custodiva
la pace.
Ed io ero piana
quasi tu fossi un santo
che placa la vana
tempesta e cammina sul lago.
Io ero un immenso
cielo d'estate
all'alba
su sconfinate
distese di grano.
E il mio cuore
una trillante allodola
che misurava
la serenità.

25 agosto 1933

Perhaps life is really
as you find it in your early days:
an eternal breeze that searches
from sky to sky
who knows what heights.

But we are like the grass of the fields
which feels the wind blow over it,
and sings in the wind
and always lives in the wind,
yet it cannot grow high enough
to halt that great flight
nor leap up from the soil
to drown itself in the wind.

Milan, 31 December 1931

The lark

After the kiss – from the shadow of the elm trees
we came out on to the road
to return home:
like tranquil children
we smiled at the future.
Our hands
holding each other
formed a stubborn
shell
that protected
peace.
And I was calm
as though you had been a saint
who placates the futile rage
of the storm and walks on the waters of the lake.
I was an immense
summer sky
stretching over endless
expanses of corn
at dawn.
And my heart
was a lark whose notes
resounded through
the calmness of the air.

25 August 1933

Pudore

Se qualcuna delle mie povere parole
ti piace
e tu me lo dici
sia pur solo con gli occhi
io mi spalanco
in un riso beato
ma tremo
come una mamma piccola giovane
che perfino arrossisce
se un passante le dice
che il suo bambino è bello.   1 febbraio 1933

Inizio della morte

Quando ti diedi
le mie immagini di bimba
mi fosti grato: dicevi che era
come se io volessi
ricominciare la vita
per donartela intera.

Ora nessuno più
trae dall'ombra
la piccola lieve
persona che fu
in una breve
alba – la Pupa bambina:

ora nessuno si china
alla sponda
della mia culla obliata –

Anima –
e tu sei entrata
sulla strada del morire.   28 agosto 1933

Modesty

If you like one of
my words
and tell me so
if only with your eyes
I burst into
a blissful smile
but I tremble
like a tiny young mother
who even blushes
if a passer-by tells her
that her child is handsome.   1 February 1933

The beginning of death

When I gave you
my pictures as a child
you were grateful: it was you said
as though I longed
to start life again
to give it all to you.

Now no one draws out
any more from the darkness
the small light
person who was
for one brief
dawn – the baby doll:

now no one bends over
the edge
of my forgotten cradle –

Soul –
you have gone
towards the road of death.   28 August 1933

Preghiera alla poesia

Oh, tu bene mi pesi
l'anima, poesia:
tu sai se io manco e mi perdo,
tu che allora ti neghi
e taci.

Poesia, mi confesso con te
che sei la mia voce profonda:
tu lo sai,
tu lo sai che ho tradito,
ho camminato sul prato d'oro
che fu mio cuore,
ho rotto l'erba,
rovinato la terra –
poesia – quella terra
dove tu mi dicesti il più dolce
di tutti i tuoi canti,
dove un mattino per la prima volta
vidi volar nel sereno l'allodola
e con gli occhi cercai di salire –
Poesia, poesia che rimani
il mio profondo rimorso,
oh aiutami tu a ritrovare
il mio alto paese abbandonato –
Poesia che ti doni soltanto
a chi con occhi di pianto
si cerca –
oh rifammi tu degna di te,
poesia che mi guardi.   Pasturo, 23 agosto 1934

Prayer to poetry

Oh poetry, you size up
my soul well:
you know if I fail and lose myself,
you who then refute yourself
and fall silent.

Poetry, I open myself to you
who are my deepest voice:
you know it,
you know I have betrayed,
I have walked over the field of gold
that was my heart,
I have trampled the grass,
ruined the earth –
poetry – that earth
where you told me the sweetest
of all your songs,
where one morning for the first time
I saw a lark fly in the calm sky
and with my eyes I tried to ascend –
Poetry, poetry you remain
my deepest remorse,
help me to find once more
my high forsaken country –
Poetry only give yourself
to the one who searches for himself
with tearful eyes –
oh make me worthy of you again,
poetry look after me.   Pasturo, 23 August 1934

Assenza

Il tuo volto cercai
dietro i cancelli.

Ma s'ancorava in golfo di silenzi
la casa,
s'afflosciavano le tende
tra i loggiati deserti,
morte vele.

Al largo,
a sbocchi d'irreali monti
fuggiva il lago,
onde verdi e grigie
su scale ritraendosi
di pietra.

Lenta vagò,
sotto l'assorto cielo,
la barca vasta e pallida:
vedemmo
in rosso cerchio crescere alla riva
le azalee, cespi muti.

Monate, 5 maggio 1935

Ora sospesa

Le case dove ogni gesto
dice un'attesa
che non si compie mai.

Il fuoco acceso nel camino
per sciogliere la nube del respiro
e in ogni cuore l'alba
di domani – col sole.

Tu – verso sera – farfalla
con le ali chiuse
tra due steli paventi
la pioggia.

30 maggio 1935

Absence

I looked for your face
behind the railings.

But the house anchored itself in a gulf
of silences,
the curtains fell limp
between the deserted galleries,
like dead sails.

On the open sea,
at the mouth of dreamlike mountains
the lake fled away,
green and grey waves
portraying themselves on stairs
of stone.

The huge pale boat
roamed slowly,
beneath the rapt sky:
growing by the shore
in a red circle, we saw
the azaleas, silent clusters.   Monate, 5 May 1935

Suspended hour

The houses where every movement
tells of a wait
that never ends.

The fire lighting in the hearth
to dissolve the cloud of breath
and in every heart tomorrow's
dawn – with the sun.

You – towards evening – butterfly
with your wings closed in
between two stems – you fear
the rain.   30 May 1935

Fine

Ritorno ed è ancora sul greto
orma di mare,
mentre l'onda si esilia.
E m'imbarca:
e saluto le rive e i colori,
sfumo nel dolce morente
tramonto,
con te mare,
ora vasta
della mia fine notturna.   8 ottobre 1936

Morte di una stagione

Piovve tutta la notte
sulle memorie dell'estate.

A buio uscimmo
entro un tuonare lugubre di pietre,
fermi sull'argine reggemmo lanterne
a esplorare il pericolo dei ponti.

All'alba pallidi vedemmo le rondini
sui fili fradice immote
spiare cenni arcani di partenza –

e le specchiavano sulla terra
le fontane dai volti disfatti.

                              Pasturo, 20 settembre 1937

End

I return and the mark of the sea
still shows on the shore,
as the wave withdraws itself.
And I embark:
and salute the shores and colours,
I vanish in the sweet fading
sunset,
with you sea,
the broad hour
of my nocturnal end.   8 October 1936

Death of a season

All night long it rained
on the memories of summer.

We went out in the dark
between the dismal thundering of stones,
standing on the brink with outstretched lanterns
to explore the danger of the bridges.

Pale at dawn we saw the swallows
drenched and motionless on the wires
looking out for secret signals to depart –

and on the ground they were reflected
in the defeated faces of the fountains.

                    Pasturo, 20 September 1937

Le montagne

Occupano come immense donne
la sera:
sul petto raccolte le mani di pietra
fissan sbocchi di strade, tacendo
l'infinita speranza di un ritorno.

Mute in grembo maturano figli
all'assente. (Lo chiamaron vele
laggiù – o battaglie. Indi azzurra e rossa
parve loro la terra). Ora a un franare
di passi sulle ghiaie
grandi trasalgon nelle spalle. Il cielo
batte in un sussulto le sue ciglia bianche.

Madri. E s'erigon nella fronte, scostano
dai vasti occhi i rami delle stelle:
se all'orlo estremo dell'attesa
nasca un'aurora

e al brullo ventre fiorisca rosai.

                              Pasturo, 9 settembre 1937

The mountains

Like giantesses they cover over
the evening:
folded on their breast their hands of stone
stare at the opening of roads, silencing
the infinite hope of a return.

Silent in their womb they nurture sons
for the absent one. (Sails called him
away – or battles. Afterwards the earth
seemed blue or scarlet to them). Now the grinding
of steps on the gravel
sends a shiver through their shoulders. The sky
flickers its white eyelids.

Mothers. And they raise their forehead, brush away
the streaks of stars from their great eyes:
to see if at the closing limit of expectation
a new dawn is born

and rosebuds bloom around their bleak protrusion.

Pasturo, 9 September 1937

Daria Menicanti

DARIA MENICANTI was born in Piacenza in 1914 and lived most of her life in Milan where she died on 4 January 1995. She went to university in that city and studied aesthetics under the direction of the then well known philosopher Antonio Banfi. In 1937 she graduated with a degree thesis on the poetry of John Keats. In that same year Menicanti married the philosopher Giulio Preti but they were mutually incompatible and separated in 1951.

One of the most striking features of Menicanti's poetry is that her first work did not appear until she was fifty and when she died some thirty years later in 1995 she had published six collections of poetry.[1] Why such lengthy silence before appearing in print? In an interview given in 1968 Menicanti says that she started to write poetry early in her life but then found that her work was incompatible with the forms of hermetic poetry that were dominant during those years.[2] In many ways this is a reply based on technical criteria but the main reason for her silence as a poet may be found in her marriage to Giulio Preti who showed little interest in her work. In a lecture given to the Gabinetto Vieusseux in 1986 in honour of Preti (who had died in 1972) entitled *Vita con Giulio*, Menicanti spoke of their common interest in aesthetics

---

1 All quotations in this chapter are taken from these editions of Menicanti's poetry. They are:

Città come (Milan, Mondadori, 1964).
Un nero d'ombra (Milan, Mondadori, Lo Specchio, 1969).
Poesie per un passante (Milan, Mondadori, 1978).
Ferragosto (Lunarionuovo, Catania, 1986).
Altri amici (Forum, Forlì, 1986).
Ultimo quarto (Milan, Scheiwiller, 1990).

2 M. Cancogni, 'Ridente e piangente', *La Fiera Letteraria*, 11.1.1968, p.1: 'Cominciai a scrivere piuttosto presto, diciamo negli anni universitari, per poi abbandonare tutto in tronco deliberatamente per ragioni inerenti alla natura della mia stessa poetica che, allora si era bloccata e rappresa nelle formule dell'ermetismo, le quali a me, di indole discorsiva, ridente e piangente, non lasciavano via di uscita. Ripresi a scrivere, di colpo nuovamente dopo aver esitato a lungo ed evitato con cura la lettura di ogni altro poeta contemporaneo per non sentirmi un'altra volta influenzata e come obbligata a una maniera che non fosse la mia.'

but noted that he was jealous of what poetry represented for her.[3] This lack of encouragement together with a feeling of incompatibility with the poetry of the time made Menicanti decide to consign her poetry to the realm of the private. Her friendship with Vittorio Sereni made her break that silence in 1964.

The cultural ferment in Milan in the Thirties had a significant impact on Menicanti's life and work. The most important aspects were her discovery of Banfi's antidogmatic philosophy together with her contact with young philosophers who were part of Banfi's circle such as Giulio Preti, Enzo Paci and Remo Cantoni. Although she chose to remain silent in the poetic sphere her intellectual and emotional curiosity extended to all areas of culture. In his work, *Linea lombarda*, Luciano Anceschi speaks of the way in which poetry, criticism and philosophy were interlinked at that time while also confirming the excitement related to the intellectual stimulation offered by Banfi to his students.[4]

A further significant stimulus for Menicanti was provided by the *linea lombarda* poetry which prevailed in Milan from the late Forties to the mid Sixties. Actively aware of the social reality and environment in which they lived, these poets established a strong bond with the city while their poetry reflected the realistic features and characteristics of the time.

The poet Vittorio Sereni was part of this movement and he had close ties with the Mondadori publishing house. It was he who first recognised Menicanti's talent as a poet and who valued her new and independent though somewhat unfashionable vein in poetry. He encouraged Mondadori to publish her poems and so, her first collection, *Città come*, was published in 1964.

The title of this work recalls the epigraph ' . . . Città come si ricordano amori' by Valéry Larbaud and its meaning becomes apparent on

3 D. Menicanti, 'Vita con Giulio', *Quaderni dell'Antologia Vieusseux* (Florence, 1987), p.9: '[. . .] Io allora stavo preparando con Banfi la mia tesi di laurea in Estetica e cominciavo ad esprimermi con le mie poesie. Era naturale che dell'una discutessimo insieme, ma delle altre, in quanto appartenenti a una mia vita troppo privata e segreta, era geloso e preferiva ignorarle.'

4 L. Anceschi, *Linea lombarda* (Varese, Magenta, 1952), p.10: 'Poesia, critica, filosofia [. . .] ognuna di esse portava in sè le altre, e tutte, con i loro mezzi diversi, volevano concorrere a dar risposta alla situazione. Furono anni fertili [. . .] nulla ci sfuggiva che tentasse o proponesse una soluzione [. . .] basterà ricordare ormai che cosa fu la scuola di Antonio Banfi per noi, un maestro, veramente un uomo che lasciava alla verità tutta la sua flessibilità, ricchezza e movimento, e non sembrava imporre nulla, anzi sollecitava in noi il nascere del nostro essere autentico. Con lui gli studi furono veramente un incanto, e una continua apertura al mondo . . . '.

reading the poems where the city of Milan is given a prominent role.
In many ways it is parallel to the importance of Trieste in the life of
Saba for whom even the most ordinary and populous place in his city
is a source of inspiration:

Caffè Tergeste, ai tuoi tavoli bianchi
ripete l'ubriaco il suo delirio;
ed io ci scrivo i miei più allegri canti.[5]

(At your white tables, Caffè Tergeste,/ the drunkard repeats his incoherence;/
and there I write my happiest poems.)

This is similar to the affection felt by Menicanti for her city, Milan, in
'Inverno al Bar Bozzi':

Qui ritrovo la luce,
qui di nuovo la gente,
qui le parole . . .   (*Città come*, p.21)

(Here again I find the light,/ the people,/ and the words . . .)

Saba describes the bond between himself and Trieste as:

La mia città che in ogni parte è viva,
ha il cantuccio a me fatto, alla mia vita
pensosa e schiva.   (*Antologia del Canzoniere*, p.61)

(My city which is alive in every part,/ has a little corner carved out for
me, for my shy/ and pensive life.)

Like Saba, Menicanti feels that she is an integral part of her city while
her love for Milan is no less powerful than his for Trieste. Her devo-
tion is frank and unambiguous in the poem 'Milano':

Tutto questo che ad altri forse è pena
angoscioso rifiuto,
quando mi eri lontana,
città di case, ospite città,
a me sempre è mancato
doluto per tutte le vene.
Questo sempre mi attendo a ogni ritorno
come un volto cercato;
un conquistato difficile amore.   (*Città come*, pp.19–20)

---

5   U. Saba, *Antologia del Canzoniere* (Turin, Einaudi, 1963), p.61.

(All this which to others is perhaps pain/ anguished rejection,/ when you were far from me,/ city of houses, welcoming city,/ I always missed/ and grieved for in my veins./ This is what I always wait for on each return/ like a sought for face;/ a difficult and conquered love.)

The presence of Milan is apparent in many poem titles, such as 'Cantilena per Porta Ticinese', 'Mattino milanese', 'I santi del Duomo', and 'Inverno al Bar Bozzi', which refer to specific geographic locations and make us aware of the importance of the city particularly in her early work. Her second collection, *Un nero d'ombra*, was also dedicated to Milan and various titles such as 'Il duomo', 'Alba a Milano', 'Via Ugo Foscolo' and '7 via Vivaio' make us aware of the city's significance in Menicanti's life. She admitted her attachment to and dependence on this city in an interview given in 1990:

Lo diceva Vittorio Sereni: la mia poesia è molto legata ad un 'ambiente'. Io non potrei avere scritto niente se non qui a Milano, nella mia casa. Quando vado via, magari anche un mese, io non scrivo una riga . . . '[6]

(Vittorio Sereni maintained that my poetry is strongly linked to a 'particular place'. I could never have written anything if not here in Milan, in my house. When I go away, even for a month, I do not write a single line . . .)

Many of these early poems are accompanied by dates and place names which refer to the time and location of their composition. Several were written from 1959 onwards and they make the reader more involved in her world – the critic Luigi Baldacci recognised that places, time and memory are part of a sentimental backdrop to Menicanti's poetry.[7]

One of the main features of her poetry is that it revolves around the contrasting themes of love and death with the accent often placed on the latter. Menicanti's introspective and often pessimistic nature is to the fore in 'Camera zero':

Da troppo tempo la sua carne rompe
in quell'ululo e tutta ne è un sobbalzo,
un rimbombo. Stenta di là a strapparsi
la povera cosa prigioniera.
Tra tutte quante morire,
questa è la difficile arte.   (*Città come*, p.74)

6 'Il fertile dubbio del grillo', un colloquio con Daria Menicanti a cura di Fabio Minazzi, in *Dal giardino all'agora*, Annuario del cinquantesimo (1942–1992) del Liceo Scientifico Statale Galileo Ferraris di Varese, 1993, p.189.

7 L. Baldacci, *Due donne ricercano le voci della memoria* in *Epoca*, n.720, 12.7.1964.

(For too long his flesh breaks into/ that howl and it is all a jolt,/ a roar. With difficulty he frees himself from there/ from that poor imprisoned thing./ Above all other things/ dying is a difficult art.)

Menicanti gives few details about herself and prefers to let the poems speak for themselves. In 'Via Prè' she admits that she longs for privacy and anonymity:

Non sempre sono stata
così autobiografica,
così ciarliera di me
a riottosi ascoltatori [. . .]
Sono qui per ognuno
anonima, in fuga.   (*Città come*, pp.14–15)

(I have not always been/ so autobiographical, so self talkative/ with unruly listeners . . . / I am here for all/ fleeing and anonymous.)

There is a light ironic tone to much of this early poetry that often hides a strong feeling of bitterness and pain:

Mi chiedi come passo il tempo. Come
vivo quassù, lontana.

Mortalmente colpita
da un triste amore per l'umanità
corro traverso gli anni
verso una meta di silenzi.

autunno 1961   (*Città come*, p.55)

(You ask how I spend my time./ How I live far away, up here./ Mortally struck/ by an unhappy love for humanity/ I race across the years/ towards a target of silences.)

For Daria Menicanti joy and happiness are found in the magical world of poetry and in the creative manipulation of words:

Dopo tanto silenzio
mi arriva di lontano
festante, fragorosa
una banda di rime,
di assonanze.

Le corro incontro
felice
fino sull'angolo.   (*Città come*, p.72)

(After so much silence/ a body of rhymes,/ of assonances/ come to me from afar/ joyful and noisy./ Happy/ I run towards them/ right up to the corner.)

In 1969, her second work, *Un nero d'ombra* was published contin-
uing many of the themes of *Città come* while a slightly more precise
portrait of the poet emerges from several of these poems as she makes
the reader party to some of her memories. In 'Via Pré' she speaks of
her longing for anonymity while now something of her memory remains
in the shadow on the footpath:

Rosee pei muri con la sera balzano
ad una ad una le finestre. Passo
di fretta come un ricordo elusivo:
sul marciapiede un nero d'ombra.   (*Un nero d'ombra*, p.9)

(One by one the windows bounce rosy/ along the walls at evening. Hurriedly/
I pass like an elusive memory:/ a dark shadow on the footpath.)

In these poems Menicanti constantly juxtaposes the themes of love
and death, day and night, prison and freedom, hope and despair. In
'Come vorrebbe andarsene' life is presented as a restless prisoner who
longs for freedom but light brings hope and with it a different image
of death:

Con la luce è più facile: rinasce
la speranza e la morte può sembrare
un'altra cosa.   (*Un nero d'ombra*, p.175)

(It is easier with light: hope/ is born again and death can seem/ like some-
thing else.)

In many ways this collection is similar to a diary filled with various
states of mind that hover incessantly between life or death, love or its
delusions. Menicanti considers the ups and downs of love with the
emphasis more frequently on the absence of love:

Ancora scrivi, ancora chiedi cosa
n'è della Daria [. . .]
Se ancora lei, la Daria, si ricorda.   (*Un nero d'ombra*, p.25)

(You still write and ask/ how Daria is faring . . . / If she, Daria, still remem-
bers.)

This love also encompasses mundane objects like the telephone which
allows immediate contact with the loved one:

Soprattutto mi piace col telefono
entrargli nella camera lontana
di là dal monte,

sentire il mio squillo
che si avventa nel buio. Poi la cara
voce fra tutte che risponde:
–Sì–i?   (*Un nero d'ombra*, p.77)

(Most of all with the phone I like/ to go to his room far away/ beyond the
mountain,/ to hear my call/ hurl itself at the darkness. Then the beloved/ voice
which answers:/ Ye-es?)

This enthusiasm alternates with ironic insults directed at the opposite
sex:

Gli uomini, tu sai,
li puoi sostituire.
Un cane
mai   (*Altri amici*, p.52)

(Men you know . . . you can/ substitute./ A dog/ never.)

Such irony also recalls the disappointments of love and the failure of
her marriage:

Natale senza di te per la prima
volta. Mi sento tra la gola e il fiele . . .   (*Un nero d'ombra*, p.88)

(Christmas without you for the first time./ I am caught between gluttony and
bile . . .)

The critic Fabio Scotto drew attention to the feeling both of soli-
darity and loneliness[8] in Menicanti's third work, *Poesie per un passante*,
which was published in 1978. On its fly cover Sergio Solmi wrote that
it was Menicanti's finest poetry to date and that it presented a con-
tinuation of the dilemma of love and death that has been a constant
feature of poetry from the early Greek lyricists right up to Leopardi.
In these poems the search for a kindred spirit takes precedence over
all else:

Lontano in qualche parte
della città anche tu mi stai cercando
smaniosamente. Io non so chi, non so
il nome.
Ma ti aspetto
in febbre e sudori   (*Poesie per un passante*, p.9)

8 F. Scotto, 'Solidarietà e solitudine nella poesia di Daria Menicanti', in *Il let-
tore di provincia*, n.86 (Ravenna, Longo), 1993.

(Far away in some part/ of the city you too are searching desperately/ for me. I do not know you/nor your name./ Feverishly perspiring/ I wait for you.)

These lines reveal the poet's solitude but also her febrile search for one who can satisfy this thirst for love. Apart from this state of mind the poet tells us little else: the distance between the two is described as 'lontano' and the place occupied by the unnamed person is 'in qualche parte della città'.

The poet's relationship and marriage to Giulio Preti provided the inspiration for *Poesie per un passante* but it is also a meditation on love and death that starts from a personal episode and moves on to a more universal consideration of these themes. Many of these poems are strikingly spontaneous and sincere, rooted as they are in the existential, sentimental and spiritual experience of the poet. In 'Morte dell'albero' death is not tragic but is seen as an inescapable and natural occurrence that has a positive tone to it:

[. . .] Ora ha finito.
Ma come è tranquilla
per gli alberi la morte,
che cosa pulita [. . .]
                Così
la cara vita ricorda   (*Poesie per un passante*, p.83)

(Now it is over./ How tranquil death is/ for the trees,/ what a clean thing [. . .] This is how / cherished life remembers.)

Pain and suffering also spring from the realisation that the search for companionship can be in vain:

[. . .] da sempre, da allora
io vo inseguendo qualcuno o qualcosa
che non vuole saperne di me   (*Poesie per un passante*, p.40)

([. . .] for ever, since then/ I am following someone or something/ that does not want to know me.)

There is a frequent use of the negative in many of these poems such as 'Non si sa', 'Non ti domando', and 'L'amore (non) è eterno':

Non può durare. Certo non durerà.
Si attacca l'amore smaniando
al tuo corpo bruciante e corre ad altre,
eterno solo in questa sua vicenda.
Il resto che si dice è peste e corna
di poveri poeti   (*Poesie per un passante*, p.13)

(It cannot last. Of course it will not last./ Love attaches itself eagerly/ to your burning body then runs to others,/ only eternal in this event./ All else that is uttered is the rubbish/ of poor poets.)

Love is the main source of inspiration in this work as it examines the many permutations of happiness, disillusionment and despair. There are lines which emphasise the attraction felt for the loved one:

Mi piacciono i tuoi larghi occhi di triste
bestia impudica   (*Poesie per un passante*, p.10)

(I like your broad eyes that are like a sad/ and shameless beast)

and lines that describe an irritable and testy relationship:

A un tratto ti rischiari nella faccia
con un alto feroce sorriso
bianco. Tu stai cercando
un piglio per litigare.   (*Poesie per un passante*, p.11)

(Suddenly your face lights up/ with a high and fierce white/ smile. You are looking/ for an excuse to fight.)

Menicanti attempts to be candid in this relationship:

Non ti domando sicurezze, mai
con te ho pensato a un amore *routine* [. . .]
Tu bada a non farmi promesse
io a non chiederne   (*Poesie per un passante*, p.12)

(I am not asking you for certainties, never/ have I thought of a routine love with you [. . .]/ Try not to make me promises/ I will not ask for them)

But such efforts are accompanied by the fear that all will end. The ultimate separation caused by death becomes a reality in 'Epigramma per noi due':

La morte giocò a lungo a rimpiattino
tra noi due. Poi ad un tratto – così dicono –
scelse il migliore   (*Poesie per un passante*, p.76)

(For a long time death played hide and seek/ between us. Then suddenly – so they say –/ it chose the better one.)

Despite the loss of the one she loves Menicanti finds some consolation in the world around her:

E subito di tutto m'innamoro
tanto ogni cosa mi risembra bella
nella sua fuga, ogni spiro, ogni insetto (*Poesie per un passante*, p.85)

(And suddenly I fall in love with everything/ and all seems beautiful once
more to me/ in its fleeing, every breath, every insect)

In the presence or absence of love the poet's solitude is mitigated by
the feeling of solidarity found in the world around her. She describes
herself as one who is light, ironic and seemingly happy:

    [. . .] una cosa
ironica leggera e all'apparenza
felice   (*Poesie per un passante*, p.53)

Ferragosto and *Altri amici*, both published in 1986, show a poet who
finds happiness and companionship among the animals and strange
creatures which populate her poems. Among them are sirens and dol-
phins, centaurs, lions and serpents, herons, seagulls, owls and crick-
ets. Some are familiar but many are strange, hybrid, often disturbing
creatures that are a 'metaphor for the hallucinations or impossible
dreams of modern man'.[9]

These works represent a change in Menicanti's poetry as she moves
away from the immediate reality of human feeling towards more abstract
and meditative themes. The title *Ferragosto* calls to mind August 15
which is generally associated with holidays and deserted Italian cities.
Unlike most of her fellow citizens who leave the city, Menicanti choos-
es to remain in the sun drenched, eerily silent city of Milan while the
apparition of a monster and hybrid creature becomes her reward for
staying behind. The opening poem presents a hybrid centaur, half
horse and half human, 'Madame Centaure', who trots around the still
streets visible only to those prepared to admire her silken tail or the
brightness of her movement. The silence of the abandoned city caus-
es the eyes of the few who remain to see mysterious and hallucinato-
ry images all around. Among these wondrous creatures is an aggressive
and threatening dantesque like chimera and a strange seductive siren.
They are accompanied by many ordinary animals and Menicanti does
not suggest or impose any structure to interpret these creatures but
allows the reader to project his or her dreams or fears, longings or
anxieties on to their images.

9 Mariella Sclafani, *Ferragosto* di Daria Menicanti, in *Lunarionuovo*, no.4, Anno
  IX, gennaio 1987, p.48.

There is also an ironic and polemical tone to many of these poems when Menicanti contrasts the freedom enjoyed by men to the way in which man can deprive animals of their liberty. Present too is the theme of the animal-like transfiguration of man. In this case the animal, normally presented in a positive light, assumes a threatening appearance often calling to mind varying aspects of human wickedness. This is well illustrated in the contrasting presentation of the serpent in the poems 'Cobra' and 'Zoo'. In 'Cobra' man is changed into an animal:

E' allora che dal collo
sboccia la bestia finora contesa [. . .]
dal nido
della solenne giacca su in alto
spinge un collo squamoso verdigno
con in cima un triangolo di testa
occhi dritti di ferro.   (*Altri amici*, p.9)

(At that point the beast/ contented until then, opens out from the neck [. . .]/ from the nest/ of the solemn jacket up pushes/ a scaly greenish neck/ topped by a triangular head/ with eyes direct and darting.)

In 'Zoo' the serpent is the victim of man and is imprisoned in a glass cage. Despite his still, flat mortal head ('la piatta fissa testa mortale') he is presented just as a sad and innocent dreamer. Here the poet's sympathy is with the animal but there are other poems in Ferragosto such as 'Pensionati', 'Cieco con cane', 'Solidarietà' and 'America latina' that show a reflective change in Menicanti's work.

Altri amici has much in common with *Ferragosto*. Although fewer poems deal with monstrous creatures of fantasy many are dedicated to plants and animals. The poet's attachment to them is evident in her deep-rooted trust apparent in the opening poem, 'Caninamente', where she deliberately uses the line, 'Quando sei solo/ Dio ti manda un cane' (*Altri amici*, p.7) that emphasises a dog's unwavering loyalty to man, a loyalty often not recognised or appreciated by the latter.

Menicanti uses original images to describe these animals. The lizard is a thin green leaf, 'sottile verdefoglia' (*Altri amici*, p.20), the glowworm a seed light, 'seme di luce' (*Altri amici*, p.40), the cockroach has his parental eyes brimming with anxiety, 'occhi di padre [. . .] pieni d'angoscia' (*Altri amici*, p.37) while the spider with his pearly black eyes gazes at the fine curly sea, 'neri occhi di perla contempla / il bel mare ricciuto' (*Altri amici*, p.18). Likewise, there is a conscious attempt to give a human dimension to the plant world:

Una sfera
pallida e trasparente è caduta
sopra le braccia aperte
dell'albero in attesa.   (*Altri amici*, p.11)

(A pale/ transparent sphere has fallen/ across the open arms/ of the waiting tree/)

and in 'Primaverile' the birches rush numerous to the river, 'accorrono in gran folla sul fiume' (*Altri amici*, p.16). Although the poet is a prey to feelings of loneliness and disappointment what is most striking is the fellowship she finds in the world of nature. Menicanti chooses the image of the festive cricket to ironically defend herself while her solidarity with these creatures provides the real freedom which only true poetry can grant:

E gli apro la guardiola. Io non ignoro
quanto amino la libertà i poeti.   (*Altri amici*, p.58)

(And I open the look-out tower for him. I do not ignore/ how much poets love freedom.)

In her final years Menicanti's attitude to life became more ironic and this is apparent in the title chosen for her last work, *Ultimo quarto*, published five years before her death. This title refers to the final quarter of life when the reality of living often takes a heavy toll on our fragile awareness of human destiny. Affection for the good features of life is accompanied by an awareness of their imminent end:

Oggi – ma anche prima di oggi –
amore dice solitudine dice
separazione strappo.   (*Ultimo quarto*, p.68)

(Today – but also before today –/ loves means separation / loneliness laceration.)

As she prepares to take her leave of life, Menicanti, now more than ever before, has a clear vision of what really counts in life and for her it is inextricably linked with what the poet has to say:

Quello che conta non è l'opinione
l'ideologia il pensiero. Quel che conta
è sempre la parola:
la vita dello scriba è una manciata
di sillabe e vocali e consonanti . . .   (*Ultimo quarto*, p.13)

(What counts is not opinion,/ ideology or thought. The word/ is what always counts:/ the scribe's life is a fistful of syllables vowels and consonants . . .)

It was appropriate that towards the end of her life, Menicanti should look to Milan, the original source of her inspiration, for a release from the despondency which tended to afflict her in old age. However, by that time, she was obviously more mature, and, chastened by life's toll, she combines a sense of place with emotions of love, requited or otherwise, with her ultimate substitution of manipulative animals for more wayward humans. She has come a full circle, with her perceptions deepening all the time, while still retaining some of the joy apparent in her earlier work. Her finely tuned talent is reflected throughout much of her poetry which shows immediacy of imagery, dexterity of appropriate language and skill in the use of various metrical forms. The reader is cajoled by the poet into reading what she has to say and then following her path through life where joy was always tempered by sadness. Menicanti's themes were not new but the way in which she expressed them was different and independent from other poets writing at that time. It was these features that won her the admiration of her peers with the critic Silvio Ramat, on learning of her death, paying her the ultimate tribute by referring to her poetry as a 'canzoniere d'amore e morte'.[10]

10 S. Ramat, 'Ricordo di Daria Menicanti' in *Il Giornale*, 4.2.1995.

Pavia

La piccola città fioca, venata
di stradine nodose, tutta a chine
verso un'acqua corriva,
la città
a lunghe torri e chiese color ocra,
col castello quadrato che si ingiglia
di trifore ed ogive
cosí improvvisamente gentili –
non più la mia città –
con insistenza oggi mi torna come
per caso. Un fresco odore d'onda
l'ha ridestata, di tiepida pioggia,
togliendola da dietro un polveroso
rovinío d'anni
dove – con pazienza
da me recisa – muta
e mi dimentica.

gennaio-marzo 1963

Epigramma 4

Mi chiedi come passo il tempo. Come
vivo quassú, lontana.

Mortalmente colpita
da un triste amore per l'umanità
corro traverso gli anni
verso una meta di silenzi.

autunno 1961

Agli Amici
1959–1963

Quando come un convitato sazio
lascerò il vostro banchetto, amici,
sola e persuasa
sola e guardinga

Pavia

The small dim city, lined
with tiny twisted streets, all sloping
towards a flowing water,
the city
with high towers and ochre coloured churches,
the square castle indented
with unexpectedly subdued
three-mullioned windows and pointed arches –
my city no more –
by chance it returns insistently to me
today. A fresh smell of waves
has re-woken it with soft rain,
removing from behind a dusty
peal of years
where – patiently
cut off by me – it changes
and forgets me.

January–March 1963

Epigram 4

You ask how I spend my time.
How I live far away, up here.

Mortally struck
by an unhappy love for humanity
I race across the years
towards a target of silences.

Autumn 1961

To my friends
1959–1963

When I will leave your banquet
friends, like a satisfied guest
stubborn and alone
wary and alone

senza salutare nessuno nessuna,
non richiamatemi indietro, per favore:
così sono stanca di tante vite
di tutte queste possibilità.
Dunque lasciatemi scendere ai morti
restare insieme con i miei morti
ricchezza della mia solitudine.
Al tempo lasciatemi, il tempo fraterno,
che su di me leggermente si chiuda.

Foglie per i morti
novembre 1963

L'è el dì di mort, alégher.
(D. Tessa)

Forse non solo qui, forse su tutto
il tiepido pianeta oramai cadono
le foglie ed è ciascuna terra involta
dentro il loro estenuarsi morire.
O dolcezza paterna di quel vento
che le adagia e raccoglie!
Qui sulle case pallide dei morti
oggi azzimate di tristi corone
il pianto cade ormai da giorni e giorni,
un fresco pianto di tranquille foglie
che va tingendo tutto il camposanto
di un festoso ed estatico vermiglio.

Per un passante

Lontano in qualche parte
della città anche tu mi stai cercando
smaniosamente. Io non so chi, non so
il nome.
Ma ti aspetto
in febbre e sudori

saluting no one
please, do not call me back:
I am so weary of numerous lives
of all these possibilities.
Let me descend therefore to the dead
to remain together with my dead ones
splendour of my loneliness.
Leave me at that time, the brotherly time,
which gently closes in on me.

Leaves for the dead
November 1963

It is all Saints' Day, let us be happy.
(D. Tessa)

Perhaps not just here, perhaps across
the luke-warm planet leaves
now fall and every land is wrapped
exhausted in its dying.
Oh fatherly sweetness of that wind
which lays them down and gathers them!
Here on the white houses of the dead
decked out today in melancholy wreaths
grief now flows for days on end,
a fresh lament of quiet leaves
colours the entire graveyard
with joyful and ecstatic scarlet.

For a passer-by

Far away in some part
of the city you too search eagerly
for me. I do not know you
nor your name.
Feverishly perspiring
I wait for you

L'amore (non) è eterno

Non può durare. Certo non durerà.
Si attacca l'amore smaniando
al tuo corpo bruciante e corre ad altre,
eterno solo in questa sua vicenda.
Il resto che si dice è peste e corna
di poveri poeti

E vedrai che

Nessuno ho conosciuto più vanesio
dell'uomo.
Accetta tutti i complimenti, tutte
le più volgari adulazioni per
della buona moneta.
E si gonfia molesto
grandeggiando per casa. Ma se vuoi
se proprio vuoi farlo felice – digli –
anche se è molle e bianco –
digli che è un grande amatore.
E vedrai che ci crede

Non si sa

Non si sa come fare con i morti:
hanno una sordità una compostezza
così elaborata, un rigore
di conclusione, di assoluti che
insieme con uno di loro
più che escluso ti senti importuno.
Non somiglia la faccia del tuo morto
a nessuna delle sue facce che
gli conoscevi amavi. Quelle
non te le sai dimenticare mai
anche se questa, l'ultima, è una somma.
Resti con lui e sei l'ospite ignorato,
sei il borghese davanti il generale

Love is (not) eternal

It cannot last. Of course it will not last.
Love attaches itself eagerly
to your burning body then runs to others,
only eternal in this event.
All else that is uttered is the rubbish
of poor poets

And you will see

No one have I known more vain
than man.
He accepts all compliments, all
coarsest flattery as if
it were true.
And he swells up bothersome
strutting round the house. But if
you really want to make him happy – tell him –
even if he is weak and white –
tell him he is a great lover.
You will see that he believes

No one knows

No one knows how to deal with the dead:
they have a deafness a studied
composure, a rigour
of conclusion, so absolute that
together with one of them
you feel uncomfortable rather than excluded.
The face of your dead one does not recall
any of his faces that you knew
and loved. You will
never forget those faces
even if this, the last one, is a conclusion.
Stay with him and you are the scorned guest,
you are in civvies before the general

che quel che dice – se pur dice e all'aria –
cose assurde e remote son le cose
che dice
buone per un'altra gente
un diverso pianeta

Lieto fine

C'era una volta che mi innamorai
di uno sino a conviverci.
Ma lui cercava una perpetua rissa
e applausi femminili al suo nome
e l'affannata attesa per ognuno
degli ambiti ritorni.
    Ora il suo battelletto se n'è andato
lontano. In compagnia di un dappoco
oggi mi annoio. Eh, sì:
meravigliosamente mi annoio

Il miracolo

Ormai poco si resta nella stanza
a parlare del tempo. È facile mentire
con lui che si fa complice. Meglio
restare guardando in silenzio.
Intanto sopra lui che all'indietro
ci sfugge insieme coi giorni
su lui fiorisce il miracolo dei vivi:
a mano a mano che muore e lui diventa
nei nostri discorsi migliore

Identità

    Questo no. Mai potrebbe
un corpo dimezzarsi e in due altri

and what he says – if he speaks in the open –
absurd and distant things are
what he says
good for another people
a different planet

Happy end

Once I fell so much in love
with a person that I lived with him.
But he always sought a continuous brawl
and female applause for his name
and the anxious waiting for each one
of the longed-for returns.
    Now his tiny boat has gone
far away. Today I am bored in the company
of someone worthless. And yes:
I am wonderfully bored

The miracle

Little time now is spent in the room
talking about the weather. It is easy to lie
when he is an accomplice too. Better
to remain and watch in silence.
Meanwhile on him who escapes
backwards from us with the days
the miracle of the living flowers over him:
as he slowly dies he becomes
better in our discussions

Identity

Not this. A body could never
divide itself and live in

convivere. È l'anima volante
che passa dall'uno nell'altro
e sul primo deposita astute
colpe ignote e rimorsi sempre vivi
mentre l'altro lo lascia fresco e bianco.
    Lo specchio, quello solo, ti rende
l'idea della tua identità
anche se incontro ti guarda *alter ego*
e in un modo simmetrico e tranquillo
di continuo fedele con te cambia

Serpente

Nulla ha che lo apparenti
con l'uomo, che gli somigli.
Silenzioso è un unico lunghissimo
ventre. Ritto si dondola
pieno di morte e ipnotizzando scatta
come col pugno il pugile. Poi cala
lento tra la polvere a cercare
pietre calde al suo sazio gomitolo

Dicembre

L'anno si accorcia: l'anno –
dicevano – sta già bruciando gli assi.
    Ma il coraggio che occorre
per accettare quello che sei stato
quello che sei – il poco che sei ora –
l'animo che ci vuole
per ricominciare tutto da capo.
Coi pochi amici ultimi e le care
cose prima che affondino
affrettati a doppiare a uscire
al largo azzurro e ignoto

another two. It is the flying soul
which passes from one body to the other
and on the first one leaves clever
unknown offenses and ever live remorse
while it leaves the other fresh and white.
    Only the mirror gives you
an idea of your identity
even if it looks at your *alter ego*
and in a quiet symmetrical way
faithful to you ceaselessly it changes.

Serpent

It has nothing in common
with man, nothing similar.
Silent it is just one long
stomach. When erect it sways
filled with death hypnotic it springs out
like a boxer with his jab. Then slowly
he collapses in the dust as he seeks out
warm stones for his satisfied coil

December

The year is shortening: the year –
they said – is already burning up the aces.
    But the courage that is needed
to accept what you have been
what you are – the little you now are –
the heart that is needed
to begin again from start.
With the few last friends and dear
possessions before they sink away
hurry on to venture out
on the blue unknown sea

Margherita Guidacci

MARGHERITA GUIDACCI's first volume of poetry *La sabbia e l'angelo* appeared in 1946 while another seventeen volumes had been published when she died in 1992.[1] Her literary career was marked by her parallel work as poet, translator and critic. In *La sabbia e l'angelo*[2] (Sand and the angel) while evoking the despair, horror and disgust caused by the recent war she nevertheless tempered such sentiments with expressions of hope and comfort:

E poi vi è anche la pietra crudele, che tronca il volo alla brezza
E su cui nulla che alla brezza risponda può germinare.

(La sabbia e l'angelo, p.15)

(And then there is also the cruel stone, which prevents the breeze taking flight,/ And on which nothing that answers the breeze can take seed.)

1 The following are the collections of poetry published by Margherita Guidacci:
   La sabbia e l'angelo (Florence, Vallecchi, 1946).
   Morte del ricco (Florence, Vallecchi, 1955).
   Giorno dei Santi (Milan, Scheiwiller, 1957).
   Paglia e polvere (Padua, Rebellato, 1961).
   Poesie (Milan, Rizzoli, 1965).
   Un cammino incerto (Luxembourg, Origine, 1970).
   Neurosuite (Vicenza, Neri Pozza, 1970).
   Terra senza orologi (Milan, Trentadue, 1973).
   Taccuino slavo (Vicenza, La Locusta, 1976).
   Il vuoto e le forme (Padua, Rebellato, 1977).
   L'altare di Isenheim (Milan, Rusconi, 1980).
   L'orologio di Bologna (Florence, Città di Vita, 1981).
   Inno alla gioia (Florence, Nardini, 1983).
   La via Crucis dell'Umanità (Florence, Città di Vita, 1984).
   Liber Fulguralis (Messina, Mela stregata, 1986).
   Poesie per poeti (Milan, Istituto di Propaganda Libraria, 1987).
   Una breve misura (Chieti, Vecchio Faggio Editore, 1988).
   Il buio e lo splendore (Milan, Garzanti, 1989).
   Anelli del tempo (Florence, Città di Vita, 1993) published posthumously.

   All references to Guidacci's poems in this chapter are taken from these texts.

2 The references to *La sabbia e l'angelo* are taken from *Poesie* (Milan, Rizzoli, 1965).

Such expressions are counterbalanced by the exhortation:

Non inchinarti alla tristezza. Essa è un evento del sogno.
Anche il tormento della pietra il tempo e il sogno consumano.
Ma ciò ch'è lieve è dell'eterno o nell'eterno si prolunga,
Poiché lievi sono le brezze ed i morti e gli angeli.
(La sabbia e l'angelo, p.21)

(Do not give in to sorrow. It is a thing of dreams./ Time and dreams also devour the torment of stone./ But what is gentle is eternal or lasts for all eternity./ Gentle too are the light breezes, the angels and the dead.)

Following the experience of the war poetry became a liberating and live force for Guidacci, 'un'esigenza di liberazione'[3] and un'alternativa alla morte'.[4] Her first collection of poetry was an attempt to free her soul from the anguish accumulated during the war years, 'un'angoscia che mi avrebbe soffocata se non fossi riuscita ad esprimerla'[5] (an anguish that would have suffocated me had I not been able to express it). She was twenty-five when she wrote those poems as she was born in Florence in 1921 and spent her formative years there and in the nearby Mugello. It was a Christian environment and one that provided her with the certainties and the detachment that were to permeate much of her subsequent writings.

Although she did her degree-thesis on Giuseppe Ungaretti at the University of Florence, Guidacci, nevertheless, remained outside the poetic forms which hermeticism had advocated, as though something had prevented her from submitting her poetry to the restraints of hermeticism. A similar independence marked her critical work while she herself attributed this feature to a love for mathematics which in turn had nurtured in her a longing for clarity of expression, a feature which characterised her entire work.

Equally important for her development as a poet was her work as a translator, especially her translation of John Donne's *Sermons*, Max Beerbohm's *The Happy Hypocrite* and later the poems of Emily Dickinson. Throughout her career she acknowledged her debt to non-Italian writers whose work she was intimately acquainted with, mainly through her translations. In John Donne's *Sermons*, for example, she discovered a sense of life moving inevitably towards death that changes all to dust but is then transcended in the celestial joy of redemption. That

3 Interview with Margherita Guidacci by L. Pupolin: 'Margherita Guidacci: poesia come liberazione e gioia', in *Idea*, 40 (1984), 2, p.39.
4 M. Guidacci, 'Dichiarazione di ragion poetica' in G. Spagnoletti (ed.), *Poesia italiana contemporanea 1909–1959* (Parma, Guanda, 1964), p.661.
5 L. Pupolin, *op.cit.*, p.39.

mirrored her own anguish caused by the war together with the isolat-
ed and melancholy period of her youth which was filled with intima-
tions of death: 'Sapevamo già di appartenere alla morte,' We already
knew that we belonged to death, she wrote, (*La sabbia e l'angelo*, p.51).
It was as if she had a mission to proclaim eternal verities and so she
had no qualms about proclaiming that:

Chi grida sull'alto spartiacque è udito da entrambe le valli.
Perciò la voce dei poeti intendono i viventi ed i morti.
(La sabbia e l'angelo, p.11)

(The one who shouts across the divide is heard by both valleys./ Therefore
both the living and the dead understand the poet's word.)

Her work as teacher and later professor of English literature and
also as translator continued down through the years while the choice
of texts for translation was always indicative of her passion for moral
and social problems. Scrupulous in her approach to translation and
fully aware of the problems and complexity of the task that faced her
she called translations *eterne spine* or eternal thorns.

Guidacci's output as a translator was phenomenal.[6] Her interest in
other literatures led her to translate also from French and Spanish
while she was responsible for the presentation in Italian of poetry from

---

6 The following are some of Guidacci's most important translations:

John Donne, *Sermoni* (Florence, Libreria Editrice Fiorentina, 1946).
Max Beerbohm, *L'ipocrita beato* (Florence, Vallecchi, 1946).
Emily Dickinson, *Poesie* (Florence, Libreria Editrice Fiorentina, 1950).
Emmanuel Monnier, *L'avventura cristiana* (Florence, Libreria Editrice Fiorentina, 1950).
George Gissing, *Sulla riva dello Ionio* (Bologna, Cappelli, 1957, 1962).
Tu Fu, *Desiderio di pace* (Milan, Scheiwiller, 1957).
Ezra Pound, *Patria mia* (Florence, Centro Internazionale del Libro, 1958).
Antichi racconti cinesi (Bologna, Cappelli, 1959).
Jorge Guillén, *Federico in persona, Carteggio* (Milan, Scheiwiller, 1960).
Henry James, *Roderick Hudson* (Bologna, Cappelli, 1960).
Joseph Conrad, *Destino* (Milan, Bompiani, 1962).
Racconti popolari irlandesi (Bologna, Cappelli, 1961).
Emily Dickinson, *Poesie e lettere* (Florence, Sansoni, 1961).
Mark Twain, *Vita sul Mississippi* (Rome, Editoriale Opere Nuove, 1962).
Poeti estoni (Rome, Abete, 1973).
Joannes Paulus II, *Pietra di luce* (Vatican City, Libreria Editrice Vaticana, 1979).
Pádraig Daly, *Dall'orlo marino del mondo* (Vatican City, Libreria Editrice Vaticana, 1981).
Elizabeth Bishop, *L'arte di perdere* (Milan, Rusconi, 1982).

cultures far removed from their Italian counterpart such as the Polish, Estonian and Chinese ones. Her access to these works was usually facilitated by existing English translations but her desire to make these works known to the Italian reading public was always dictated by an affinity of spirit she felt with these writers. In many of her translated works we find echoes of Guidacci's key images in poetry – wind and sand, grass and rain, stones and sea, light and darkness, land and sky, rivers and water: they are all natural elements of a physical life that is acutely conscious of death and which Guidacci considers to be an essential element of this transient life on earth. One of the distinguishing features of her poetry is the faith she places in a certain future. Even in *Neurosuite*, which explores the dramatic reality of the mentally disturbed, such conviction and faith can be found in the final poem, 'Ostrica perlifera' (Pearl oyster), of the collection. A striking empathy for the problems of her fellow creatures makes Guidacci proclaim:

Dio mi ha chiamata ad arricchire il mondo
decretandone il semplice strumento:
basta un opaco granello di sabbia
e intorno il mio dolore iridescente!   (*Neurosuite*, p.97)

(God has called me to enrich the world/ by naming the simple instrument:/ only a grain of sand/ and around it my deriding sorrow.)

The influence that her research as a translator had on her work as a poet is evident yet again in the poems published in 1977 entitled *Il vuoto e le forme* (Void and form). In this collection there is a poem that she wrote in English and which she presented to the families of two young mountain-climbers killed in the Bolivian Andes in 1973. That awareness of the sorrows and blows which life may bring (such as isolation, mental illness, the sense of loneliness and void, the loss of loved ones) was something Guidacci shared having experienced many of those events in her personal life. For many this could have been a devasting and inexplicable loss but it was one that curiously urged Guidacci to offer some form of possible consolation to the bereaved. Such awareness made her express her own faith in the future through this gesture of solidarity with a family shattered by sudden and violent death. There is a strong sense of the Christian hope in an after-life in the final line of this poem:

The mountain
was their Tabor, we trust, as well as their Calvary:
for there they saw the face of the Lord.

(*Il vuoto e le forme*, p.59)

In the same way that Guidacci selected texts for translation that reflected her own poetic sensitivity, so too the themes chosen for expression in her poetry are ones that highlight her concern for fellow-men in their passage through life, though the Christian certainty often seems fragile in her early work.

In *Morte del ricco* she focuses on self-induced destruction by man himself. In the Biblical story of Lazarus and the rich man there is a sign of contradiction, a key to justice. The drama of the rich man is the drama of the one who has broken a sacred bond: damnation and eternal punishment are the forms of judgment which correspond to that betrayal expressed on earth through the blindness of the flesh, the greedy longing for pleasure and possessions that silences fraternal love and which are shown to be the real root of human ruination though the example is a lesson to all. Man's injustices to man are transferred from the individual to a universal level. In *Morte del ricco*, as elsewhere, Guidacci's poetry is the expression of this psychological tension that is voiced in a very direct manner. The choral parenthesis in the structure of this poem marks a new feature in Guidacci's poetry while also reiterating the themes of life and death, always essential subjects in her poetry.

On one occasion when discussing her poetry Guidacci said that it was similar to the singing of birds which have a voice that can be harmonious but also discordant. Her poetry amidst the neo-hermeticism and the neo-symbolism of the 1960s tended to strike an isolated chord leaving her bewildered and also prone to silence. While still convinced of her message she realised that her audience was unreceptive. The frustration finally erupted in a series of poems which appeared in the early 1970s: *Neurosuite* and *Un cammino incerto* (An uncertain path) in 1970 and *Terra senza orologi* (Land without clocks) in 1973. A sense of disillusionment permeated these poems and she highlights the absurdity which she sees in the world around her, though that in turn concentrates her vision on the social reality of her own existence and that of many others. While she always had a social conscience, her disillusionment sharpened her appreciation of contemporary social problems though also casting doubts on the divine rationale of these phenomena. That reality now assumed a greater role in her poetry and she became increasingly aware of the need to overcome the tensions between the physical and the metaphysical, and not just through a religious vision of faith but through an appreciation of a rationale to be found in the immediate situation.

Her statements on the confusion and problems of modern man have a universal echo but also certain distinctive features which point to the value of a poetry which tries to be of benefit to all. It is with this awareness that she interprets the dramatic condition of men seen in an existential and historical dimension. Any wavering of faith obliges her to seek a human explanation of reality. The result is some fine poetry, a new equilibrium which, while not denying her earlier themes, is now anchored in history and not exclusively confined to the metaphysical.

In *Un cammino incerto*, the forms of expression are barer and more discreet than in earlier works. The title itself is quite explicit. Doubt had increased her sense of drama and this in turn is evident in expressions of anguish that reflect the poet's own uncertainty at that time:

Sopra quanti miracoli
getta luce
quello che non avviene!'[7]

(Over how many miracles/ is light cast/ by that which does not happen!)

Such lines also recall in many ways the *male di vivere* expressed by Montale in *Ossi di Seppia* (Cuttlefish bones) but in Guidacci the emphasis changes. When she says 'Che posso fare se non posso sperare da sola?' (what can I do if I am unable to hope on my own? *Un cammino incerto*, p.38) she makes way for a final hope of forgiveness:

L'ultimo riposo sarà
Come un grande perdono, coltre d'umida nebbia, per tutti'.
(*Un cammino incerto*, p.40)

(The final rest will be/ Like a great pardon not denied anyone.)

It was in this climate of tension that the seeds of *Neurosuite* (published later in 1970) were sown. *Un cammino incerto* had already undermined the strength of faith reflected in her earlier works, uncertainty being the first step towards fear and terror. *Neurosuite* marks the lowest point in that descent though its closing verses also reveal a glimmer of light. Set against the grim background of a neurological clinic, these poems are dedicated 'a quanti conobbero le acque oscure agli scampati ai sommersi' (*Neurosuite*, p.7), to those who experienced the dark waters, the survivors and the victims.

The work is doubly symbolic because, although it refers in individual poems to particular situations, there is an overall image of a milling universe divided between the squalor of darkness and the desperate longing for light. Certainty has, once again, given way to doubt.

7 The quotation is taken from the poem *Miracoli* later published in *Incontro con Margherita Guidacci*, Scarperia (Fi) (Cassa rurale ed artigiana del Mugello, 1986), p.19.

And yet at the end of this painful voyage among those who are mentally alienated Guidacci reiterates the rights of all to the dignity and freedom best expressed by the poet. In 'Ostrica perlifera' the poetic voice, first instinctively, then consciously, is seen as a haven of salvation, an alternative to death. The act of poetry, which is often the voice of sorrow is now the only freedom that may be possible for man.

By the mid 1970s Guidacci's outlook was being shaped not only by her earlier unquestioning faith but also by reflections on the world around her, leading to a greater confidence in man's ability to mould events, for better or for worse. Faith is no longer a trusting abandonment to one's Maker, but the expression of the will to live and act knowing that what we do will be judged in the end.

The presence of two contrasting faiths, one in the human, the other in a transcendental sphere, marked a new stage in the growth of Guidacci as a poet and are highlighted in *Il vuoto e le forme* published in 1977. In the opening lines of this collection she states:

Il vuoto si difende.
Non vuole che una forma lo torturi.   (*Il vuoto e le forme*, p.13)

(The void defends itself./ No form must torment it)

while elsewhere she says:

Abbi pazienza, abbi pazienza!
Chi ha fermato la barca non può fermare l'acqua.
L'acqua prosegue il suo cammino, potente, irresistibile.
L'acqua chiede altre barche, e noi gliele daremo.
                    (*Il vuoto e le forme*, p.24)

(Be patient, be patient!/ Those who have blocked the boat cannot stop the water./ The water follows its course, strong, irresistible./ The water asks for other boats and we will supply them.)

Art makes man the author of his own release with structure and form as liberating agents. In *Il vuoto e le forme* Guidacci appears to have passed from despair to hope and in the process she rekindled most of her youthful optimism which had provided her with the confidence and self assuredness to face the future. She became more convinced of the merits of poetry and of the value of the poet. Another poem in this collection contains lines addressed by her to the poet Pablo Neruda after his death where she wrote:

Sfolgorante, tremenda
è la tua vita, Pablo.
E sopra il rogo che hanno preparato
ai tuoi versi, rifulge
l'inconsunta natura di fenice.   (*Il vuoto e le forme*, p.23)

(Radiant and wonderful/ is your life, Pablo./ While the unsullied nature of the phoenix/ shines over the bonfire/ they prepared for your poetry.)

Here Guidacci's poetry is a tribute to a search for truth where the light of what is absolute increases our consciousness of what is ephemeral.

The best example of that changed mood is to be found in the work *Inno alla gioia* (Hymn to joy) published in 1983. Her style had become more succinct with the passing years as she became more convinced that simplicity and clarity were essential for communication with a wider readership. In the notes that accompany these poems Guidacci tells us that she was obliged to select this title despite the formidable analogy between it and the Schiller-Beethoven combination because it was the only relevant title for her work. If such a title had not existed, she said, she would have been obliged to invent it (*Inno alla gioia*, p.83). The whole impetus of this work can be found in the symbolic quotation from the Spanish poet Jorge Guillén that is used by Guidacci to introduce these poems.[8] She calls the quotation an *epigrafe* and presents it in Italian translation:

Abito l'amore. Mi avvolge
Solare, il vento profondo
Di una felicità respirabile.   (*Inno alla gioia*, p.83)

(I live with love. The deep wind/ and sun surround me/ with palpable happiness.)

It is the exact opposite of the dark and sorrowful areas of human experience found in *Neurosuite* and *Un cammino incerto*. This happiness is almost a delirium, the joy of loving and being loved makes her feel that she owns the earth: 'Perché ti amo possiedo la terra' (*Inno alla gioia*, p.37). The anguish of absence and torment are overcome in a hymn to light and joy. The reader of *Neurosuite* would now find it hard to remember the long dark cavern which gave birth to ecstasy – like an underground river that breaks free as it enters the sea and which is even more beautiful because of the mystery that earlier hid it from view.

8 The original Spanish is:
   Habito el amor.
           Me envuelve,
   Solar, el viento profundo
   De una dicha respirable.   (*Inno alla gioia*, p.13)

Il nostro amore fu un fiume carsico [. . .]
Ed ora, ecco, risorge e corre libero alla foce
sotto un cielo stupito della sua ricomparsa. (*Inno alla gioia*, p.26)

(Our love was like a river in Carso [. . .]/ Now, here it re-appears, runs freely
to the river mouth/ beneath a sky astounded by its re-appearance.)

Inno alla gioia opens with lines dedicated to the loved one but they
seem to go beyond the opening sequence and reach the state of love
which she considers to be the secret of happiness and of joy. In an
accompanying note (*Inno alla gioia*, p.83) Guidacci tells us that these
verses were part of one of her earliest poems and were not written for
anyone in particular but simply for her love of love and under the influ-
ence of the English metaphysical poets whom she had then just dis-
covered. Almost forty years later she came across these lines and placed
them at the beginning of this book because it seemed to her that it was
their natural resting place. To cross time and space is the real secret
of joy with love changing passions, feelings, images and thoughts into
light. The loved one is both the object and the place of love, similar
to a gate of love that opens out to all the world:

Il mio amore che nasce
in te, non finisce
in te. Sei la porta d'amore
attraverso cui passo
incontro all'universo, tendendo a tutto le braccia.

                              (*Inno alla gioia*, p.42)

(My love which is born/ of you, does not stop/ at you. You are the gateway of
love/ through which I step/ to meet the world, reaching out my arms to every-
one.)

The feeling that love will not die but will be eternal returns here with
renewed vigour:

Poiché tu sei eterno ed io sono
eterna [. . .]
sarà eterna la nostra gioia.   (*Inno alla gioia*, p.30)

(Because you are eternal and I am eternal [. . .]/ our joy will be eternal.)

Like an invisible presence in the path of life this love will bring joy to
future generations. The language used here by Guidacci is simple and
clear and is the most appropriate form for poetry which now coun-
teracts the trials of existence with the joy of living: life is rooted in the
light of what lies beyond.

1989 saw the publication of *Il buio e lo splendore*, Guidacci's last collection of poems published some months before a stroke which left her practically immobile until her death in 1992. As in previous works, Guidacci furrowed her own path independently of current trends. She returns once more to the dramatic verbal form in the monologues of the Sibyls that open this work. She attempts to divine the enigma of the Sibyl and initiates an intimate conversation with celestial bodies such as Rigel and Betelgeuse in which these silent companions of man's life lose some of their coldness and seem to pay attention to the fragile creatures who inhabit this world. The ensuing joy of sharing one's innermost secrets with the silent inhabitants of the sky dominates these pages. Guidacci's searching through the firmament is a metaphorical transposition of her endless search for the meaning of human existence. It is through the intervention of poetry that darkness has now given way to brightness.

Margherita Guidacci was working on further poems when illness curtailed her creative career though she had already chosen the apt title, *Gli anelli del tempo* (The rings of time) for them. On her death they were bequeathed to a friend in Florence and were published in 1993.[9] In this final chapter of her earthly life, like Montale in *Ossi di Seppia*,[10] Guidacci compared herself to the agave plants which flower once every one hundred years and then die:

> la breve festa nuziale
> al sole e al vento, celebrata da sciami
> d'api d'oro – poi, subito, la morte.   (*Anelli del tempo*, n.10)

(the short nuptial banquet/ in the sun and in the wind, celebrated by swarms/ of golden bees – then, suddenly death appears.)

Like humans, plants too have a limited life span and disappear from the terrestial horizon. In this and other poems we are aware of Guidacci's search for the essential and her tireless quest for truth. Despite her fears and hesitations the desire to prepare for that encounter with the One who closes the final ring of time is now more insistent as He will in turn open out that same ring to encompass infinite brightness. That she was on the verge of life was clear to Guidacci. While choosing the *stella cadente* or falling star as an emblem of our fleeting human existence, she justified its transience by that 'bright flash' which illuminates the dark sky:

9 *Anelli del tempo* (Florence, Città di Vita, 1993). The book is not paginated and the poems are indicated by number.
10 See *Scirocco* in Eugenio Montale, *Tutte le poesie* (Milan, Mondadori, 1977), p.97: 'ora son io/l'agave che s'abbarbica al crepaccio/dello scoglio . . . '

Alcuni desideri si adempiranno,
altri saranno respinti. Ma io
sarò passata splendendo
per un attimo. Anche se nessuno
mi avesse guardata
risulterebbe ugualmente giustificato –
per quel lucente attimo – il mio esistere.   (*Anelli del tempo*, n.48)

(Some wishes will be fulfilled,/ some will be rejected. But I shall have passed by/ resplendent for a moment. And even if no one/ watched me, my existence/ – for that dazzling moment – / shall still be justified.)

Earlier in her career Guidacci said that: 'la poesia non ha pace finché non ha trovato l'espressione unica e insostituibile per dire quello che aveva da dire'[11] (poetry will not rest until it finds that single inimitable expression that will let it say what it has to say). Throughout her poetic career Guidacci strove to achieve this objective and her poetry was an attempt to cast light where previously darkness had been found and we can sense a new confidence in her final work which was the result of a lifetime of probing and questing. In 1988 Guidacci published a series of short poems in Italian based on the Japanese *haiku* format which she had first become acquainted with in English translation.[12]

This unique poetic form provided her with a more precise vehicle to articulate her philosophy of life. In the last of her Italian *haiku*-type poems composed shortly before her stroke, she found apt expression for her life-long message:

Il chiaro giorno
    corre incontro alla notte,
        la notte all'alba.   (*Una breve misura*, p.77)

(The clearest daytime/ rushes on to meet the night/ night leads on to dawn.)

It would be hard to find a more suitable closure.

11 'La poesia non ha pace' in *Uomini e libri*, Milan, 16 n.79, giugno–luglio 1980, p.45.
12 *Una breve misura* (Chieti, Vecchio Faggio, 1988) contains Guidacci's haiku-type poems.

Furono ultime a staccarsi le voci

Furono ultime a staccarsi le voci. Non le voci tremende
Della guerra a degli uragani,
E nemmeno voci umane ed amate,
Ma mormorii d'erbe e d'acque, risa di vento, frusciare
Di fronde tra cui scoiattoli invisibili giocavano,
Ronzìo felice d'insetti attraverso molte estati
Fino a quell'insetto che più insistente ronzava
Nella stanza dove noi non volevamo morire.
E tutto si confuse in una nota, in un fermo
E sommesso tumulto, come quello del sangue
Quando era vivo il nostro sangue. Ma sapevamo ormai
Che a tutto ciò era impossibile rispondere.
E quando l'Angelo ci chiese: 'Volete ancora ricordare?'
Noi stessi l'implorammo: 'Lascia che venga il silenzio!'

Giorno dei Santi

Giorno dei Santi e il cielo di Novembre
Riflesso nell'asfalto delle vie
Inondate di pioggia, due grigiori
Paralleli ad opprimere lo sguardo
Dovunque cerchi fuga. La città
Sembra di piombo e cenere, ed il crudo
Lampo dei fari rende più spettrali
I visi dei passanti. Lente scorrono
Le ore in questo scroscio
D'acqua, tra schizzi brevi
Di fango e il volteggiare
Di foglie marce dai giardini. È arduo
Oggi pensare al Paradiso; tutto
Ci riconduce e prostra sulla terra.
Occorre troppa fede a superare
L'alta barriera di tristezza. Facile
Sarà invece domani, nella scia
D'una stagione di disfacimento,
Ricordare la fine d'ogni carne.

The last to move away were the voices

The last to move away were the voices. Not the terrible voices
Of war and hurricanes,
Nor human and beloved voices,
But the babbling of grass and water, the laughter of wind,
Leaves rustling where invisible squirrels used to play,
The joyful buzz of insects over many summers
And even that insect that buzzed the more insistently
In the room where we did not wish to die.
And everything confused in a single note, in a firm
and subdued contrast, like that of blood
When our blood was yet alive. But we already knew
It was impossible to respond to all of that,
And when the Angel asked us: 'Do you still want to remember?'
We ourselves implored him: 'Let silence come!'.

All Saints Day

All Saints Day and the November sky
Reflected on the surface of the roads
Inundated by rain, two parallel
Greynesses that oppress one's gaze
Wherever it seeks flight. The city
Seems of lead and ash, and the hard
Glare of headlights makes more ghostly
The faces of passers-by. Slowly the hours
Move by under this downpour
Of water, between short splashes
Of mud and the tossing about
Of rotten garden leaves. It is difficult
Today to think of Paradise; everything
Brings us to, prostrates us on the ground.
Too much faith is needed to overcome
The high barrier wall of sadness. Instead
Tomorrow it will be easy, in the path
Of a season of decay,
To remember the ending of all flesh.

La morte

Questo lavoro è terminato. Nella notte eterna
Arderà il ricco con le sue memorie
Mentre Lazzaro riposa nel seno d'Abramo.
Altro lavoro mi attende. La morte non ha sosta.
Più operosa del cielo e dell'inferno
Tutto raccolgo quanto il Giudizio poi separa.
Prima che il fiume di fuoco
Dividesse Epulone da Lazzaro
Il mio fiume più vasto
Entrambi li travolse.
Ora riprendo il mio corso, tutto toccando come il vento,
Seguendo come lui leggi non fatte da uomini.
Mi precede il terrore, mi circonda la tenebra.
Al mio passaggio le creature
In silenzio si coprono il volto
Quasi le sfiori il lembo della veste
Di Dio, agitata dall'uragano.

Il tuo linguaggio è indecifrabile

Il tuo linguaggio è indecifrabile
Per noi, sia che ti udiamo
Parlarlo senza posa
O ti vediamo con dita abbaglianti
Scriverlo sulla rena.
Ed anche la risposta è indecifrabile
Che ti rendiamo. Qual parte di noi
Era conchiglia od alga, uno sfuggente
E lucente riverbero, e conobbe
Te meglio dell'umano mondo e ora
Si lascia trasportare nelle anse
Della tua voce, o riposa contenta
In mezzo ai tuoi geroglifici?

Madame X

Io non sono il mio corpo.
Mi è straniero, nemico.

Death

This work has ended. The rich man
Will burn with his memories in the eternal night
While Lazarus rests against Abraham's breast.
I have other work to do. Death has no respite.
Busier than heaven or hell
I collect all that the Judgment then divides.
Before the river of fire
Separated the rich man from Lazarus
My greater river
Had engulfed them both.
Now I continue my path, like the wind I touch all,
Like it I follow laws not made by men.
Terror precedes me, darkness surrounds me.
As I pass by all creatures
Silently cover their face
In case the hem of the Lord's garment,
Buffeted by the hurricane, might touch them.

For us your language is indecipherable

For us your language is indecipherable
Whether we hear you
Use it without airs
Or see you write it
With dazzling fingers on the sand.
And our reply for you
Is indecipherable too. Which part of us
Was shell or seaweed, a fleeting
Shining reflection, and it knew
You better than the human world
And now is carried in the loops
Of your voice, does it rest contented
There among your hieroglyphics?

Madame X

I am not my body.
To me it is alien, an enemy.

Ancora peggio è l'anima,
e neppure con essa m'identifico.

Osservo di lontano
le rozze acrobazie di questa coppia,
con distacco, ironia –
con disgusto talvolta.

E intanto penso che la loro assenza
sarebbe più guadagno che dolore:
questa e altre cose . . . Ma mentre le penso,
io chi sono, e dove?

La madre pazza

Noi con gli stracci smessi del passato
ci costruiamo un presente.
Come una bambola piena di segatura
lo stringiamo al petto,
teneramente lo culliamo.
Cosí la madre pazza, mia vicina,
parla con un fanciullo
da molto tempo sparito in mezzo ai fiori,
e intanto volta indignata le spalle
all'uomo grigio, flaccido ed affranto
che quel fanciullo è diventato
e che la supplica invano
di riconoscerlo.

Nero con movimento

Ombre convulse intorno ad una fiamma,
neri brandelli di nubi strappate,
erba dolente, frustata dal vento,
e l'orrore
di uccelli prigionieri in una rete
che premono col petto impazzito
sbattendo l'ali tra le maglie
in un volo sempre abortito, un impeto

My soul is worse,
Nor can I identify with it.

From a distance I note
The uncouth acrobatics of this couple,
With detachment, irony –
Sometimes with revulsion.

And meanwhile I think their absence
Would bring more gain than grief:
This and other things . . . But while I think of them,
Who am I, and where am I?

The insane mother

With the cast-off rags of the past
we build a time in the present.
Like a sawdust-filled doll
we clasp it to our breast,
tenderly we cradle it.
And so my neighbour, an insane mother,
speaks to a boy
long since vanished among the flowers,
meanwhile, indignant, she turns her shoulders
on the grey, flabby, prostrate man
that boy has now become
and who, in vain, begs her
for recognition.

Black with movement

Nervous shadows round a flame,
black strips of torn clouds,
weeping grass, whipped by the wind,
and the horror
of birds imprisoned in a trap
against which, crazed with grief, they press their breast
beating their wings between the meshes
in a flight that always fails, an assault

senza tregua nè foce (il cacciatore
già da un cespuglio vicino li spia
con allegria feroce).

Versi per un prigioniero

Abbi pazienza, abbi pazienza!
Chi ha fermato la barca non può fermare l'acqua.
L'acqua prosegue il suo cammino, potente, irresistibile.
L'acqua chiede altre barche, e noi gliele daremo.

Abbi pazienza, abbi pazienza!
Chi ferma l'uomo alla frontiera non può fermare gli uccelli.
La verità ha grandi ali, ed oltre tutte le barriere
ne giunge il battito.

Abbi pazienza, abbi pazienza!
Chi t'incatena non incatena la tua anima.
La libertà risplende anche sul volto della morte
a chi lottò per una terra piú umana.

Questa pausa

Dopo l'ebbrezza, dopo la tempesta
questa pausa.
                    Tu pensami
come un gabbiano ad ali tese sull'aria,
pronto a tuffarsi, ma ancora
prodigiosamente immobile
tra cielo e mare, proclamando
di entrambi, nel suo breve corpo,
il luminoso equilibrio.

Il girasole

A quest'ora si desta il girasole
nel tuo giardino e volge il capo ad oriente

without relief or outlet (from a nearby
hedge the hunter has already spied them out
with fierce delight).

Verses for a prisoner

Be patient, be patient!
Those who have halted the boat cannot halt the water.
The water follows its course, powerful, irrestible.
The water looks for other boats, and we will supply them.

Be patient, be patient!
Those who halt the man at the border cannot halt the birds.
Truth has huge wings, and its wingbeat
vibrates beyond every barrier.

Be patient, be patient!
Those who chain you down cannot chain your soul.
Freedom shines out even on the face of death
for those who have battled for a more humane world.

This pause

After the rapture, after the storm,
this pause.
                    Think of me
as a seagull with wings outstretched on air,
ready to plunge, yet
marvellously still,
set between sea and sky, emphasising
for both, in its short-lived body,
their brilliant harmony.

The sunflower

At this hour the sunflower wakes
in your garden and turns its eyes to the east

per seguire poi il sole nel suo giro
fino al tramonto, fedelmente.

Anch'io mi desto e subito rivolgo
a te il pensiero. L'amore è il mio astro,
di cui segna le ore, tutto il giorno,
la mia segreta meridiana.

Meteore d'inverno

Stelle fugaci, delfini del cielo,
con voi viaggia la mia anima,
un guizzo luminoso nelle onde
turchine della notte,

verso i lontani amici desiderati
che forse scorgono il segno, e pensando
con la mia stessa nostalgia
a dolci ore passate insieme

pregano ci sia dato un nuovo incontro,
ed è già esaudimento la preghiera:
il simultaneo affetto, nella scia della stella,
ci stringe in un abbraccio immateriale.

Giorno delfico

Dopo la notte stellata, l'attesa
piena di gioia (ho rifiutato
il sonno, l'insidia dei sogni,
perché il filo perfetto della memoria
non s'impigliasse nei loro labirinti)
ecco, dai ripercorsi anni d'amore
a questa tesa anima, che a te
si volge illimpidita dal silenzio,
come sorge splendente
il nostro giorno delfico!

to follow the sun faithfully in its journey
as far as sunset.

I wake up too and straight away I turn
my thoughts to you. Love is my star
whose hours are marked, all day,
by that secret sundial.

Winter meteors

Falling stars, dolphins of the sky,
my soul travels along with you,
a luminous flicker in the cobalt
waves of the night,

towards the distant, beloved friends
who see its track, perhaps, and think
with the same nostalgia
of lovely hours spent together.

They pray that we might meet once more,
and the prayer is heard already:
the love we feel, in the trail of the stars
binds us in an incorporeal embrace.

Delphic day

After the starry night, the waiting
full of joy (I have rejected
sleep, the snare of dreams,
so that the perfect thread of memory
would not be lost in their labyrinths)
here, from the repeated years of love
to this tense soul which confused
by silence turns to you,
how splendid breaks
our delphic day!

Anelli del tempo

Degli anelli del tempo, che si aggiungono
sempre nuovi, furono alcuni così stretti
che ne ricordo solo l'orrore di soffocare.
In altri, larghi e informi, vagai smarrita
senza un sostegno a cui aggrapparmi. I più,
pallidamente indifferenti, si ammucchiavano
gli uni sugli altri, subito saldandosi
senza nemmeno un segno di sutura.
Solo a pochi e per poco è tollerabile
riandare. Ma almeno questo, l'ultimo,
di cui oggi si chiude il cerchio, resta perfetto
nel mio cuore: cornice d'oro intorno
a uno specchio di gioia. Chiedo solo
di serbar quest'immagine. E che a te
uno stesso fulgore la riveli
e la circondi, allo scader dell'ora,
nel tuo specchio gemello.

A un meraviglioso discepolo

Io; sprofondata nel silenzio, attendo
ora le tue parole che, levandosi in volo
come stormo d'uccelli dal lontano orizzonte,
vengono a rincuorarmi. Mentre ascolto
viaggiano di nuovo le Galassie
nel mio universo, la terra si copre
di fiori e d'erbe, i fiumi
accolgono i colori dell'aurora
e li recano al mare, nelle loro
acque amorose. S'empie di speranza
ogni vuoto. Così potenti aleggiano
e dolci, su di me, le tue parole
che più non sento pena
se le mie sono morte.

Rings of time

Of the rings of time, always new ones
adding themselves on, there were some so tight
that I remember only the horror of suffocation.
In others, shapeless, wide, I wandered lost
with nothing to catch hold of. Most of them,
pale and indifferent, piled themselves
one on top of the other, instantly blending
without even a sign of stitching.
Only to a few and only for a while is it tolerable
to think back. But this one, at least, the last,
whose circle will close today, stays perfect
in my heart: a frame of gold around
a mirror of joy. I ask only
to preserve this image. And that for you
the same radiance may reveal
and circle it, at the close of day,
in your identical mirror.

To a wonderful disciple

Absorbed in silence, I wait now
for your words which, lifting up in flight
like a flock of birds from the far horizon,
come to cheer me up. As I listen
the Galaxies travel again
through my universe, the earth covers itself
with grass and flowers, the rivers
welcome the colours of the dawn
and bring them to the sea in their
loving waters. Every void fills up
with hope. And so, sweet and powerful
your words blow gently over me
who now feels no more pain
if my words have died.

Anniversario con agavi

Questo giorno, che fu d'amore e lacerazione
tanti anni fa, ci vede ora camminare
insieme su sabbie e rocce, la tua mano
aiutandomi nei passi difficili
e il tuo sguardo orientando il mio, verso l'alta
barriera d'agavi e di canne,
limite di nord-est al litorale.
'Ecco – mi dici – sono queste', e indichi
le cinque agavi ormai pronte,
dopo la quasi centenaria attesa,
all'incredibile fioritura. Racchiuso
nel suo grosso uovo bruno, ogni fiore-fenice
si prepara ad erompere in un volo
estatico: la breve festa nuziale
al sole e al vento, celebrata da sciami
d'api d'oro – poi, subito, la morte.
Osserviamo le agavi protendersi
al loro compimento, nello slancio
degli steli, indomabile, e la resa
delle foglie già esauste, che immolarono
ogni linfa all'unico fine e si ripiegano
come vele ammainate. Qualcosa in noi
profondamente, quasi perdutamente,
risponde a quello slancio, a quella resa.
Io sento un nodo alla gola e rimango
in silenzio. Tu dici piano: 'Anche le piante
hanno il loro destino'.

Sull'orlo della visione

Notte – albero, nido – notte da cui mi è tanto
faticoso staccarmi, presa tra un'ala bruna
ed un grande barbaglio, saprò muovermi
sotto un cielo di luce, tra le forme
che, per me ignote, avanzano? O vorrò
chiudere gli occhi, rifugiarmi ancora
in te?

Anniversary with agave plants

This day, full of love and torment
many years ago, now sees us walk
together over sand and rocks, your hand
helping me across the trying parts
and your gaze guiding mine towards the
high barrier of agave plants and reeds,
on the north-east confines of the coast.
'Here they are' you say, and point out
the five agave plants now ready,
after a one hundred year wait almost,
for that amazing flowering. Closed
in its large brown ovum, each phoenix-like flower
prepares to burst into an ecstatic
flight: the short nuptial banquet
in the sun and in the wind, celebrated by swarms
of golden bees – then, suddenly death appears.
We see the agave plants lean forward
towards their completion, the explosion
of the stalks, unyielding, and the surrender
of the leaves already spent, which sacrificed
every sap – for just one purpose then fold themselves
like lowered sails. Something inside us,
deeply, almost hopelessly,
answers that explosion, that surrender.
I feel a knot in my throat and stay
silent. Softly you say: 'Plants too
have their destiny'.

On the edge of vision

Night – tree, nest – night that I leave behind
with great difficulty, caught between a brown wing
and great dazzlement, will I know how to move
beneath a sky of light, among these forms
unknown to me, advancing? Or will I want
to close my eyes, seek refuge once again
in you?

Biagia Marniti

BIAGIA MARNITI has played an active role in many areas of Italian culture over the last fifty years. A librarian by profession she also worked as editor, translator, literary critic, prose writer and poet and has published several poetry collections since the early Fifties.[1] Born in 1921 in the town of Ruvo in Apulia some years later her parents moved to Bari and then to Rome which became her adopted city and where she has lived, more or less intermittently, since the years of her adolescence. Nevertheless, her links with the area and culture of Apulia are a vital lifeline and her pseudonym Marniti was specially chosen to express her attachment to her place of birth. Although the family name was Masulli she decided to select the pseudonym Marniti for a number of reasons:

Come molti sanno *Marniti*, anche se non appartiene all'onomastico locale, è il mio pseudonimo scelto consapevolmente. Volli abbinare nell'inventarlo qualche elemento del mio cognome Masulli, con un richiamo alla mia terra d'origine. Così conservai la sillaba iniziale *Ma*, pensando alla Puglia, in alcune zone arida, spesso argillosa e calcarea, l'immagine della *marna* mi portò a Marniti, la cui liquida vibrante ben si accompagna alla labiale e alla palatale di Biagia, nome di battesimo che mi piacque conservare perché insolito in una donna.[2]

(As many know, Marniti, even if it does not figure among local surnames, it the pseudonym which I deliberately chose for myself. In creating it I wanted to combine something from my family surname, Masulli, with some aspect

1 Biagia Marniti's main poetry collections are:
  Nero amore rosso amore (Milan, Fiumara, 1951).
  Città, creatura viva (Caltanissetta, Sciascia, 1956).
  Più forte è la vita (Milan, Mondadori, 1957).
  Giorni del mondo (Caltanissetta, Sciascia, 1967).
  Il cerchio e la parola (Caltanissetta, Sciascia, 1979).
  La ballata del mare e altre poesie (Riccia-Rome, Associazione Turistica 'Pro Riccia', 1984).
  Il gomitolo di cera (Caltanissetta, Sciascia, 1990).
  Piccola sfera (Bari, La Vallisa, 1992).
  Racconto d'amore (Milan, Greco e Greco, 1994).

2 *Biagia Marniti racconta se stessa* in *Idea*, a.46, n.8–9, agosto–settembre 1990, p.41.

of the place I came from. Therefore I retained the initial syllable *Ma* when remembering Apulia which is arid in some places and often calcareous and clayish, while the image of the *marna* [marl stone] led me to the formation of *Marniti* whose vibrant liquid consonants go well with the labial and palatal sound of Biagia, the baptismal name which I was anxious to retain because it is seldom given to a woman.)

Marniti's first collections of poetry were *Nero amore rosso amore* (Black love red love, 1951) and *Città, creatura viva* (City, live creature, 1956): the first a collection of poems written between 1941 and 1949 while the second contains poems composed between 1950 and 1956. In 1957 Mondadori published *Più forte è la vita* (*Life is stronger*), in its renowned poetry series 'Lo Specchio' with an introduction by the distinguished poet Giuseppe Ungaretti.

Marniti was awarded a degree in archaeology from the University of Rome and then followed a postgraduate course in Italian literature given by Giuseppe Ungaretti. This was a turning point in her career as it gave her the opportunity to show him some of her poems previously published in little known journals. Struck by the directness of her work and by her poetic and linguistic skills Ungaretti encouraged her to continue writing poetry. In his introduction to *Più forte è la vita* he mentions the features that struck him most in these poems:

Quella spontaneità [. . .] quel loro rispondere a necessità di canto che, nella poesia, non saprei per quale aberrazione, oggi si considera spesso non indispensabile qualità, ma quasi difetto.[3]

(That spontaneity [. . .] their response to lyrical necessity which, in poetry, for what aberration I cannot say, is often considered not an indispensable quality, but almost a defect.)

Ungaretti also drew attention to the main theme of *Più forte è la vita* which is love. It describes the enthusiasm of incipient love that is soon followed by disappointment and the death of an emotion that has no hope of reciprocity. It is a love which makes the reader fully aware of the highs and lows of its experience. What is striking is the dignified manner in which Marniti presents the opposing sentiments of hope and despair together with the absolute control of her own feelings that are indicative of her inner strength, her ability to start all over again which is one of the principal features of her later poetry. What is particularly relevant in this context is the real meaning of the title *Più forte è la vita*. The title indicates that life is stronger than love and that life always remains at a level that is above and superior to love.

3   G. Ungaretti, Preface to B. Marniti, *Più forte è la vita*, *op.cit.*, p.9.

For the critic Arnaldo Bocelli Marniti's poetry draws its strength from her experience as a woman and her contact with the world around her, the memory of Apulia, the exhilaration of love but also the despair which causes the poet to close in on herself and on occasion to adopt an ambiguous and hostile attitude towards that world which yet constantly draws her towards it.[4]

The opening poem of *Più forte è la vita* marks Marniti's attachment to her native Apulia and her solidarity with its inhabitants:

Odore di terra nera,
arsa da secoli da morti e da vanghe
ti sento ancora nell'aria di montagna [. . .]
Sole che stende immoti i campi
i fichi bianchi
il mare ondoso a riva
l'affanno del contadino felice
nelle rughe . . .   (*Più forte è la vita*, p.13)

(The smell of black soil,/ scorched for centuries by the dead and spades/ I still can feel you in the mountain air [. . .]/ The sun casting stillness over the fields/ the white fig trees/ the sea waves by the shore/ tiring the labourer happy/ even in his wrinkled skin . . .)

For Marniti these childhood memories of Apulia are an endless store of memory, 'una valigia senza fondo',[5] that often highlight the draw between memory, affection and reality:

Terra di Puglia
che nel mio sangue bruci la cenere
la disperazione degli avi,
il cuore ti chiama amore sconosciuto [. . .]
Forse un giorno tornerò alla mia collina
tra ulivi e mandorli cinerini nel sole d'estate,
ai braccianti agli artigiani
fra l'odore del basilico e garofani rossi.
Per il mondo la vita ora mi conduce.   (*Più forte è la vita*, p.117)

---

4   A. Bocelli, *Letteratura del Novecento*, serie seconda (Caltanissetta-Rome, Sciascia, 1980), pp.287–288: 'Il contenuto della sua poesia non è desunto dalla letteratura, ma dalla sua vita di donna, fervida di sensi e innamorata della sua terra (la Puglia), della natura e soprattutto dell'amore, ma anche pronta a chiudersi, o rinchiudersi, in sé, a farsi pensosa e triste, con un che di duro, di ostile verso quel mondo che pur è il suo costante richiamo'.

5   Intervista a A. Jurilli, *Il Rubastino*, a.IX, n.1, aprile 1984, p.13.

(Land of Apulia/ burning in my blood the ashes/ the despair of my forefathers,/ unknown love my heart calls you [. . .]/ One day perhaps I will return to my hill/ in the summer sun among the ash-grey olive and almond trees/ to the labourers and artisans/ to the perfume of basil and red carnations./ For life now leads me round the world.)

In Marniti's poetry the memories of her early life in Apulia are remarkably insistent and she proudly notes what it is that makes the people of her native area different from others:

Nata da terra vulcanica
di fiumi azzurri di grotte aperte
ricca d'ulivi e vento
nulla temo . . .   (*Città, creatura viva*, p.9)

(Born from volcanic soil/ with blue rivers and open caves/ rich with olive trees and wind/ I fear nothing . . .)

That love of the past is reiterated in another poem where the poet longs for Apulia and the simple features it had to offer:

Siamo altri figli
perché in noi è il fresco sangue delle zolle
ancora umide di lacrime.
Io sono con i contadini del paese ove nacqui.
                                   (*Città, creatura viva*, p.6)

(We are other sons/ because in us is flows the fresh blood of clods/ still wet with tears./ I am with my homeland peasants.)

With remarkable ability Marniti analyses her personal emotions and highlights their sensuality and fragility when poetic images, often not related, follow each other in quick succession:

Io spero di fiorire all'alba.
Che tu mi prenda
Amore, carne viva,
usignolo di verde pino.
Sciolta arenaria
la roccia è infranta
o dolcissima fiamma.
Azzurri occhi, acqua di cristallo,
il tuo corpo è terra infinita
ove il morbido seme germoglia.   (*Più forte è la vita*, p.45)

(I hope to blossom at dawn./ Take me/ my Love, living flesh,/ nightingale of the verdant pine tree./ Melted sandstone/ the rock is shattered/ oh sweetest flame./ Blue eyes, clear water,/ your body is endless land/ where the soft seed germinates.)

The same image of blossoming is reiterated in the lines:

Sboccia il mio fiore
sull'odorante piano . . .   (*Più forte è la vita*, p.46)

(My being opens out/ on to the scented plain).

But Marniti's sense of place is not confined to memories of Apulia; she also absorbs the generic qualities of nature in her portrayal of human emotions especially love. This contact with nature sharpens Marniti's perception of love which finds new vigour in its images and rhythms. When feeling runs high love is perceived as a moment when the good things of this world are offered in abundance:

Sono terra che uomo ha scavato.
Ora porto radici di albero e fiori.
Sua sarà l'uva e la spiga
perché il seme piú alto germogli.   (*Più forte è la vita*, p.55)

(I am the earth dug by man./ Now I bear tree roots and flowers./ It will have grapes and spikes/ for the seed to sprout higher.)

The image of the tree which puts down deep roots is a symbol of the link between the present and the past and the perennial link between life and poetry:

A te diedi un mandorlo fiorito.
Il ramo messaggio era d'amore.
Ormai non risplende di pallide pupille,
ma lo sguardo che in te chiudo
senza parlare
affonda piú della radice
che spinse quel ramo alla sua vita.   (*Più forte è la vita*, p.54)

(I gave you a flowering almond tree./ The branch with its message of love./ It shines no more with pale pupils,/ but the look which I direct at you/ without words/ goes deeper than the root/ which brought that branch to life.)

But this sense of place even in its wider context is not sufficient to sustain her when beset by the despair of unfulfilled love. In *Giorni del*

mondo (Days of the world) published in 1967, the story of the passion
for the person met and loved from adolescence to maturity is alluded
to. This love is full of quandaries and dilemmas as it hovers between
light and darkness while the realisation that the poet has been cast
aside makes her aware of the nothingness that follows elation and
despair. While the contrast between her native Apulia and her adopt-
ed city Rome is a dialectical one the delusion which love brings leaves
her with the bitter realisation that all that remains are the tormented
memories of the past and the uncertain hope for the future.

   In *Giorni del mondo* the days referred to are the routine days of life
that follow each other relentlessly. Having stated her belief that life is
superior to sorrow and that it must not allow itself be submerged by
anguish, Marniti writes about these days which mark our passage
through life. What they are exactly is revealed in the penultimate poem
of this collection:

Giorni del mondo,
anche quando silenziosi e quieti
lasciate che ciascuno costruisca
il suo orizzonte dopo l'uragano,
una speranza sempre recidete,
quella di ieri e, forse, di domani.   (*Giorni del mondo*, p.79)

(Days of the world/ even when silent and calm/ you allow everyone build/ his
horizon after the storm,/ you always cut off a hope,/ that of yesterday and,
perhaps, tomorrow.)

The serenity of yesterday contrasts with the aridity and despair of today:

Il mio ricordo è fredda luna
che indaga campi arati.
Luna, il tuo cercare è tristezza,
voci perdute che vento
sussurra all'orecchio.   (*Più forte è la vita*, p.78)

(My recollection is a cold moon/ that searches over tilled fields./ Moon, your
searching is sadness,/ lost voices that the wind/ whispers in the ear.)

The light of the moon is spectral and highlights the absence of the
object of the poet's affection. The flowering of love in every sense is
now contrasted with love that is anguish and cruelty. Similar to the
harsh nature imagined by Leopardi, Marniti's world now displays its
cruel and damaging aspects:

Amico dall'occhio luminoso
nel cui sguardo risplendeva amore,
reso mi hai pietra cardo spina
infissa lama nello smunto cuore.   (*Più forte è la vita*, p.79)

(Bright eyed friend/ whose gaze reflected love,/ you have reduced me to stone
thistle thorn/ plunged a blade into my pale heart.)

Elsewhere, Marniti seems consumed by an inner struggle as she attempts
to find some spiritual peace when she appears to be the victim of brood-
ing melancholy:

Ho perduto la verginità, madre mia,
ho perduto il cuore, amico.   (*Più forte è la vita*, p.49)

(I have lost my virginity, mother,/ I have lost my heart, friend.)

Many of these poems are almost void of reference to the surrounding
world while the accent rests firmly on the present which recalls the
eternal cycle of emotions:

Batte la tristezza il suo tamburo
violenta risuona alle orecchie
ruota avida nei pensieri.
Siede vicina e mi tormenta.   (*Città, creatura viva*, p.31)

(Sadness beats its drum/ rings out harshly in the ears/ revolves greedily in the
mind./ It sits nearby and torments me.)

The grief caused by the disappointment of love can be devastating:

Senza saluto amore mi ha lasciata
e vagabondo sola per le strade.   (*Più forte è la vita*, p.66)

(My love left me without word/ alone I wander through the streets.)

The regret for what has been and now is no longer, finds expression
in the following lines:

Ascolto ancora la tua voce
e i passi lenti sul selciato.
Chiamarti vorrei,
ma anche l'eco non risponde più.   (*Più forte è la vita*, p.72)

(I still hear your voice/ and your slow footsteps on the flagstones./ I would
like to call you,/ but even the echo no longer answers.)

These sentiments are accompanied by the realisation that the poet has been cast aside to remain alone with her memories. The despair experienced at no longer being loved, at being obliged to suppress her longings and desires is given eloquent and incisive expression in the metaphor of the mechanical repetition of life itself:

Il mio dolore ritorna
e senza speranza girano gli orologi.
Conosco strade alberi case,
ma nulla è vile come un uomo.   (*Più forte è la vita*, p.82)

(My grief returns/ and the clocks move on without hope./ I know roads trees houses,/ but nothing is as cowardly as a man.)

Here the title of *Più forte è la vita* assumes a new dimension and makes us aware of the poet's determination to recover from the defeat inflicted on her by love. Despite the despair such disappointment may bring she remains resolute in her affirmation of the energy and faith which life, even if divorced from place rather than love, may offer the individual. The final section of *Più forte è la vita* emphasises the seriousness of the promise which the poet makes to herself when she says:

Qualcuno batte alla mia porta,
è il vento, non aprire.
Una mano dall'altana fa cenni,
è l'onda del ramo, non trasalire.
Ma giunta è l'ora di scendere,
d'entrare nella vita un'altra volta.   (*Più forte è la vita*, p.135)

(Someone is knocking at my door,/ it is the wind, do not open./ A hand beckons from on high/ it is the wave of the branch, be not startled./ But the time has arrived to come down,/ to enter life once more.)

Marniti is determined more than ever to involve herself again in the ebb and flow of life, ever hopeful but also timorous of possible negative consequences in the future. Determined to universalise rather than personalise her own experience she generalises it and declares herself a citizen of an ideal world:

Ti guardo città, sei il mondo
ma se carezzo lontano
un tramonto, un fiore,
un colore, il cielo fra i tetti,
uomini bianchi donne negre,
la mia città è il mondo.   (*Più forte è la vita*, p.138)

(City, I watch you, you are the world/ but if I caress a distant/ sunset, a flower,/ a colour, the sky among the rooftops,/ white men black women,/ my city is the world.)

Still, despite the optimism created by her attachment to life, there can be no doubt that these melancholy set backs left their mark. She was forced to live with the feelings of missed opportunities and lost hopes that led to pessimism but bravely she accepted these by trying even harder to rekindle her grasp of life, so that this condition was fleeting.

For Mario Sansone these moments of transitory pessimism make us acutely aware of Marniti's verbal skills in the presentation of her poetry and the role played therein by the poetic word:

Quando la Marniti scriveva questa sua poesia era l'epoca in cui la parola era elevata a mito, ad un livello che si disse anche magico, ad una funzione metafisica. La parola invece con cui parla la Marniti non ambisce a metafisica o a magia: ha funzione magica solo nel senso che rivela la coscienza a se stessa, e la libera dalle angosce di quel suo 'tempo' [. . .] La parola è il *logos*, [. . .] è [. . .] il restituirsi alla vita. La dialettica che muove internamente tutta quanta l'opera della poetessa e la ravviva e la caratterizza è precisamente questo fondo di cose perdute, di dolore che si ristora e si rileva nell'impegno del vivere.[6]

(Marniti wrote this poem at a time when the word had been raised to a mythical, almost magical level and it had a metaphysical dimension. The word used by Marniti has no pretensions either on the metaphysical or magical level: its only magical function is the way in which it reveals its own consciousness and it frees it from the anxieties of that time [. . .] The word is the *logos*, [. . .] it [. . .] brings itself back to life. The dialectics which operate in the entire work of this poet, which enliven and characterise it is precisely this store of things that are lost, of grief which restores and stands apart in its commitment to life.)

Sansone sees a definite line running through these early works and refers to them as a trilogy where *Più forte è la vita* is the story of Marniti's struggle between life and love, *Giorni del mondo* is the place where she discovers her real self while *Il cerchio e la parola* (*The circle and the word*) is more a book of liberation than one of utter desolation.[7]

Il cerchio e la parola opens with an emblematic composition which shows particular maturity in Marniti's poetry:

6   Mario Sansone, *Rilettura di Biagia Marniti*, 'Otto/Novecento', V, marzo-aprile, 1981, pp.314–315.
7   M. Sansone, p.318.

La solitudine
ora mormora parole assurde,
ora reclina il capo ad un colloquio,
ad un amore che dinega.
Se le gridiamo contro
la sua risposta è un'eco.
Ma forse è tempo
d'abbandonare la terra,
e nella vicenda dei mondi,
trovare altro regno.   (*Il cerchio e la parola*, p.5)

(Solitude/ now whispers absurd words,/ now cuts off everything,/ denying me love too./ If we shout out in opposition/ the reply is but an echo./ It is perhaps the moment/ to leave the earth,/ and in the succession of worlds,/ to find another kingdom.)

These images are suitably vague, impersonal and tantalisingly disturbing. The poet's determination to prevail is apparent in the final lines where she speaks of her possible search for an 'altro regno'. Even in those moments of despair Marniti never loses sight of her link with the world. While reflecting the influence particularly of the Hermetic poets in her concise and symbolic language she manages to stay outside all the trends and currents that characterised Italian poetry in the second half of this century while at the same time creating poetry that is notable for its dignity, frankness and moral courage.

But will that continue? Will she still find refuge through absorption in life? It is indeed doubtful in view of her more recent scepticism about man's intrinsic nature and its manifestations in the many evils and cruelties apparent in today's world. Her latest works, *Il gomitolo di cera* (The coil of wax) and *Piccola sfera* (1992) (The small sphere)[8] deal with the evil of this world and the blindness of all who 'corrono già folli/ verso una meta di morte', they run already mad/ towards an object of death, (*Il cerchio e la parola*, p.39) and who, yet, are strangely alive in a world that is all dust and ashes, 'cenere e polvere' (p.42). *Il gomitolo di cera* highlights the poet's quasi-certainty that the search for truth and the real meaning of life is one that does not lead anywhere. Many of the poems are full of engaging antitheses which accentuate the poet's uneasiness:

I giorni scompaiono
volatili fossili,
e ovunque sorge un muro

8   The 'small sphere' is a reference to the smallness of the planet earth when
    viewed by the astronauts from outer space.

visibile invisibile
ove la ragione si scontra
e cogliere la verità
è raggio che rapido
scivola nel cielo.   (*Il gomitolo di cera*, p.19)

(The days disappear/ winged fossils,/ and everywhere a wall rises up/ visible invisible/ where reason collides/ and finding the truth/ is like a ray that quickly/ passes in the sky.)

The title *Il gomitolo di cera* represents the existential uncertainty caused by the impossibility of freeing oneself from the violence that has dominated the closing decades of this century:

Non so ritrovare l'essenza,
l'abracadabra
che infranga l'abulica indifferenza.
Uomini e donne
ci sorridiamo ambiguamente
ed io cerco il gomitolo di cera
che mi aiuti ad uscire
dal labirinto del secolo che preme.   (*Il gomitolo di cera*, p.58)

(I cannot find my being,/ the abracadabra/ which might crush that weak indifference./ Men and women/ we smile ambiguously at each other/ and I look for the coil of wax/ which may help me exit/ from the pressing labyrinth of this century.)

There is an obvious fear of the world in Marniti's poetry where she declares her disaffection in a society where old values disintegrate and 'fuochi striscianti avanzano/ nel mondo impazzito', slithering fires advance/ in an insane world (*Il gomitolo di cera*, p.37). Acutely conscious of the uneasiness and isolation which this century offers she expresses her dilemma in the following lines:

Muoversi?
Con il vento.
Comunicare?
Con la pioggia.
Tacere?
Con la neve.
Chi amare?
La notte.   (*Il gomitolo di cera*, p.27)

(To move oneself?/ With the wind./ To communicate?/ With the rain./ To stay silent?/ With the snow./ Who to love?/ The night.)

The concept of time is fundamental in this work and is often presented in the guise of metaphor. She tells us that 'i giorni scompaiono/ volatili fossili,' days disappear/ flying fossils (*Il gomitolo di cera*, p.19), that 'lo spartiacque degli anni si alza', the watershed of years rises up (p.24), or she refers to her suspended autumn, 'il mio sospeso autunno' (p.30). These thoughts cause her to ask the anguished question that remains unanswered:

Mia vita dove sei
sfiorita fra le dita
di giorni grevi?   (*Il gomitolo di cera*, p.56)

(Oh life, where are you/ withered between the fingers/ of oppressive days?)

Linked with the awareness of time is the consciousness of death which is epitomised in the image of the old man who sits motionless while his thoughts return to his youth:

Si siede e attende la morte
il vecchio dagli allentati tendini [. . .]
Si rivede ragazzo, poi atleta
e sorride.
Il sole abbronza le sue mani e il volto.
Fu. Esiste. Dove andrà.   (*Il gomitolo di cera*, p.20)

(He sits and waits for death/ this old man with loosened tendons [. . .]/ A boy once more he sees himself, then an athlete/ and he smiles./ Hands and face tanned by the sun./ He was. He exists. Where will he go to?).

In *Piccola sfera,* her most recent work, Marniti imagines herself already outside this world and she looks at the planet earth from a distance ironically referring to it as a *piccola sfera* which swings haughtily in space. Her request for a sign from those invisible forces remains unanswered as has already happened in *Il gomitolo di cera*, p.34: 'Tu . . . / chiami senza risposta' (You . . . / call out and there is no reply). This silence causes Marniti to introduce the myth of the Athenian Aglaurus who, changed into stone by the god Mercury, calls out unheeded:

Voglio urlare ma non grido,
pietra lavica divento
e sconvolta come il vento
rotolo verso un cielo che non ho.   (*Piccola sfera*, p.9)

(I want to cry out but I do not shout,/ I am turning into a stone/ of lava and deranged like the wind/ I roll towards a sky I have not got.)

No longer can she call on Apulia or on the healing power of nature to allay the suffering and melancholy caused by her alienation from today's world. Distance and time have made Apulia more remote for her, forcing her to content herself with the implications of spending so long in the Roman urban environment that has produced so much of what she considers deplorable in modern life. Nevertheless, she has not lost faith in the invigorating powers of life itself or in the solace to be found in the cosmic perception of that life, both of which continue to sustain that indomitable spirit that has been such a characteristic of her entire existence. In the closing lines of *Solitudine Duemila*, Marniti says that, despite all, her final wish is to try to discover the enduring strength of the universe:

Solitudine duemila
a me presto vicina [. . .]
Aspetto ancora le parole
che mi aiutino a scoprire
l'inviolata forza dell'universo.   (*Piccola sfera*, p.23)

(Loneliness of the new millennium/ soon near me [. . .]/ I still wait for those words/ which may help me discover/ the indomitable strength of the universe).

Sono terra che uomo ha scavato.

Sono terra che uomo ha scavato.
Ora porto radici di albero e fiori.
Sua sarà l'uva e la spiga
perché il seme piú alto germogli.

Siamo altri figli

Siamo altri figli
perché in noi è il fresco sangue delle zolle
ancora umide di lacrime.
Io sono con i contadini del paese ove nacqui
con gli operai della città in cui vivo
con gli ingegni che non temono l'avvenire.
Uomini senza fiato
piegano le rosse viti dell'autunno.
Ma siamo pini ed abeti
larici colpiti dal sole ricchi di rami
racconta il semplice amico.
Dal ferro trarrò scintille,
nostro è il cuore del mondo
e la vita il lento cavo
che unisce la terra.
Se batti scriverò come un angelo
e a lui simile apocalisse
sarà la verità.

Mia terra

Mondo sulle spalle ti porto.
Terra sulle spalle mi pesi.
A volte la tua mano non sento
gigantessa dal cuore d'uccello,
ma tu sei la mia terra
e il cuor del mondo m'affanna
poiché il mio è caos d'amore

I am the earth dug by man

I am the earth dug by man.
Now I bear tree roots and flowers.
It will have the grapes and spikes
for the seed to sprout higher.

We are other sons

We are other sons
because in us is the fresh blood of clods
still moist with tears.
I am with my homeland peasants
with the workers in the city where I live
with the minds who do not fear the future.
Breathless men
bend the red autumnal vines.
But we are pines and fir trees
branchy larches beaten by the sun
says our simple friend.
I will draw sparks from the iron,
ours is the heart of the world
and life the slow cable
which unites the earth.
If you hit me I will write like an angel
and truth will be
similar to an apocalypse.

My land

World on my shoulders I bear you.
Earth on my shoulders you weigh.
At times I do not feel your hand
giantess with the heart of a bird,
but you are my land
and the heart of the world troubles me
for mine is the chaos of love

senza speranza.
Non ho saggezza,
la mente non ha legge
e dormire è appena una liberazione.

Tristezza e buio

Tristezza e buio,
è questo il mio destino.
Vita che passi come nube al sole
senza calore e morte
come muro che non ha spazio, vivo
e pietra non si muove.

Dura pietra voglio rimanere

Dura pietra voglio rimanere
sulla strada che mi allontana.
Sarò lapide umana
senza falso segno di voce.
Così il pazzo cuore riposerà
senza incerti abbandoni.

Roma, città sul verde fiume

Riportami primavera,
la città assorta nelle luci della sera
i caffè ombrosi di fumo
la nebbia del suo mattino.
Città sul verde fiume
sei l'amore che non ha più fiaba
la lettera che temo vada smarrita
gli uomini senza pane e casa
nel cerchio della vita.

that has no hope.
I have no wisdom,
the mind has no law
and to sleep is barely liberation.

Sadness and darkness

Sadness and darkness,
this is my fate.
Life you pass by quickly
without warmth and death
I live like a wall that has no space,
and no stone moves.

I want to remain a hard stone

I want to remain a hard stone
on the road which distances me (from you).
I will be a human tombstone
with no false voices.
And so the insane heart will rest
without fear of uncertain abandonment.

Rome, city on the green river

Springtime bring back to me
the city absorbed in evening lights
the cafes shrouded with smoke
its morning mist.
City on the green river
you are the disenchanted love
the letter that I fear will be lost
the men without bread and home
in the circle of life.

Nuova ed incauta,
quasi ignorando che non si torna indietro
sfilo e riprendo la mia tela.
Poesia donami il canto
che sgretoli il nostro tempo
ove affoga ogni calore umano,
illumina la nostra palude
questo jazz della morte,
brucia l'ipocrisia
la bontà è stanca.
Sul mare conduci tu il mio grido
corallino gabbiano, onda,
trinchetto della bianca nave,
in alto vessillo di pace.

Il mio ricordo è fredda luna

Il mio ricordo è fredda luna
che indaga campi arati.
Luna, il tuo cercare è tristezza,
voci perdute che vento
sussurra all'orecchio.
Arsa d'amore
la tua stessa luce ti divora
e simile a me
ti consumi in attesa dell'alba.

Demone o luce

Se fuoco incandescente il corpo
si risveglia e brucia
demone o luce, castità senza speranza,
tu sei il rifugio.
Ondeggiano le carezze del ricordo,
farfalle in voluttuosa danza,
amore abita lontano.
Conosco i cieli, i mari

New and imprudent,
ignoring almost that we do not go back
I undo and redo my canvas.
Poetry present me with the song
which may shatter our time
where all human warmth drowns,
light up our marsh
this jazz of death,
burn hypocrisy
decency is tired.
Lead my cry over the sea
coral seagull, wave,
foremast of the white ship,
on high like a banner of peace.

My memory is a cold moon

My memory is a cold moon
that moves over ploughed fields.
Moon, your searching is sadness,
lost voices that the wind
whispers in the ear.
Ablaze with love
your same light devours you
and like me
you exhaust yourself waiting for the dawn.

Demon or light

If the body that incandescent fire
wakes up and burns
demon or light, virtue without hope,
you are my haven.
The caresses of memory hover,
butterflies in a voluptuous dance,
love lives far away.
I know the skies, the seas

del mio antico guerriero,
nella solitudine mi lego alla terra.
Ascolto il fiume
la città fra le sue rive
i treni che fuggono via,
sgomitolo la mia vita
ed in silenzio prego
che la mia voce dica.

Filo spinato

Muoversi?
Con il vento.
Comunicare?
Con la pioggia.
Tacere?
Con la neve.
Chi amare?
La notte.
Ignota ai molti
estranea agli altri
ogni volto sempre più si allontana.
Non io: verso le cose e gli uomini
mi tendo come su un filo spinato.
Ma il secolo fa il vuoto intorno
e forse il futuro è già cominciato.

La tregua

Nel vento viene la morte
e veloce in un soffio ti chiama;
la schivi con un giuoco infantile
lungo il muro del cortile.
La morte ti richiama,
incontro tu le porgi
il ramo oscillante di un ulivo.

of my ancient warrior,
I bind myself in loneliness to the earth.
I listen to the river
the city between its banks
the trains which rush away,
I unravel my life
and pray in silence
that my voice may speak.

Barbed wire

To move?
With the wind.
To communicate?
With the rain.
To stay silent?
With the snow.
Who to love?
The night.
Unknown to most
alien to others
each face moves further away.
Not me: towards things and men
I reach out as though across barbed wire.
But the century creates a void all around
and perhaps the future has already begun.

The truce

Death comes in the wind
and quickly in a breath it calls you;
you dodge it with a childish game
along the courtyard wall.
Death calls you again,
against it you offer
the quivering branch of an olive tree.

La sindone

L'animo si è così asciugato
che non percepisco le parole umane,
ormai eco lontana di conchiglie.
E se una sindone mi asciuga
il volto affaticato,
da inquiete ombre
l'ombra della morte più mi si affianca.

La solitaria

(seduta sulla scogliera)

Sei il mio unico smeraldo
mare profondo,
e la mia perduta ametista,
crepuscolo di tremula marina
che l'animo sbianca ai naviganti.
Quando sei silenzioso
neppure mormori
e sembri senza lacrime
finché non si alzano a cattedrale
i tuoi marosi,
i bagliori ghiacciati delle tue spade.
Ti feconda anche la luna
che fa crescere e decrescere,
amore e pena,
l'incantata distesa.
L'ondeggiare merlettato e marezzato
mi riveste e mi tiene compagnia,
ma appena sarò veramente stanca
mi arrenderò alle tue acque,
tornerò al tuo fluido.
Ora, ascolto le voci
dei tuoi visibili, invisibili
abitanti e le frementi onde
e l'antico cantico.

The shroud

My heart has so dried up
that I do not feel human words,
now just a distant echo of shells.
And if a shroud dries
my weary face,
from restless shadows
the shade of death comes closer to me.

The lonely one

(seated on the cliff)

You are my only emerald
deep sea,
and my lost amethyst,
twilight of trembling marine shore
which pales the minds of sailors.
When you are silent
you do not murmur
and seem devoid of tears
until your breakers,
cathedral-like rise up
the frozen flashes of your swords.
The moon too fecundates you
as it increases and decreases
love and torment,
the enchanted sea expanse.
Laced and marbled swaying
bedeck and keep me company,
but whenever real weariness touches me
I will give myself to your waters,
I will return to your fluidity.
Now, I listen to the voices
of your visible, invisible
inhabitants and the quivering waves
and the ancient canticle.

Maria Luisa Spaziani

MARIA LUISA SPAZIANI was born in Turin in 1924 and has been actively involved in the field of Italian culture for well over forty years. In that time she has produced an impressive amount of poetry,[1] has written for the theatre,[2] worked as a literary critic[3] and translated several French, German and English authors into Italian.[4] Professor of French at the University of Messina until 1994, she also founded the Montale Centre in Rome both to commemorate the Italian Nobel poet and to foster an appreciation of poetry not just in Italy but worldwide. One of Italy's best known contemporary poets she is well known outside Italy thanks to various translations of her work in the field of poetry and theatre.

1 Maria Luisa Spaziani has produced the following collections of poetry:

Le acque del Sabato (Milan, Mondadori, Lo Specchio, 1954).
Il gong (Milan, Mondadori, 1962).
Utilità della memoria (Milan, Mondadori, Lo Specchio, 1966).
L'occhio del ciclone (Milan, Mondadori, Lo Specchio, 1970).
Transito con catene (Milan, Mondadori, Lo Specchio, 1977).
Poesie (Milan, Mondadori, 1979).
Geometria del disordine (Milan, Mondadori, Lo Specchio, 1981).
La stella del libero arbitrio (Milan, Mondadori, Lo Specchio, 1986).
Giovanna D'Arco (Milan, Mondadori, Oscar, 1990).
Torri di vedetta (Milan, Crocetti, 1992).
I fasti dell'ortica (Milan, Mondadori, Lo Specchio, 1996).

In 1992 she published *Donne in poesia* (Marsilio, Venezia), a series of imaginary interviews with twenty women poets who lived in the nineteenth and twentieth centuries.

All references to *Le acque del sabato*, *Il gong*, and *L'occhio del ciclone* in this chapter are taken from the above mentioned edition of *Poesie*.

2 The text of *Giovanna D'Arco* (1990) has been adapted for theatre. She has also written *La Ninfa e il suo Re* (1992) and a one act play *La vedova Goldoni* (1994).

3 Her best known critical works are:

Ronsard fra gli astri della Pléiade (Turin, 1972).
Il teatro francese del Settecento (Rome, 1981).
Il teatro francese dell'Ottocento (Rome, 1982).
Il teatro francese del Novecento (Messina, 1984).

4 She has translated the work of many authors into Italian. Of these the best known are Wolfgang Goethe, Marguerite Yourcenar and Michel Tournier.

In her first poetry collection, *Le acque del Sabato* (Waters of Saturday), published in 1954, Spaziani presents a series of themes, situations, symbols and phrases which reappear in later collections in a richer, more mature and more independent context. The city of Paris, particularly the Latin Quarter, plays a prominent role in her early poetry with frequent references to its unusual ambience of university and student life that are often accompanied by the strong visible and audible presence of people from North Africa and the Near East. In 'Marzo in rue Mouffetard' she lists some of these features that catch both the eye and ear:

Stoccafissi, incunaboli, archibugi,
lardo di foca, cembali, damaschi,
sopra il fiume di paprike e cannella.   (*Poesie*, p.46)

(Dried cod, incunabula, harquibuses,/ seal fat, cymbals, damasks,/ over the river of cinnamon and paprika.)

Prominence is also given to the theme of winter which contrasts strongly with the warmth of summer and which heartlessly lays bare our human loneliness:

Come un grumo di sangue
quest'ora buia al tempo si rapprende [. . .]
E' notte e inverno. E tu sei morto, amore.   (*Poesie*, p.45)

(Like a clot of blood/ this dark hour congeals in time [. . .]/ It is night and winter. And you, my love are dead.)

The poems of *Le acque del Sabato* have links with the Hermetic movement in Italian poetry but, writing in the Fifties, Spaziani's Hermeticism is limited to the confines of ideological integrity and affinity for the form and style of language this poetry had to offer. Although many of her themes deal with the idea of death, unlike hermetic poems, hers often point in new directions that transcend the realm of solitude. In addition she establishes a link between personal experience and poetry thereby creating a firm bond between the poet and the reader while still retaining her independence as a poet.

The titles of several of her collections have an oxymoron-like dimension to them: *Utilità della memoria* (Usefulness of memory) and *L'occhio del ciclone* (The eye of the cyclone), *Transito con catene* (Transit with chains), Geometria del disordine (Geometry of disorder) and *La stella del libero arbitrio* (The star of free will). The ambivalent poetic allusiveness of these titles allows her adopt a whole range of symbols, figures and allegories that clearly indicate the influence of Eugenio

Montale on her poetry. The relationship between these two poets is
well documented both in Spaziani's poetry and in the numerous let-
ters in her possession which Montale wrote to her over a period of
twenty years.[5] Montale called her his *volpe* or fox and in his poem 'Da
un lago svizzero' Montale spells her name acrostically in the first let-
ters of its opening lines.[6]

Her talent as a poet was soon recognised and when *Il gong* was pub-
lished in 1962 the critic Emilio Cecchi spoke of the link between her
poetry and the experience of the individual, the striking immediacy of
her language and the vibrant structural rhythm of her poems.[7] What
is personal is presented as symbolic and the images used are concise
and effective within the parameters of traditional poetic melodic metre.
This talent is apparent in the finely worked *terzine* of 'Il fuoco dipin-
to' (the painted fire):

Ci scambiammo tesori senza prezzo.
Sprecai genio e speranze, notti e fede
per lanciare quel ponte luminoso.

Raggiungerti è impossibile a ritroso.
Ogni passo s'impiglia – o serpe, o fogna –
nella fitta gramigna del disprezzo.   (*Poesie*, pp.67–68)

(We exchanged treasures with no price./ I wasted genius and hopes, nights
and faith/ to launch that radiant bridge./ To reach you backwards is impos-
sible./ Each step becomes entangled – serpent or sewer – / in the thick couch
grass of contempt.)

5 Spaziani confirmed the existence of these letters in an interview given to the
   Corriere della Sera on June 26, 1986. For further details of her relationship
   with Montale see S. Guarnieri, *L'ultimo testimone* (Milan, Mondadori, 1989),
   pp.50–55.
6 E. Montale, *La bufera e altro* (Milan, Mondadori, Lo Specchio, 1957), p.101:
   Mia volpe, un giorno fui anch'io il 'poeta
   assassinato': là nel noccioleto
   raso, dove fa grotta, da un falò;
   in quella tana un tondo di zecchino
   accendeva il tuo viso, poi calava
   lento per la sua via fino a toccare
   un nimbo, ove stemprarsi; ed io ansioso
   invocavo la fine su quel fondo
   segno della tua vita aperta, amara,
   atrocemente fragile e pur forte.
7 E. Cecchi, *Corriere della Sera*, 23.12.1962: 'S'afferma sempre più impetuosa
   una vena lirica che sgorga direttamente dalla *situazione* [. . .] si esprime con
   la più esemplare immediatezza verbale e nella più vibrata struttura ritmica.'

Similar frankness is displayed in 'Il fuoco dipinto' when Spaziani asks:

Ti ricordi la luna così bianca
del quattordici luglio? No, perdona.
Per me sola esalava quell'incenso.

Sera di Carnevale. Mi capivi
nell'ombra accanto alla finestra? Il pianto
mi sfrangiava i colombi, astratte lune.   (*Poesie*, pp.68–69)

(Do you remember the white moon so white/ on the fourteenth of July? No,
excuse me./ That incense was perfumed only for me./ Evening of Carnival.
In the darkness/ beside the window, did you understand me? The tears/ fringed
my eyes, abstract moons.)

The main theme of *Le acque del Sabato* and *Il gong* is that of the jour-
ney through the contingencies of life and time:

Ma qui il tempo fu vivo, fu *presente*,
fu il tanghero che impone il pagamento immediato.
L'imprecisione delle ore si fece allucinante chiarezza
e il tormento mi rose, instancabile, come una marea.

Ora so cos'è vivere: un gioco crudele
che inchioda profonda ogni fibra alla ruota del tempo.
                        (*Poesie*, p.50)

(But here time was alive and present,/ it was the lout who insists on instant
payment./ The inaccuracy of the hours became dazzling brightness/ and like
a tide, the torment gnawed at me, relentless./ Now I know what it is to live:
a cruel game/ which nails every fibre deep down to the wheel of time.)

The precariousness of fleeting moments is repeated in the lines:

L'estate in gloria che su queste strade
per me ha brillato un giorno, ora sepolta
mi mulina le ceneri sul cuore.   (*Poesie*, p.45)

(The glory of summer/ that shone one day for me/ on these roads, now buried/
twirls its ashes on my heart.)

The awareness of our fragility increases the anxiety that an all engulf-
ing silence may ultimately encircle the human species:

tu hai creato per noi questo silenzio
ardente strepitoso sterminato . . .   (*Poesie*, p.72)

(For us you have created this silence/ burning noisy endless . . .)

There is no prospect of rebirth here and reality or truth which stand for death, love or loneliness now dominate. However, when faced with death, man retains his lucidity and it is here that poetry obtains some form of utopian revenge:

La radice d'un fiore bianco e giallo
stranamente ramifica nel cuore.
La rugiada vi piange i suoi cristalli
verdi e pesanti come perle antiche.

E' nato dentro un foglio di quaderno
bianco come un paese nevicato.
Io rinasco con lui, splende il passato
su per lo stelo altissimo, in eterno.   (*Poesie*, p.58)

(The root of a white and yellow flower/ branches curiously in the heart./ The dew spreads out its crystal hues/ heavy and green like antique pearls./ Born inside the sheet of a copy/ white as a snow-covered landscape./ I am born again with it, the past/ shines up along the high stem, for eternity.)

In *Utilità della memoria* memory is useful in the way in which it interacts between present and past while the introspective analysis of events that it fosters may ultimately offer some form of deliverance. In *Il gong* memory can have both a positive and negative dimension to it:

Memoria, fiorita prigione [. . .]
Sei l'aria fresca su un deserto, sei
il deserto d'un cielo senz'aria.   (*Poesie*, p.54)

(Memory, flowering prison [. . .]/ You are the fresh air over a desert,/ you are the desert of a sky without air.)

The attempt to recall the past through the use of memory in many of these poems would appear to suggest that memory has a significant value when it attempts, as Silvio Ramat asserts, to become the 'transcriber of our longings and desires'.[8] Memory itself is incapable of restoring the past but the word or metaphor lasts the test of time and allows the poet document what happens all around. Poetry uses metaphors to define and decipher both human existence and its own relationship to the world:

8 S. Ramat, *Storia della poesia italiana del Novecento* (Milan, Mursia, 1976), p.668: 'Possiamo collocare nell'ambito del "desiderio" tutto quanto ci è noto finora della poesia di Maria Luisa Spaziani.'

Dicono i marinai, quegli ormai vecchi
lupi di mare che sugli usci fumano
pipe portoricane, che fra tutti
i ricordi tremendi dei tifoni
e l'ululo di morte dei naufragi,
nulla atterrisce più di quella calma
che per ore si crea al centro stesso
della tregenda: l'occhio del ciclone.   (*Poesie*, pp.93–94)

(Sailors say, those now elderly/ sea wolves who smoke Puerto Rican/ pipes
on the doorsteps, that of all/ the fearful memories of typhoons/ and the howl-
ing of death in shipwrecks,/ nothing is more terrifying than that calm/ that
forms for hours right at the centre/ of the tumult: the eye of the cyclone.)

Spaziani's faith in the restorative powers of poetry is well documented:

La poesia è la mia vita. E' gioia, è controveleno che esorcizza la tristezza e il
dolore, è illuminazione. Chi sente la poesia è come se avesse un organo in
più, che gli permette di comprendere la vita dal punto di vista intellettuale e
sensibile insieme. In questo senso la poesia salva la vita [. . .] la poesia è stu-
pore, scoperta, meraviglia.[9]

(Poetry is my life. It offers joy, it acts as counter poison to exorcise sadness
and sorrow, it offers inspiration. For those who listen to poetry it is like hav-
ing an extra organ which allows them understand life both from an intellec-
tual and tangible point of view. In this way poetry saves our life [. . .] poetry
stands for wonder, discovery and astonishment.)

Although this statement dates from 1990 it is apparent that the con-
viction of the intrinsic value of poetry is one that Spaziani has always
believed in and applied to her poetry down through the years. For the
critic Giacinto Spagnoletti Spaziani's poetry reflects an intuitive belief
in the hidden powers of poetry that are particularly apparent in the
harmonious forms of language used in her poetry.[10]

From *Utilità della memoria* onwards Spaziani's language is bared of
most autobiographical elements, there is a fusion of past and present

---

9 'A colloquio con la poetessa Maria Luisa Spaziani' in *Tuttolibri*, 17.10.1993.
10 G. Spagnoletti, *Storia della letteratura italiana del Novecento*, (Rome, Newton
   Compton, 1994), p.667: 'La Spaziani [. . .] ha un sicuro intuito delle vir-
   tualità nascoste nella poesia, che per lei non è soltanto lettura del mondo, ma
   anche canto, armonia del dicibile.' (Spaziani displays a sound intuition of the
   hidden virtuosity of poetry which is not only a reading of the world for her
   but it is also a song, the harmony of what can be expressed.)

and the eye of the poet is firmly fixed on what lies beyond. The use of metaphor with all its various meanings spread throughout the poetic text is present both in *L'occhio del ciclone* and *Transito con catene*. The diversity of themes in *Transito con catene* is striking as Spaziani includes subjects that often seem to have little in common such as DNA, Assisi, death, love, a trip to Corinth, an earthquake and the madness of Nietzsche in Turin. Spaziani binds all these micro texts together in the overall context of a macro text in this movement away from what is traditional in poetry to the more uncertain realm of the experimental. The contrast of opposites ranging from the void to profusion is also apparent in the way in which Spaziani intersperses short poems with long ones, makes statements and poses questions that bring the material back to the realm of human life and to the role that individuals play therein:

E io, se mai morissi, non ditemi che invento,
che affabulo, che esagero. Il cuore s'incaverna
                              solo per abitudine.
                                   (*Transito con catene*, p.23)

(And were I to die, do not tell me that I invent,/ narrate, exaggerate. It is only out of habit/ that the heart dies.)

Spaziani has never been drawn to the more fragmented style of poetry, so favoured by many poets in the second half of this century. She opts instead for a balanced and controlled verse that imposes its own rigour and discipline. The importance of the written word is quintessential for her, and, in the opinion of the poet Jolanda Insana, Spaziani's writing emphasises the vehicle rather than the object of communication.[11]

The critic Luigi Baldacci is convinced that her 'aggressive and active femininity'[12] has a virile dimension that is responsible for upturning the traditional roles particularly in the poem 'Viaggio a Corinto':

Eri una pagina bianca, un'argilla informe,
un fascio di forze vaghe che chiedevano un ritmo.
T'ho foggiato a Corinto, nel lume della luna,
con gesti carezzevoli di antico vasaio.   (*Transito con catene*, p.87)

(You were a blank page, shapeless clay,/ a sheaf of vague forces in search of rhythm./ I shaped you in Corinth, in the light of the moon,/ with the loving gestures of an old potter.)

11 J. Insana, *Maria Luisa Spaziani* in *Novecento, I Contemporanei* (Milan, Marzorati, 1979), p.9122.
12 M.L. Spaziani, *Poesie*, pp.18–19.

Baldacci's assertion is confirmed by Spaziani who rightly insists on having the term 'poeta', meaning poet, applied to her as opposed to the term 'poetessa', meaning woman poet, which in many ways implies that poetry written by women is necessarily second rate. She also says that second rate male poets should therefore be called 'poetessi'.[13]

La stella del libero arbitrio, published in 1986, shows Spaziani continuing to link contradictory terms in the title chosen for these poems: what is mobile (the star) runs counter to what is immobile (free will), order is contrasted with chaos, the present with the future. The title of one of the subsections, *Inutilità della memoria*, contrasts sharply with the title of the earlier collection *Utilità della memoria* and it once more queries the usefulness of memory and its relationship to poetry. Memory can be both beneficial and harmful while poetry records its salutary and damaging aspects. Equally, this title could simply mean that memory does not serve any useful purpose:

L'onda degli anni belli, quante carogne di gatti
in vortici trascinava che appaiono ninfee [. . .]
Evita la troppa coscienza: quel tuo fiume di fiori
potrebbe alla lunga svelarsi la cripta dei Cappuccini.

(La stella del libero arbitrio, p.35)

(How many rotting cat carcasses did the breaker of those fine years/ drag through whirlpools and now they look like water-lilies [. . .]/ It avoids too much intellect: in the end/ your river of flowers could show itself to be the Capuchin crypt.)

These lines aptly describe our often ambiguous attitude towards the past as we attempt to suppress its horrors and reveal its delights. Memory may offer the illusion of being able to confine oblivion to the recesses of the past and this coincides with the same gratifying but deceptive victory of poetry over death:

Ogni pagina scritta
è una vittoria su di lei. (Bisogna
ringraziare chi inventò questa favola.)   (*La stella del libero arbitrio*, p.32)

(Each written page/ is a victory over it. (We should/ thank the one who invented this fable.)

Spaziani's communication with the reader is clear and unambiguous and is reiterated in the introduction to these poems:

13 Spaziani/Profilo: 'Io sono un poeta. I poetessi cercateli fra gli uomini' in 'Il Resto del Carlino', 18.2.1990.

Se uso la parola è per pregarti
di ascoltare il mio fondo silenzio.
Non c'è ancora un linguaggio (o s'è dimenticato)
per tradurre ciò che a te ho da dire.   (*La stella del libero arbitrio*, p.13)

(If I use the word it is to ask you/ to listen to my deep silence./ As yet there
is no language (or it has been forgotten)/ to translate what I have to say to
you.)

Poetry allows the poet express her innermost thoughts even though
what is said may offer little comfort to the reader. The element that
dominates in the later poems of this collection is the bright guiding
star of poetry that gives meaning to life:

La poesia è il solco che s'apre fra i marosi,
trincea di paradiso verso la terra promessa.
                                         (*La stella del libero arbitrio*, p.93)

(Poetry is the wake that opens out among the breakers,/ the front line of heav-
en towards the promised land.)

In the epigraph written in honour of the poet Eugenio Montale, Spaziani
attempts to show that poetry gives a real meaning to life while the
poet's message can transcend death:

Viandante illuminato fra tante ombre in marcia,
solo hai perso, morendo, la tua mortalità.
                                         (*La stella del libero arbitrio*, p.96)

(Enlightened traveller among so many shades on the march,/ dying, you have
only lost your mortality.)

In this case the star or 'stella' serves as a guide both for the poet and
poetry alike while Spaziani is convinced that the poet possesses a spe-
cial instinct which can determine the direction in which the free will
may be directed. Acutely aware of the gloomier aspects of life and of the
disillusionment that often accompanies hope Spaziani shares the senti-
ment expressed by Dylan Thomas that a good poem can change the
universe.
    The story of St. Joan of Arc is a fascinating one that has engaged
the attention of many authors over the centuries. It has been presented
for the theatre by George Bernard Shaw, Friedrich Schiller and Jean
Anouilh and put to music by Giuseppe Verdi and Arthur Honegger.
Maria Luisa Spaziani too has been captivated by the figure of Joan of
Arc and in 1990 she dedicated the poem, *Giovanna d'Arco*, to her. It
is subtitled a 'romanzo popolare in sei Canti in ottave e un Epilogo'

(a popular novel with six cantos in octaves and an epilogue) and marks the encounter between Giovanna, the heroine, and Maria Luisa, her interpreter. In the cantos describing Giovanna's adventures Spaziani uses the classical Italian octave with 1416 hendecasyllabic lines – a verse form seldom used by Italian poets in this century. Few modern poets have shown any attention for historical subjects but Spaziani's interest in Giovanna is a lifelong one:

Mi sono innamorata di Giovanna d'Arco quando avevo dodici anni [. . .] e in tutti questi decenni non ho mai smesso di pensarla, immaginarla, amarla, voltare e rivoltare la sua storia alla ricerca dei molti misteri della sua biografia. E' stata la presenza più costante e illuminante della mia vita.[14]

(I fell in love with Joan of Arc when I was twelve [. . .] and in all these decades I have never stopped thinking, imagining and loving her. I have turned her story backwards and forwards to try and solve the many mysteries of her biography. Her presence has been the most faithful and rewarding of my life.)

This story flows fluidly and dramatically while the verses lend themselves naturally to the drama of the story. As Giovanna is dragged away to be burned at the stake she says:

Fui trascinata a piedi, incatenata
e legata al cavallo di un francese
complice dei nemici. Tutti urlavano
'Strega, ti bruceremo', ma un silenzio
per me planava fra la terra e il cielo.
Solitudine immensa. Così Cristo
nell'orto di Getsémani. Inciampavo
sulle aguzze macerie del mio sogno. (Canto IV)

(*Giovanna d'Arco*, p.56)

(I was dragged on foot, chained/ and tied to the horse of a Frenchman/ an accomplice of the enemy. They all shouted/ 'Witch, we will burn you', but for me/ a silence hung between heaven and earth./ Enormous loneliness. As it was for Christ/ in the garden at Gethsemane. I stumbled/ over the sharp ruins of my dream.)

In this work Spaziani investigates the possibility that the heroine may have been helped escape from the burning at the stake, continued the war against the English and married a fellow soldier Robert Des Armoises who fully respected Giovanna's vows of virginity. In Spaziani's poem Giovanna dies in a fire caused by sparks that accidentally set her clothes alight as she lay asleep at night. Spaziani is not

14 Interview with Maria Luisa Spaziani in *Alleanza*, n.1, 1990, p.15.

alone in querying whether Joan of Arc actually died at the stake and this new version of her life which she offers does not diminish the saint's stature in any way.

Spaziani's re-interpretation has much in common with the so-called 'dissident thesis' regarding Joan's life which many have subscribed to in France in recent years. In Spaziani's poem Giovanna is the saint who bears a sword and everything about her is poetry in action. Indeed Spaziani sees Giovanna as another *alter ego*. Mature beyond her years, intelligent and courageous, Giovanna's destiny is unique and she stands out as a remarkable woman far removed from the traditional clichéd representation of women in general. For the critic, Silvio Ramat, Spaziani's approach to the subject shows courage and independence as she attempts to cast some light on the different controversies and the variations of free will and fate associated with Giovanna's life.[15]

The themes of travel and memory appear once more in *Torri di vedetta* (Look out towers), a short collection of poems published in 1992. Places such as Liguria, Provence, Paris, and people like Montale are remembered in these poems where every movement between reality and illusion becomes an escape, a sort of protective self distancing from the cares of daily life. The poems have a mask-like quality to them as they act as look out towers that warn of the dangers ahead. In the poem 'Viaggio Verona-Parigi' provisional plans, intense nostalgia and future hopes are all alluded to:

Le vibrazioni più profonde, eccole
affidate ad arpeggi di otto versi.
Tutto quanto è profondo ha la maschera.
Chi non gioca non prega.   (*Torri di vedetta*, p.45)

(The deepest vibrations, are here/ entrusted to eight verse arpeggios./ All that is deep has a mask./ The one who does not gamble does not pray.)

One of the most significant contributions made to our understanding of women poets and poetry in recent years was provided by Spaziani's *Donne in poesia*, which presents a series of imaginary interviews with twenty women poets. The real novelty of this work lies in its dramatic and theatrical recreation of the personality and work of some of the finest woman poets who have lived over the last one hundred and fifty years. Spaziani's objective is to give them a voice after death and also to provide a critical re-evaluation of their work. She attempts to give them back that voice cut off by death and to allow them live their lives once more through these interviews.

15 *Forum Italicum*, Vol.24, No.2, Fall 1990, p.270.

The poets chosen for interview come from a variety of cultural and intellectual backgrounds: the French poets Marceline Desbordes-Valmore and Simone Weil, the Russian Anna Achmatova and Marina Tschetaeva, the Chilean Gabriella Mistral, the Argentinian Alfonsina Storni and the American Emily Dickinson. Among the Italian poets she selects are Ada Negri, the little known Luisa Giaconi and Antonia Pozzi, who, in 1938, at the age of twenty six committed suicide in the very same year in which Alfonsina Storni took her own life thousands of miles away in another country.

These encounters are structured around the interviewer, the poet and others who were close to the ferments and who help provide additional details for each individual story and its historical context. In this way Spaziani provides key insights into the life of each poet and the way in which these women lived their life and spoke of it in their poetry. A short biographical note is given for each one and Spaziani also includes some of their poems. What most of these women have in common is lack of success as poets, misfortune, poverty and unhappiness in love. When speaking of the way in which women writers can be neglected in the histories of literature Spaziani makes the narrator in the Vittoria Aganoor Pompilj episode say that, in this respect, one should bear in mind the warning offered by the Arabs of never to be born a woman: 'mai nascere donne' (*Donne in poesia*, p.53). Spaziani, however, attempts to show that these women were real heroines in life who often struggled to achieve some form of emancipation from the dominance of the other sex.

Donne in poesia provides a number of exemplary texts that show how poetry can reflect both deep suffering and real joy. It reflects on the relationship of female identity to poetry and as such provides a vital key to Spaziani's own affinity with poetry. *Donne in poesia* is, to a certain extent, Spaziani's own autobiography as she empathises fully with much of what these women have to say. At the end of this work the lesson she imparts is that poetry, whether written by men or women, needs to be approached with passion and understanding in order to fully understand what it is the poet has to say. It is a lesson that also aptly summarises Spaziani's dedication to the cause of poetry.

While Spaziani is critical of the use of memory and its potential for distortion she nevertheless has drawn on it for much of her writing – this is a problem for her because of her awareness of the pitfalls of drawing heavily on the past – but she has found it rewarding. Her memories of Paris, Corinth, Rome and other places and particularly her memory of Montale has enriched her poetry and her greatest endorsement of that contribution is her memorable work, *Donne in Poesia*, which by its nature relies exclusively on memory.

Come un grumo di sangue

Come un grumo di sangue
quest'ora buia al tempo si rapprende.
Più nessuna barriera mi difende
dal vento amaro.

L'estate in gloria che su queste strade
per me ha brillato un giorno, ora sepolta
mi mulina le ceneri sul cuore.

È notte e inverno. E tu sei morto, amore.

Lettera 1951

Natale altro non è che quest'immenso
silenzio che dilaga per le strade,
dove platani ciechi
ridono con la neve,

altro non è che fondere a distanza
le nostre solitudini,
sopra i molli sargassi
stendere nella notte un ponte d'oro.

Sono qui, col tuo dono che mi illumina
di dieci stelle-lune,
trasognata guidandomi per mano
dove vibra un riverbero
di fuochi e di lanterne (verde e viola),
di girandole e insegne di caffè.

Van Gogh, Parigi azzurra . . .
                              Un pino a destra
per appendervi quattro nostalgie
e la mia fede in te, bianca cometa
in cima.

Like a clot of blood

Like a clot of blood
this dark hour congeals in time.
No barrier protects me now
from the bitter wind.

The glory of summer that shone for me
one day on these roads, now buried
twirls its ashes over my heart.

It is night and winter. And you, my love, are dead.

Letter 1951

Christmas is just an immense
silence that spreads through the streets,
where blind plane trees
laugh with snow,

it is only a fusing of our loneliness
at a distance
stretching a bridge of gold at night
over the soft gulf weeds.

I am here, with your gift which brightens me
with ten star moons,
in a dream guiding myself by hand
there to the trembling reflection
of fires and lanterns (green and violet),
Catherine wheels and cafe signs.

Van Gogh, Paris in its azure hue . . .
                          A pine tree to the right
to hang up four yearnings
and my faith in you, white comet
at the top.

La Via Crucis

La bronchite stanotte mi trasforma
in una quercia carica di neve.
Crocifissa alla terra con radici
di debolezza e brividi,
sento i rami che grevi si curvano
sotto il peso di mille cristalli.

Conobbi un giorno un ragazzetto, molto
piú malato di me.
Respirava a fatica, ed un veliero
insabbiato pareva nel suo letto,
ma il suo pensiero in alto era il rigogolo
sulla cima dell'olmo fulminato.

Questa notte lo penso, io che so bene
che presto guarirò.
E simile mi sento a quel fedele
che vidi a Bruges nel suo manto di lontra.
Guardava una *via Crucis* e si sforzava
d'immaginare il fiele e ogni tormento.

E forse oscuramente anche sentiva
che non soltanto il Cristo delle icone
il passo sterminato delle tenebre
lo varca in nostro nome.

da '*Il mare*'

Io mi ricordo onde che s'infrangono
molto più forti rapide violente
contro scogli giganti alla cui vetta
non si leva nemmeno per scongiuro
mai la mano dell'uomo. Ne ricordo
l'orgoglio ed il candore, l'inesausta
potenza nel creare cattedrali
che nessun occhio sfiorerà nel tempo,
che rifiutan preghiere, e che nel rombo
millenario riscoprono la musica

Via Crucis

Bronchitis tonight transforms me
into an oak tree heavy with snow.
Crucified to the ground with roots
of weakness and tremors,
I feel the branches which bend laden
beneath the weight of a thousand crystals.

One day I met a young boy, far
more ill than I.
With difficulty he breathed, and in his bed
was like a boat run aground,
but his mind on high was like the golden songbird
on top of the ravaged elm tree.

Tonight I think of him, I who well know
that recovery is near for me.
I feel similar to that devout one
I saw in Bruges in his otter mantle.
He was looking at a *Via Crucis* trying
to imagine the gall and all the pain.

And perhaps he also felt obscurely
that not only the Christ of the icons
passes over the threshold into
the endless darkness in our name.

from 'The sea'

I remember waves that break
ever stronger, quick and violent
against rocks so huge whose peak
no human hand could touch
not even under spell. I remember
their pride and purity, their tireless
power to create cathedrals
that no eye will touch in time,
that rebuff prayers, and that in
the millenary roar rediscover the music

che fu prima dell'Arca, che la terra
espresse singhiozzando eppur rapita
nel suo stesso morire.

Avatar

Già per la quarta volta hai racceso il tuo volto,
cavaliere trentenne, Avatar, grazia di fonte eterna.
Quando io dico *tu* non sei né tu né gli altri
ma un'ombra bella, un'eco in fondo alla caverna.

Sono la creatura del cui genio sei segno,
silenzio, corrosa bellezza, arco spezzato nell'oltremare.
Solo è degno di leggerti chi tre volte ha varcato la morte,
chi solo di acque profonde nutrì la sua sete di amare.

Preistoria

Giaceva il seme in un sonno profondo d'argilla,
il magma della mia vita era non-vita.
I soli in travaglio velava una palpebra immensa,
il verbo attendeva l'epifania dell'alfabeto.

Preistoria sepolta, ruota che non scorreva,
il sangue si ricorda di te, dolce grembo materno.
Senza di te, silenzio, sarebbe flauto o tromba
puro delirio sotto campana vuota.

Senza di te l'amore, stelo cieco di clorofilla,
non sarebbe un'altera vittoria sui marosi del nulla.
Il grido in vetta al piacere è coscienza tua
che di ogni carezza fa storia all'ombra dell'eterno.

Inutilità della memoria

Nell'odore dei fieni c'è il passato
stratigrafato, un Céroli di te.
L'inebriarsi ingenuo, il ricordarlo,
il ricordare che l'hai ricordato.

that sounded before the Ark, that the earth
voiced in sobs yet entranced
in its own dying.

Avatar

Already for the fourth time you have lit up your face again,
thirty year old knight, Avatar, charm of eternal spring.
When I say *you* it is neither you nor the others
but a fine shade, an echo in the depth of the cave.

I am the creature and you the sign of my genius,
silence, corroded beauty, broken arch beyond the sea.
Only he who has brushed thrice with death deserves to read you,
only he who of deep waters nourished his thirst for love.

Prehistory

The seed lay in the deep dormant clay,
the magma of my life was no life.
A huge eyelid hid the suns in anguish,
the word waited for the epiphany of written words.

Buried prehistory, wheel that did not glide,
the blood remembers you, sweet maternal bosom.
Without you, silence, it would be flute or trumpet
sheer rapture beneath an empty bell.

Without you, love, blind stem of chlorophyll,
would not have a stately victory over the tides of nothingness.
The cry atop pleasure is your conscience
which singles out each caress in the shade of eternity.

Impotence of memory

In the scent of hay the past
is stratified, a silhouette[1] of you.
The guileless inebriation, remembering it
the remembering that you have remembered it.

1 Mario Cèroli is a contemporary Italian sculptor who carves wood silhouettes.

Ogni anno il profumo è diverso,
a poco a poco l'olfatto svaniva.
Più eroica la memoria si accaniva,
più forte si aggrappava.

Nell'odore dei fieni ancora transita
mia madre (e i nostri successivi cuori).
Si trasforma la vita nell'immenso
salone di un museo senza odori.

Viaggio a Corinto

Eri una pagina bianca, un'argilla informe,
un fascio di forze vaghe che chiedevano un ritmo.
T'ho foggiato a Corinto, nel lume della luna,
con gesti carezzevoli di antico vasaio.

Nel viaggio di andata (la nave attraccava a Corfù)
non parevi che un'ombra, un flabello di cineree fantasie.
   Ma nelle tue stelle era scritto quel piccolo marchio di fuoco
del quale, da complici esperti, fra noi non si fece parola.

La casa del sacro recinto, dove Paolo parlò,
era un relitto sbattuto in marosi di grilli.
Nemmeno lui quella notte ci avrebbe detti pagani:
l'amore è la chiave di cieli difficili e alti.

Ora il tuo marchio in fronte mi sgrana alfabeti infiniti,
sbiadiscono antiche sapienze, dal mare risorgono nuove,
il tuo silenzio è una Venere di gocce primigenie
che musica lo spazio in gamme di squillante blu.

Non dalla tua materia nasce la tua bellezza,
non dalla mano di calma che a ogni gesto ti crea.
Acqua di tanta grazia ha sorgenti lontane,
è l'ermetica nenia del pope, è le tue labbra chiuse.

Each year the scent is different,
the sense of smell slowly disappeared.
Memory more heroically stuck doggedly to it,
it clutched on stronger.

In the scent of the hay my mother
still passes through (and our varying hearts).
Life transforms itself in the huge
vaulted room of a museum devoid of scent.

Journey to Corinth

You were a blank page, shapeless clay,
a sheaf of vague forces in search of rhythm.
I shaped you in Corinth, in the light of the moon,
with the loving gestures of an old potter.

On the outward journey (the ship moored in Corfu)
you seemed but a shade, a fan of ashen fantasies.
But in your stars was written that small brand of fire
and, like expert accomplices, we never mentioned it.

The house in the hallowed enclosure, where Paul spoke,
was a wreck beaten up by capricious breakers.
Not even he would have called us pagans on that night:
love is the key to lofty and difficult skies.

Now the mark on your forehead reveals endless words for me,
Ancient wisdom pales, new ones rise from the sea,
your silence is a Venus with primeval drops
that fills the space with music in ranges of intense blue.

It is not from your subject that your beauty springs,
not from the soothing hand which creates you with each gesture.
Water of such grace has distant springs,
it is the hermetic dirge of the priest, your closed lips.

Sempre più raramente

Sempre più raramente sentiamo gli angeli cantare.
Il mondo trabocca di esorcismi, un motore li umilia,
un jet gli lacera le ali, la nostra povera fretta
ci spezza l'onda lunga, la rete con cui si catturano.
Sono come le Ninfe al tramonto dell'era pagana,
rifugiate in caverne, in boscaglie,
così intimidite e braccate da odiare il loro stesso fulgore.
Non sbarriamo del tutto ai messaggeri
i nostri sensi, le porte dell'anima.
Ci colpiscono con carezze a tradimento
fra un urlo e uno stridore: un alito verde di vento,
una cresta di nuvola, un presagio
o poche note del concerto in re.
Discretissimamente chiedono la nostra attenzione.
Non si respinge il desiderio di un condannato a morte.

La Lucerna

Il poeta con il suo diadema di solitudine
è un'oliva schiacciata nel frantoio.
Potesse al mondo una lucerna sacra
brillare grazie a lei.

Oggi la grandezza si misura a metri, a centimetri,
badate bene a darle un altro nome.
Adagio e senza grazia si discende
verso la logorante logosfera.

Siamo scintille di un gran fuoco d'artificio,
spolverio, scoriandolio, sfrigolio,
traccia per poco ancora incandescente
di comete defunte.

Ever more rarely

Ever more rarely do we hear the angels sing.
The world overflows with exorcisms, a motor humiliates them,
a jet tears their wings, our pitiful haste
breaks the long wave for us, the net used to catch them.
They are like Nymphs at the close of the pagan era,
sheltering in caves, in undergrowth,
so intimidated and hounded they hate their own radiance.
We do not block our senses completely
on the messengers, the doors of our soul.
They strike us and caress us treacherously
between a howl and screech, a green puff of wind,
a crest of cloud, an omen
or a few notes of the concerto in D.
Most discreet they look for our attention.
You cannot ignore the wish of one condemned to death.

The oil lamp

The poet with his lonely tiara
is an olive crushed in the oil mill.
Would that a sacred oil lamp could shine
in the world thanks to it.

Greatness today is measured in meters, centimetres,
be careful to give it an other name.
Slowly and without grace we go down
towards the wearing logosphere.

We are sparks of a huge firework,
dust clouds, scattered squibs, hissing,
for a short white yet hot trail
of departed comets.

La stella del libero arbitrio

Risplendente avventura, ultima musa d'Occidente,
molla scattante, genietto annidato nei gesti dell'uomo,
gentile, violenta, perduta, mio erratico fiore,
memorabile stella d'ogni libero arbitrio –

I miei fratelli e figli poco sanno di te,
sono formiche in fila, carne e grisaglia d'autobus,
portiamo marchiate sul petto come bestie al macello
le sedici cifrette del codice fiscale –

In sogno qualcuno ti scopre, sei una rosa mistica
di forma e di odore sfumanti oltre i limiti del turchino,
il sangue rosso di mille Tamerlani,
l'ippogrifo che punta a sconvolgenti lune –

Ogni pista, ogni oceano, ogni cielo, ogni mente
si striano di reticolati, di divieti –
tutti noi siamo Gulliver legati da leggi e laccetti,
e impossibile è scioglierli, nella ressa dei nani.

Epigrafe per Montale

Viandante illuminato fra tante ombre in marcia,
solo hai perso, morendo, la tua mortalità.

A Montale
il 12 settembre 1981

Tu ti cancelli e subito in altre forme ti annunci,
falsetto sapienziale di nebbia allegra,
antica palma adolescente, tremula
in un bemolle di acque strane.

The star of free will

Sparkling adventure, final muse of the West,
lively spring, tiny genie hidden in man's gestures,
kind, violent, lost, my erratic flower,
memorable star of every free will –

    My brothers and children know little about you,
    like ants in a row, meat and grisaille of a bus,
    marked on our chest like beasts for slaughter we carry
    the sixteen numbers of the tax code –

Someone discovers you in a dream, you are a mystic rose
in shape and perfume fading beyond the boundaries of turquoise,
the red blood of a thousand Tamerlanes,
the hippogriff who heads towards perturbing moons –

    Every track, every ocean, every sky, every mind
    stripe themselves net-like, with prohibitions –
    we are all Gullivers tied up by laws and tiny strings,
    impossible to undo them, in the host of dwarfs.

Epigraph for Montale

Enlightened traveller among so many shades on the march,
dying, you have only lost your mortality.

To Montale
12 September 1981

You erase yourself and instantly appear in other forms,
sapiential falsetto of happy fog,
ancient adolescent palm, trembling
in a flat of strange waters.

La tua scomparsa è scandalo, è messaggio
che sconvolge interiori meridiani,
coinvolge il futuro e trascina
pitósfori, bufere e termitai –

Potrà mai dileguarsi il tuo passo
per chi eredita quegli impervi segreti?
Il meglio della seppia è l'osso.
Il resto è per i cuochi.

Dove arrivano i glicini del libero arbitrio?

Dove arrivano i glicini del libero arbitrio?
E sono, io, arbitra di alzare questa mano?
Eleggendo i tuoi occhi, li ho davvero scelti
o qualche flauto emetteva Diktat?

Attenta ai flauti, così bravi a stregare.
Ti cullano. Ti svegli dentro un sogno.
E poiché ti carezza, quel Diktat
sembra il tralcio del libero arbitrio.

Your death is an outrage, a message
which perturbs interiors meridians,
it implicates the future and sways
pittosporum shrubs, storms and termites' nests.

Will your footprint ever be able to disappear
for the one who inherits those impervious secrets?
The best part of the cuttlefish is the bone.
The rest is for the cooks.

Where does the wisteria of free will reach?

Where does the wisteria of free will reach?
And am I free to raise this hand?
Selecting your eyes, have I really chosen them
or was it some flute voicing Diktat?

Be wary of flutes, so able to bewitch.
They beguile you. You awaken in a dream.
And because it caresses you, that Diktat
seems to be the offshoot of free will.

Amelia Rosselli

ONE OF THE MOST original and independent of all Italian poets in this century was Amelia Rosselli who was born in 1930. Her mother, Marion Cave, was English, of Irish descent, while her father was the Italian patriot Carlo Rosselli. He was actively opposed to the Fascist regime and for his safety and that of his family was forced to leave Italy and go to live in Paris in 1929. While in exile he continued to support the antifascist movements in Italy and Spain. Amelia was born in Paris and when she was seven her father and his brother Nello, who also lived in Paris, were tracked down and assassinated by Fascist gunmen.

The life of the Rosselli family was certainly conditioned by this traumatic event. Her mother never seemed to recover fully and the family led a wandering, rootless life in the years that followed. Amelia's first language was French but she always spoke Italian with her father and uncle. Three years after their death, when the Nazis invaded France, the family moved to England and there she learned English. With the worsening of the war they moved to the States and were joined there by Carlo's mother and Nello's wife and family. Amelia's first contact with Italy was when she returned to Florence after the Italian Liberation in 1946. Soon after she was forced to return to England and continue her education there as her American school qualifications were not recognised in Italy.

This second sojourn in England was decisive because there she discovered music for the first time and, having completed her secondary school studies, decided, much to her mother's dismay, to continue with the study of music and composition. She returned once more to Italy in 1948 and while there her mother died and so Rosselli was forced to find work as a translator, an occupation she continued for much of her life. Her mother had suffered from poor health, particularly in the years following her husband's assassination, but the swiftness of her death left Amelia, still a teenager, bereft of both parents. Her first nervous breakdown occurred shortly afterwards and for the rest of her life she suffered from a variety of nervous and other illnesses.

In these early years Rosselli's main interest and research was centred on music while her first poems date from 1952. Her study included the area of composition and music theory while this propensity for music plays a significant role in her poetry. Rosselli published a number of prose and poetry collections between 1964 and 1992.[1]

The progress made by the right wing party, *Alleanza Nazionale*, in the Italian elections in the early Nineties certainly increased her fear of persecution. With the passing years her state of mind became increasingly fragile and her sense of despair more acute. She took her own life on 11 February 1996.

Rosselli's linguistic formation was both complex and anomalous while her musical interests dominated her literary ones until the early 1960s. Her early friendship with the Southern Italian poet, Rocco Scotellaro,[2] was also important. They shared a common interest in politics and he made her aware of the political and social problems plaguing the Mezzogiorno. Scotellaro too had been a victim of politics. A member of the Socialist Party he was elected Mayor of his home town Tricarico when he was twenty three. He was unjustly charged with embezzlement and imprisoned in 1950. Released from prison he died in Naples in 1953 and his premature death marked the loss of yet another close friend. His book *Contadini del Sud* (Peasants of the South), which was published posthumously, had a significant impact on Rosselli's formation.[3] His concern and affection for his fellow workers and the impact of his poetry on hers is apparent particularly in the following lines from *Impromptu*:

1 POETRY

Variazioni belliche (Milan, Garzanti, 1964).
Serie ospedaliera (Milan, Il Saggiatore, 1969).
Documento 1966–1973 (Milan, Garzanti, 1976).
Impromptu (Genoa, San Marco dei Giustiniani, 1981).
Appunti sparsi e persi (1966–1977) (Reggio Emilia, Aelia Laelia edizioni, 1983).
La libellula (1958) (Milan, SE Studio Editoriale, 1985). This publication also included *Serie ospedaliera* (1969). (Abbreviated to *La libellula* in this chapter.)
Antologia poetica, a cura di Giacinto Spagnoletti (Milan, Garzanti, 1987). (Abbreviated in this chapter to *Antologia poetica*.)
Sonno–Sleep (1953–1966) (Rome, Rossi e Spera, 1989).
A bilingual edition with poems in English by Rosselli translated in to Italian by Antonio Porta). (Abbreviated in this chapter to *Sonno–Sleep*.)
Sleep–Poesie in inglese (Milan, Garzanti, 1992).
A bilingual edition with poems in English by Rosselli translated in to Italian by Emmanuela Tandello). (Abbreviated in this chapter to *Sleep*.)

PROSE

Primi scritti (1952–1963) (Parma, Guanda, 1980). (Abbreviated in this chapter to *Primi scritti*.)
Diario ottuso (1954–1968), (Rome, IBN Editore, 1990)

2 Rocco Scotellaro (1923–1953).
3 For further information on Scotellaro and Rosselli see Giacinto Spagnoletti's interview with Rosselli in *Antologia poetica*, p.154.

Difendo i lavoratori
difendo il loro pane a denti
stretti . . .   (*Impromptu*, pp.16–17)

(I defend the workers/ I defend their living with/ clenched teeth . . .)

Well aware of the unsettled nature of her early formative years with
its consequent diversity of linguistic background Rosselli often spoke
ironically of this period in her life:

Nata a Parigi travagliata nell'epopea della nostra generazione
fallace. Giaciuta in America fra i ricchi campi dei possidenti
e dello Stato statale. Vissuta in Italia, paese barbaro.
Scappata dall'Inghilterra paese di sofisticati. Speranzosa
nell'Ovest ove niente per ora cresce.   (*Antologia poetica*, p.35)

(Born in Paris afflicted in the epic of our deceptive/ generation. Laid out in
America among the rich fields of landowners/ and of the federal State. Lived
in Italy, a barbarous country./ Escaped from England, country of the sophis-
ticated. Full of hope/ in the West where nothing now grows.)

A further frank description of herself aptly illustrates both her spirit
and melancholy nature:

Io contemplo gli uccelli che cantano ma la mia anima è
triste come il soldato in guerra.   (*Antologia poetica*, p.36)

(I gaze at the birds that sing but my soul is/ sad like the soldier at war.)

The most unusual feature of Rosselli's poetry has to be what Silvio
Ramat calls her 'triplice sottofondo linguistico'[4] (triple linguistic back-
ground). This is also mentioned by Giovanni Giudici in his introduc-
tion to *Impromptu* (1981) which was reproduced in Spagnoletti's
Antologia poetica in 1987. There is no doubt that this unusual linguis-
tic background singled Rosselli out in the field of modern Italian poetry
and provoked both positive and adverse reactions among readers and
critics alike.

Rosselli describes her *Primi Scritti* 1952–1963[5] as an exercise in
poetry before opting for a particular language as her main medium for

4 *Poesia*, IX, n.93, marzo 1996, p.21.
5 Published by Guanda, Milan, 1980.

expression. *Primi scritti* (First writings) consists of prose in English and poems in Italian and it was not until 1963 that she finally opted for Italian as a medium for the poems of *Serie ospedaliera* (Hospital series). For Rosselli English represents the language of religion, French that of surrealism and 'rebellion to the gods' while Italian stands for what is both concrete and rhythmical. With her passion for music and having opted for residence in Italy it was almost inevitable that she should select Italian as her main language of expression though she subsequently wrote a series of poems in English that were entitled *Sleep* and which were later translated into Italian. A curious example of Rosselli's early writing in English is the following passage:

After coying with my grandmother I sent a flat letter to England: the two weeks holidays must wheeze into permanent residence. Our eighteen years had a will which smelt of ambition and pride so we cut with our grandmother and gathered ourselves to the country, screaming tid-bits to the deaf but affectionate aunt. Here the light is molten lead yet would not melt the void, kept under key. Our soul coughed in private [. . .] Pirouette, pirouette my pet, peck down the lordy halls of soul, its skotland skirted owners dead, deep dead, blow their dust [. . .] The hall, the whole, the hole, I want to recite and desire our desire to shaft up colombed columned miraculously!

(*Primi Scritti*, pp.9–11)

The initial part of this extract refers to Rosselli's request to her mother, then resident in England, to be allowed extend her stay in Italy with her paternal grandmother. Here Rosselli experiments with English and pushes it in directions which reflect expressions more typical of French and Italian but which sound decidedly strange though nevertheless comprehensible in English. In the second part she seems to enjoy the sounds and effects created both by alliteration and the repetition of words which are similar in sound though different in meaning and spelling.

An idea of Rosselli's approach to the composition and rhythm of her poetry is given in *Spazi Metrici* (Metrical Spaces), which Spagnoletti included in his *Antologia*, where she openly discusses the connection between music and poetry:

Una problematica della forma poetica è stata per me sempre connessa a quella più strettamente musicale, e non ho in realtà mai scisso le due discipline, considerando la sillaba non solo come nesso ortografico ma anche come suono, e il periodo non solo un costrutto grammaticale ma anche un sistema.

(*Antologia poetica*, p.75)

(For me one of the problems of the poetic form has always been strictly linked to a musical one, and in fact I have never separated the two disciplines as I consider the syllable not just an orthographic link but also a sound, and the sentence not just a grammatical construction but also a system.)

Rosselli attempts to give musical resonance to much of her compositions and so she uses letters, syllables, words, phrases and sentences to achieve this effect:

Le inquadrai in un tempo-spazio assoluto. I miei versi poetici non poterono più scampare dall'universalità dello spazio unico: le lunghezze ed i tempi dei versi erano prestabiliti, la mia unità organizzativa era definibile, i miei ritmi si adattavano non ad un mio volere soltanto ma allo spazio già deciso, e questo spazio era del tutto ricoperto di esperienze, realtà, oggetti e sensazioni [. . .] la mia metrica se non regolare era almeno totale [. . .] la mia ritmica era musicale . . .   (*Antologia poetica*, p.78)

(I placed them within absolute time and space. My poetry lines could no longer escape from the universality of single space: the length and time of the verses were pre-arranged, my organisational intent was clear, my rhythms responded not just to my wishes but to the space already decided and this space was completely filled with experiences, reality, objects and sensations [. . .] my metre though not regular was almost complete [. . .] my rhythm was musical . . .)

With this clear plan Rosselli began to write and much of her poetry, when recited, reflects her effort to provide musical scansion within the poems themselves. Equally curious is her statement regarding the length of the lines and the placement of words within these lines:

Nello stendere il primo rigo del poema fissavo definitamente la larghezza del quadro insieme spaziale e temporale; i versi susseguenti dovevano adattarsi ad egual misura, a identica formulazione. Scrivendo passavo da verso a verso senza badare ad una qualsiasi priorità di significato nelle parole poste in fin di riga come per caso.   (*Antologia poetica*, p.79)

(When laying out the first line of the poem I firmly established both the spatial and temporal length of the overall picture; the verses which followed had to adapt in similar fashion both in length and expression. When writing I went from verse to verse without paying attention to any priority of meaning in the words placed as though by chance at the end of the line.)

The final composition in *Variazioni belliche* is a good illustration of a poem where the length and rhythm of the lines is determined by the opening one:

Tutto il mondo è vedovo se è vero che tu cammini ancora
tutto il mondo è vedovo se è vero! Tutto il mondo
è vero se è vero che tu cammini ancora, tutto il
mondo è vedovo se tu non muori! Tutto il mondo
è mio se è vero che tu non sei vivo ma solo
una lanterna per i miei occhi obliqui. Cieca rimasi
dalla tua nascita e l'importanza del nuovo giorno
non è che notte per la tua distanza. Cieca sono
ché tu cammini ancora! cieca sono che tu cammini
e il mondo è vedovo e il mondo è cieco se tu cammini
ancora aggrappata ai miei occhi celestiali.

(Antologia poetica, p.74)

(All the world is widowed if it is true that you still walk/ all the world is wid-
owed if it is true! All the world/ is true if it is true that you still walk, all the/
world is widowed if you do not die! All the world/ is mine if it is true that you
are not alive but just/ a lantern for my crooked eyes. I remained blind/ from
your birth and the importance of the new day/ is only night for your distance.
I am blind/ because you still walk! I am blind as you walk/ and the world is wid-
owed and the world is blind/ if you still walk clutching to my heavenly eyes.)

What strikes the reader here is the circular, almost musical move-
ment, where the repetition of words such as *mondo*, *vedovo*, *solo*, *sono*
and *cieco* stand out in the text and become the dominant chords which
Rosselli wants to awaken in the reader's mind.

Rosselli's first poems appeared, with an introduction by Pier Paolo
Pasolini, in Elio Vittorini's literary review *Menabò* in 1963. They num-
bered twenty four and in his introduction Pasolini spoke of a feature
that had struck him forcibly in these poems, viz. the accidental or
Freudian lapsus which he considers a distinguishing and unique fea-
ture in her poetry: 'I lapsus sono in fondo l'unico fatto che rende ques-
ta lingua storicamente o almeno correntemente determinata',[6] (The
lapsus are essentially the only thing that make this language histori-
cally or at least currently special.)

This lapsus can consist of Italian phrases where an English word is
willingly or incorrectly used in place of an equivalent in Italian. Rosselli
speaks of a 'retrograde amore', (*Antologia poetica*, p.43) 'tantrums
segreti' (*Antologia poetica*, p.98) and of one who will wave 'nonsensi'
(*Antologia poetica*, p.97). In her epilogue to *Sleep* Emmanuela Tandello
points out that even when Rosselli writes in English the basis is always
Italian and it often breaks though consciously or unconsciously in the
English text. Tandello uses examples that show the close parallel in
sound or meaning between the Italian and English words: 'shallop' for

6 *Il Menabò*, n.6 (Turin, Einaudi, 1963), p.66.

'scialuppa', 'shind' for 'scindere', 'fall drit into the mire' for 'cadere dritta nel fango' (*Sleep*, p.216). The examples are numerous and another marked one is the 'fence of spine' which is so similar to the Italian 'recinto di fil spinato':

you seem to hear angels mocking you,
you seem to cry out look the stars!
and run out rapid against a fence of spine.   (*Sonno-Sleep*, p.12)

(sembri udire angeli deriderti/ sembri gridare guarda le stelle!/ e correre fuori rapida contro un recinto di fil spinato.)

In 1989 a *plaquette*, entitled *Sleep–Sonno*, containing twenty poems written in English between 1953–1966 and translated into Italian by Rosselli's friend and mentor, the poet Antonio Porta, were published together with drawings by the artist Lorenzo Tornabuoni. In 1992 the entire text of these poems, numbering eighty eight, were published by Garzanti with a parallel translation in Italian by Emmanuela Tandello.

The influence of the metaphysical poets and particularly John Donne is apparent in these poems especially when Rosselli speaks of religion, absence, regret and love and projects an acute and ironic perception of herself:

Am I a turnip? a string of pearls
or the safe ground on which to bear
weights?   (*Sleep*, p.162)

(Sono una rapa? un filo di perle/ o il terreno sicuro sul quale sopportare/ pesi?)[7]

Here too neologisms or lapsus often accompany Rosselli's bleak outlook on life:

o the shallops put out to sea and we remain ashore
gnawing into the salt bread of
disaster . . .   (*Sleep*, p.34)

(o le scialuppe calate in mare e noi restiamo a terra/ rosicchiando il pane salato/ del disastro . . .)

Love does not bring solace and is depicted as something 'that entire/ devotes its time to solitude!'   (*Sleep*, p.74)

(che intero/ dedica il suo tempo alla solitudine!).

---

  7 All translations in Italian that are taken from *Sleep–Poesie in inglese* are by
    Emmanuela Tandello.

Looking within her heart the poet describes herself frankly and dis-
armingly as one who is courageous yet fragile:

> I am he that thinks too
> much, and my wordings are severed from
> this your human bondage – or are they
> not, roaming the field in search of this
> high blessing?   (*Sleep*, p.190)

(Io sono colui che pensa/ troppo, e il mio parolare è stroncato/ da questa tua
umana schiavitù – oppure non è/ che siano, le parole, vaganti per i campi in
cerca di questa/ alta benedizione?)

Rosselli's first collection in Italian *Variazioni belliche* (1964) (Martial
variations) consists of a series of poems which follow the ideas expressed
in *Spazi Metrici* where the lines are spread out evenly across the page
with the thought or rhythm repeatedly proposed to the reader almost
like variations of a musical theme:

L'inferno della luce era l'amore. L'inferno dell'amore
era il sesso. L'inferno del mondo era l'oblio delle
semplici regole della vita: carta bollata ed un semplice
protocollo. Quattro letti bocconi sul letto quattro
amici morti con la pistola in mano quattro stecche
del pianoforte che ridanno da sperare.   (*Antologia poetica*, p.46.)

(The inferno of light was love. The inferno of love/ was sex. The inferno of
the world was the forgetfulness/ of the simple rules of life: official paper and/
simple protocol. Four beds four dead friends/ face downwards on the bed
with the pistol in their hand/ four piano bars which rekindle hope.)

The association of ideas is often unexpected and Rosselli likes to play
on the association of phonic sounds as with 'lattante' and 'latitante'
in these lines:

L'alba si presentò sbracciata e impudica; io
la cinsi di alloro da poeta: ella si risvegliò
lattante, latitante.

L'amore era un gioco instabile; un gioco di
fonosillabe.   (*Antologia poetica*, p.47)

(Dawn showed itself sleeveless and wanton; I/ crowned her with the poet's
laurel: breast-fed and fugitive/ she woke up./ Love was a tireless game; a game
of/ phonosyllables.)

This manipulation and often distortion of language is deliberate as the poet challenges the established canons of poetry and reality, feelings and ideas with the language at her disposal. Like it or not it is the distinguishing feature that makes her poetry independent from that of all other poets and she continues this approach in her second collection *Serie ospedaliera* (1969). With these poems she also included *La libellula* (1958), (The dragonfly), where the central theme is freedom. There are two distinct parts to this collection as the poems which follow *La libellula* are completely separate from it. The hospital is the backdrop for the language which seems to search for a cure after the devastation wrought on it by the *Variazioni belliche*. Rosselli seems to become increasingly convinced of the futility of the task of attempting to express herself adequately:

Morta ingaggio il traumatologico verso
a contenere queste parole: scrivile sulla
mia perduta tomba: 'essa non scrive, muore
appollaiata sul cestino di cose indigeste
incerte le sue manie'.   (*La libellula*, p.47)[8]

(Dead I enlist the traumatised verse/ to contain these words: write them on/ my lost tomb: 'she does not write, she dies/ crouched over the wastebasket of indigestible things/ her manias uncertain.')

Many of the poems in this collection tend to be less dense, more relaxed and show greater variation in the use of verse forms:

Avvezza al sogno, al sonno, al sole
avanzare spogli di gloria, un tichettio
di scarpe sul selciato.   (*La libellula*, p.59)

(Used to dream, sleep, the sun/ advancing free from glory,/ a clicking of shoes on the flag stones.)

Striking in this text is Rosselli's propensity for the sibilant and musical sound of 's' whether accompanied by vowel or consonant.

In 1976 Rosselli published *Documento* (1966–1973) and in it the theme of love returns constantly. Love has an elevating yet often devastating effect on the poet as she admits in the poem 'La passione mi divorò giustamente' (Passion quite rightly devoured me). The dilemma for her is the attempt to

8 Although *La libellula* was written in 1958 and *Serie ospedaliera* in 1969 they were republished together in 1985 as A. Rosselli, *La libellula* (Milan, SE Studio Editoriale, 1985). All references in this chapter refer to this edition.

Distinguere la passione dal

vero bramare la passione estinta
estinguere tutto quel che è

estinguere tutto ciò che rima
con è: estinguere me, la passione

la passione fortemente bruciante
che si estinse da sé.

Estinguere la passione del sé!
estinguere il verso che rima
da sé: estinguere perfino me

estinguere tutte le rime in
'e': forse vinse la passione
estinguendo la rima in 'e'.   (*Antologia poetica*, pp.119–120)

(To distinguish passion from/ real yearning dead passion/ to extinguish all that is/ to extinguish all that rhymes/ with 'è': extinguish myself, passion/ strongly burning passion/ that extinguished itself./ To extinguish the passion of self!/ to extinguish the verse that rhymes/ with self: to extinguish even myself/ to extinguish all the rhymes in/ 'e': perhaps passion won/ by extinguishing the rhyme in 'e'.)

The informal, conversational tone of these lines recalls Mengaldo's definition of the spoken tone or 'scrittura-parlato' (Mengaldo, p.995) that is so characteristic a feature of Rosselli's poetry. Having written *Impromptu* in 1981 Rosselli, both for health and other reasons, no longer felt able to write anything new from then until her death in 1996. Although further publications did appear[9] they all contained work written prior to the early Eighties. Giacinto Spagnoletti's *Antologia poetica* (1987) presents a good selection of poems from her previous work in addition to a reprint of *Spazi Metrici*. One of its most valuable features is the long interview it records where Rosselli frankly recounts the most important moments in her life and their impact on her.

In *Spazi Metrici* Rosselli stated that she paid little attention to the meaning or type of word placed at the end of the line and this reveals yet another feature that sets her poetry apart from that of contemporary Italian poets as many lines strangely terminate either with monosyllables, single or combined prepositions. Certain sections of *Impromptu* illustrate this tendency well:

9 See note 1.

Il borghese non sono io
che tralappio d'un giorno all'
altro coprendomi d'un sudore
tutto concimato, deciso, coinciso
da me . . .

Nel verso impenetravi la
tua notte, di soli e luci
per nulla naturali, quando

l'elettrico ballo non più
compaesano distingueva tra
che era fermo e chi non

lo era.   (*Impromptu*, pp.15–16)

(I am not the bourgeois one/ who hobbles from one day to/ the other covering myself with sweat/ all fertilised, settled, agreed/ by me . . . / Inscrutable in verse/ your night, of suns and light/ no way natural, when/ the electric dance no longer of my village/ distinguished between/ what was still and who was/ not.)

When writing poetry Rosselli also felt there was a significant difference between poetry written by hand and poetry that was type-written. The hand being slower than the mind, had a retarding effect on her writing which the speedier typewriter did not. In *Spazi Metrici* Rosselli said:

Nello scrivere a mano invece che a macchina non potevo [. . .] stabilire spazi perfetti e lunghezze di versi [. . .] scrivendo a mano si pensa con più lentezza [. . .] Ma scrivendo a macchina posso per un poco seguire un pensiero forse più veloce della luce. (*Antologia poetica*, pp.80–81)

(Writing by hand rather than by typewriter I was unable [. . .] to establish perfect space and length of verse [. . .] you think slower when writing by hand [. . .] But when typing I can for a short while follow a thought faster perhaps than light.)

Amelia Rosselli's poetry has not had an easy passage within the circles of Italian literary criticism. With her early non Italian cultural and linguistic background she neither adhered to nor fitted into the various schools and trends of poetry so favoured by many critics and few paid attention to her poetry in the Sixties or early Seventies. Her early poetry was written in the Sixties when linguistic experimentalism was dominant and although she had some contact with the Gruppo 63 her poetry was neither shaped nor influenced by any of these groups. The fact that much of her poetry written in the Sixties and Seventies was not published until the Eighties is already indicative of the early lack of recognition of her work in Italy at that time.

The first significant evaluation of her work came in 1978 when Pier Vincenzo Mengaldo in his seminal work *Poeti italiani del Novecento* cast aside the historiographical perspective to poetry that had previously dominated and evaluated poetry for what it had to say, its links with reality and its innovative use of language. At last Rosselli's work approximated to some of these requirements. Mengaldo valued Rosselli's linguistic independence, saw it as her outstanding quality and included her as the only woman poet in his anthology. Of her language he says that it is

Una scrittura, o piuttosto una scrittura-parlato, intensamente informale, in cui per la prima volta si realizza quella spinta alla riduzione assoluta della lingua della poesia a *lingua del privato*, che si ritrova quindi in non pochi poeti post-sessantotteschi [. . .] la poesia è qui vissuta anzitutto come abbandono al flusso buio e labirintico della vita psichica e dell'immaginario . . . [10]

(A writing, or rather a spoken writing, extremely informal, where for the first time that force towards the absolute reduction of the language of poetry to the language of the private takes place, which is found therefore in quite a few poets writing since 1968 [. . .] here poetry is lived above all as a surrender to the dark and labyrinthine stream of the psychic life and the imaginary . . .)

In an interview with Rosselli in 1995,[11] in which she recalled her troubled childhood and later painful experiences, she confirmed the agony which had been so much part of her existence and of her ensuing poetry. The passage of time had not assuaged that mentality while her foreboding for the future could now be interpreted as a presentiment of the horror to come. Nevertheless, she was still imbued with the poignancy of the poetic message and while she may not have written poetry in recent years she had not lost sight of the relevance of that medium. It was therefore hardly a coincidence that in her final despairing act she should have taken her own life on the same day and month chosen by the poet Sylvia Plath[12] for her suicide some thirty three years earlier.

10 *Poeti italiani del Novecento*, a cura di Pier Vincenzo Mengaldo (Milan, Mondadori, 1978), p.995.
11 Interview between Amelia Rosselli and Catherine O'Brien, Rome, 16 March 1995.
12 Sylvia Plath (Boston 27.10.1932 – London 11.2.1963)
   In 1991 Rosselli wrote an article on the instinct of death and pleasure in Plath's work: *Istinto di morte e istinto di piacere in Sylvia Plath*, published in *Poesia*, IV, 1991. Rosselli also translated many of Plath's poems into Italian.

Contiamo infiniti cadaveri. Siamo l'ultima specie umana.

Contiamo infiniti cadaveri. Siamo l'ultima specie umana.
Siamo il cadavere che flotta putrefatto su della sua passione!
La calma non mi nutriva il sol-leone era il mio desiderio.
Il mio pio desiderio era di vincere la battaglia, il male,
la tristezza, le fandonie, l'incoscienza, la pluralità
dei mali le fandonie le incoscienze le somministrazioni
d'ogni male, d'ogni bene, d'ogni battaglia, d'ogni dovere
   d'ogni fandonia; la crudeltà a parte il gioco riposto attraverso
il filtro dell'incoscienza. Amore amore che cadi e giaci
supino la tua stella è la mia dimora.

     Caduta sulla linea di battaglia. La bontà era un ritornello
che non mi fregava ma ero fregata da essa! La linea della
demarcazione tra poveri e ricchi.

Il soggiorno in inferno era di natura divina

Il soggiorno in inferno era di natura divina
ma le lastre della provvidenza ruggivano nomi
retrogradi e le esperienze del passato si facevano
più voraci e la luna pendeva anch'essa non più
melanconica e le rose del giardino sfiorivano
lentamente al sole dolce. Se sfioravo il giardino
esso mi penetrava con la sua dolcezza nelle ossa
se cantavo improvvisamente il sole cadeva. Non
era dunque la natura divina delle cose che scuoteva
il mio vigoroso animo ma la malinconia.

Il corso del mio cammino era una delicata fiamma

Il corso del mio cammino era una delicata fiamma
d'argento, o fanciullezza che si risveglia quando
tutte le navi hanno levato àncora! Corso della
mia fanciullezza fu il fiume che trapanò un monte
silenzioso contro un cielo scarlatto. Così si

We count endless corpses. We are the last human species.

We count endless corpses. We are the last human species.
We are the corpse that floats putrefied on its passion!
Composure did not nourish me the summer heat was my desire.
My pious desire was to win the battle, the evil,
sadness, nonsense, recklessness, the plurality
of evil nonsense recklessness the administration
of every evil, every good, every battle, every duty
every nonsense: cruelty apart the secret game through
the filter of recklessness. Love love you fall and lie
supine your star is my abode.

    Fallen on the line of battle. Goodness was a refrain
which did not dupe me but it diddled me! The line of
demarcation between poor and rich.

The sojourn in hell was divine in nature

The sojourn in hell was divine in nature
but the slabs of providence roared out retrograde
names and the experiences of the past were becoming
more voracious the moon too hung free
from melancholy and the roses in the garden faded
slowly in the sweet sun. If I brushed close to the garden
its sweetness went through me to my bones
if I sang suddenly the sun would sink.
It was not therefore the divine nature of things that roused
my vigorous feeling but melancholy.

The course of my path was a delicate flame

The course of my path was a delicate flame
of silver, oh childhood that wakes up when
all the ships have weighed anchor! The course of
my childhood was the river that pierced a mountain
silent against a scarlet sky. And so

svolse la danza della morte: ore di preghiere
e di fasto, le ore intere che ora si spezzano
sul cammino irto e la spiaggia umida, il ghiaccio
che muove.

Quanti campi che come spugna vorrebbero

Quanti campi che come spugna vorrebbero
arricchire il tuo passato, anche il
tuo presente soffocato.

Quante viuzze del tutto pittoresche
che tu vorresti tramutare in significato

dell'essenza di questa tua sofferenza.

Ma geme nell'essenza della tua sofferenza
un desiderio di sonno o di carne. Oh

come i merli tacciono! Hanno confuso
la tua idea della pace con il tramonto

che offrì ai tuoi occhi penduli solo
un sofisticato sequestro della tua brama
d'essere solo, e te stesso.

I fiori vengono in dono e poi si dilatano

I fiori vengono in dono e poi si dilatano
una sorveglianza acuta li silenzia
non stancarsi mai dei doni.

Il mondo è un dente strappato
non chiedetemi perché
io oggi abbia tanti anni
la pioggia è sterile.

the dance of death took place: hours of prayers
and of pomp, the full hours that now break up
over the jagged journey and the damp beach, the ice
that moves.

How many fields like a sponge would like

How many fields like a sponge would like
to enrich your past, your
stifled present too.

How many alleys so picturesque
that you would like to signify

the essence of this your suffering.

But in the essence of your suffering groans
a longing for sleep or flesh. Oh

how the blackbirds fall silent! They have confused
your idea of peace with the sunset

that offered your hanging eyes just
a sophisticated seizure of your yearning
to be alone, and you yourself.

Flowers come as a gift then open out

Flowers come as a gift then open out
sharp surveillance silences them
never tire of gifts.

The world is a wrenched out tooth
do not ask me why
today I am so old
rain is sterile.

Puntando ai semi distrutti
eri l'unione appassita che cercavo
rubare il cuore d'un altro per poi servirsene.

La speranza è un danno forse definitivo
le monete risuonano crude nel marmo
della mano.

Convincevo il mostro ad appartarsi
nelle stanze pulite d'un albergo immaginario
v'erano nei boschi piccole vipere imbalsamate.

Mi truccai a prete della poesia
ma ero morta alla vita
le viscere che si perdono
in un tafferuglio
ne muori spazzato via dalla scienza.

Il mondo è sottile e piano:
pochi elefanti vi girano, ottusi.

Per Gianfranco

Non ho voglia di morire oggi, non ho nemmeno
speranza di morire oggi: sono in piena
attività cerebrale; sono come gli altri –

candida, della tua morte fiorita d'oltretombe
della tua morte offerta a premio, del

tuo intimidito sorriso giovanile, della
tua sfacciataggine sicura e spretata. Sono

sicura tu cambierai registro, sono sicurissima
che non mi amerai neppure là, dove vai
e dove andrò io, vivente. Sei mai sicuro

tu di questa stessa cosa, faccenda, delirante
sicurezza d'invecchiare?

In search of dead seeds
you were the faded union I was searching for
to steal the heart of another and then use it.

Hope is doubtlessly irreparable harm
coins ring out crude in the marble
of the hand.

I convinced the monster to retire
to the clean rooms of an imaginary hotel
in the woods were small embalmed vipers.

I disguised myself as a priest of poetry
but I was dead to life
the entrails that lose themselves
in a brawl
you die from it swept aside by science.

The world is subtle and flat:
few elephants wander around, slow-witted.

For Gianfranco

I have no wish to die today, not even
a hope of dying today: I am in full
cerebral activity; I am like others –

innocent, of your death flowering in the afterlife
of your death offered as a prize,

your shy youthful smile, your
sure and unfrocked impudence. I

am sure you will change register, and very sure
you will not love me even there, where you go
and where I will go, alive. Are you ever sure

of all this same thing, the delirious
certainty of growing old?

('Non sono sicura d'esserti vicino, mai
ho sicurezza intera di te, che spiando
mi ragguagli o raggiungi . . . Competizione!
la vita senza guinzagli, garbugli, gola
o freschezza impervia'. Deliravo, e mi
misi ad armeggiare per correggere questo

vizio . . . di saperti armato di sapienza
di saperti lontano un quarto di miglia

come se tutta la sapienza al mondo potesse
sbranar cani come io già sto facendo, come
io già farò, riposandomi in questa baracca
riposandomi in questa ricerca di te che muori

quasi allegramente. – Perché, tanto sorriso
e tanta educazione? Nei sorrisi arrabescati

del vino fluente e secco, superbo il
vino ma mista la miscela!

E sono morta oramai vicino al tuo scoccare
frecce intere per il mio parmigiano, nel
ridere di vita e morte interezza e spugna
non ho più nulla da dire, come te, che
spari o sparisci).

(a Pier Paolo Pasolini)

E posso trasfigurarti,
passarti ad un altro
sino a quell'altare
della Patria che tu chiamasti
puro . . .

E v'è danza e gioia e vino
stasera: – per chi non pranza
nelle stanze abbuiate
del Vaticano.

('I am not sure I will be near you, never
completely sure of you, who equals or
catches up with me in spying . . . Competition!
life without leads, confusion, gluttony
or inaccessible freshness'. Delirious,
I fussed about to correct this

vice . . . knowing you were armed with wisdom
knowing you were distant a quarter of a mile

as if all the wisdom of the world could
tear dogs apart as I am already doing,
and will do, resting in this hovel
resting in this search for you who die

almost with joy. – Why, such a smile
so much good breeding? In the arabesque smiles

of dry flowing wine, the wine is top class
but the mixture blended!

And now I am dead close to the darting
of your arrows for my parmesan,
in the laughter of life and death entirety and sponge
I have no more to say, like you, who
strike or disappear).

(to Pier Paolo Pasolini)

And I can transfigure you,
pass you to another one
up to that altar
of the Fatherland that you called
pure . . .

And there is dance joy and wine
this evening: – for those who do not dine
in the darkened rooms
of the Vatican.

Faticavo: ancora impegnata
ad imparare a vivere, senonché
tu tutto tremolante, t'avvicinavi
ad indicarmi altra via.

Le tende sono tirate, il viola
dell'occhio è tondo, non è
triste, ma siccome pregavi
io chiusi la porta.

Non è entrata la cameriera;
è svenuta: rinvenendoti morto
s'assopì pallida.

S'assopì pazza, e sconvolta
nelle membra, raduna a sé
gli estremi.

Preferii dirlo ad altra infanzia
che non questo dondolarsi
su arsenali di parole!

Ma il resto tace: non odo suono
alcuno che non sia pace
mentre sul foglio trema la matita.

E arrossisco anch'io, di tanta esposizione
d'un nudo cadavere tramortito.

Tutto il mondo è vedovo se è vero che tu cammini ancora

Tutto il mondo è vedovo se è vero che tu cammini ancora
tutto il mondo è vedovo se è vero! Tutto il mondo
è vero se è vero che tu cammini ancora, tutto il
mondo è vedovo se tu non muori! Tutto il mondo
è mio se è vero che tu non sei vivo ma solo
una lanterna per i miei occhi obliqui. Cieca rimasi
dalla tua nascita e l'importanza del nuovo giorno
non è che notte per la tua distanza. Cieca sono
ché tu cammini ancora! cieca sono che tu cammini

I laboured: still busy
learning how to live, until
you all trembling, came near
to show me another way.

The curtains drawn, the violet
of the eye is round, it is not
sad, but since you were praying
I closed the door.

The maid did not come in;
she fainted: discovering you dead
she turned pallid.

She dozed off, crazed, beside herself
in person, gathers the essentials
to herself.

I preferred to say it to another infancy
rather than this swaying
on arsenals of words!

The rest falls silent: I hear
no sound that is not peace
as the pencil quivers on the sheet.

And I too blush at such exposure
of a naked comatose corpse.

All the world is widowed if it is true that you still walk

   All the world is widowed if it is true that you still walk
all the world is widowed if it is true! All the world
is true if it is true that you still walk, all the
world is widowed if you do not die! All the world
is mine if it is true that you are not alive but just
a lantern for my crooked eyes. I remained blind
from your death and the importance of the new day
is only night for your distance. I am blind
because you still walk! I am blind as you walk

e il mondo è vedovo e il mondo è cieco se tu cammini
ancora aggrappato ai miei occhi celestiali.

Must I tire my mind out

Must I tire my mind out
with absurd tyrannies, when
obviously the seaside roars
to tell far better stories
in a crash of lovingness?
Must I walk the plain or
the sea shore, with such
uncanny unreasoning, as
is yet mine? Must I wait,
stand, pray, and not answer
any of the bells tolling
pleasantly out to sea? When
the foremost bell rang sharp
out again or thrice she
drove the elephant by its
white tail to the sea shore
and had it grasp the single
utter meaning of the spell
the sea could cast.

and the world is widowed and the world is blind if you walk
still clutching to my heavenly eyes.

Devo proprio sfinire la mia mente

Devo proprio sfinire la mia mente
con assurde tirannie, quando
ovviamente il mare ruggisce
nel dire assai più belle storie
in uno schianto d'amore?
Devo proprio camminare per la pianura o
pel bordo del mare, con tal
irreale sragionare, come
tal è ancora il mio? Devo proprio aspettare,
sopportare, pregare, e non rispondere
ad alcuna delle campane risuonanti
piacevolmente al largo del mare? Quando
la più vicina campana risuonò aspra
due volte o tre essa
trascinò l'elefante per la sua
bianca coda ai bordi del mare
e l'ebbe a comprendere l'unico
assoluto significato dell'incanto
il mare potesse proiettare.

Alda Merini

IN 1984 THE SCHEIWILLER publishing house produced *La Terra Santa*, a collection of forty poems by Alda Merini accompanied by an introduction to her poetry by Maria Corti. The attention of the critics had been drawn again to one of the finest and most curious of contemporary Italian poets. Since 1984, Alda Merini has written a considerable amount of prose and poetry all of which bears witness to the stormy creative activity that has been intrinsically linked to her troubled career as a poet.

Her experience of life is inextricably linked to her destiny as a poet and it is difficult to try and ascertain how much each has influenced the other. What is certain, however, is that there has been a constant link between her writing and her experience of life over many decades while her experience makes us acutely aware of the vagaries of favour and acceptance within poetic circles in Italy in the second half of this century. Despite the fact that her poetry had been valued by poets and critics such as Giacinto Spagnoletti, Giuseppe Ungaretti, Giorgio Manganelli, Maria Corti and Giovanni Raboni the fact remains that Merini has often been relegated to the periphery, passed over or accorded token recognition within the field of contemporary Italian poetry. Fortunately, in the closing decade of this century her poetry has received the critical acclaim which it deserves.

Alda Merini was born in Milan in 1931 and her talent as a poet was first recognised by the critic Giacinto Spagnoletti who included two of her poems in his *Antologia della poesia italiana 1909–1949* published that same year. Her first collection, *La presenza di Orfeo*,[1] was published in 1953 and included poems written from the age of sixteen to

---

1 A. Merini, *La presenza di Orfeo* (Milan, Scheiwiller, 1993). This volume includes *La presenza di Orfeo* (1953), *Paura di Dio* (1955), *Nozze romane* (1955) and *Tu sei Pietro* (1962). In 1993 Alda Merini was awarded the Librex Guggenheim Eugenio Montale prize for poetry. Unless otherwise stated all references in this chapter are taken from these editions of Merini's poetry.
   Since 1980 Alda Merini has published the following works:

Destinati a morire (Poggibonsi, Lalli, 1980)
Le rime petrose (Edizione privata, 1981)
Le satire della Ripa (Taranto, Laboratorio Arti Visive, 1983)
Le più belle poesie (Edizione privata, 1983)

twenty. At that early stage Alda Merini had already evaluated her human and poetic self and realised that her insatiable need for love imposed impossible strains on a normal life:

Io vivo nello spazio di un amplesso:
tu stesso mi maturi senza accorgerti
sotto il tepore delle tue carezze . . .   (*La presenza di Orfeo*, p.15)

(I live within the space of an embrace:/ without realising it you mature me/ in the warmth of your caresses . . .)

But in these early poems she still had hope that was a reflection of her spontaneous nature and her gift for natural expression which for the critic Giovanni Raboni is 'un dono, di un talento espressivo clamorosamente "naturale"'(*Testamento*, p.10):

Ora che io riposo
nella certezza del tuo ritorno
e sento che l'ore
si caricano d'aspettazione [. . .]
accordo questo tormento
alla notturna carità di un suono.   (*La presenza di Orfeo*, p.35)

(Now that I take rest/ in the certainty of your return/ and feel that the hours/ overburden themselves with expectancy . . . / I tune in this affliction/ to the nocturnal kindness of a sound.)

She herself recognised this talent as a

Mirabile linguaggio che trascorre
dalle limpide acque alla vibrata
forza dell'inumana profezia!
            (*Paura di Dio in La presenza di Orfeo*, p.42)

(Wondrous language which passes/ from the limpid waters to the excited/ strength of inhuman prophecy!)

   La Terra Santa (Milan, Scheiwiller, 1986)
   L'altra verità, Diario di una diversa (Milan, Scheiwiller,1986)
   Fogli bianchi (Cittadella, Biblioteca Cominiana, 1987)
   Testamento, Antologia 1947–1988, a cura di G. Raboni (Milan, Crocetti, 1988)
   Delirio Amoroso (Genoa, Il Melangolo, 1989)
   Il tormento delle figure (Genoa, Il Melangolo, 1990)
   Vuoto d'amore (Turin, Einaudi, 1991)
   Ipotenusa d'amore (Milan, La Vita Felice, 1992)
   La palude di Manganelli o il monarca del re (Milan, La Vita Felice, 1993)
   Titano amori intorno (Milan, La Vita Felice, 1994)

a view also endorsed by the critic Giacinto Spagnoletti who stressed the link between Merini's poetry and spiritual love poetry when he wrote:

'La poesia spirituale d'amore ha sempre trovato in Alda un linguaggio fermo, austero, drammaticamente irto.'[2]

(In Alda's [work] spiritual love poetry is always expressed in a firm, austere, bristling and dramatic language.)

Her second collection of poetry *Paura di Dio*, published in 1955, revealed a poet fully aware of the ability of the poetic word to highlight what is basic and integral in life itself. The closing lines of her poem 'San Francesco' show us how close she can be on occasion to the ideals and aspirations of this type of poetry:

L'uomo non soffre attorno a sé una fine,
ma io ho un chiaro disegno
di povertà come una veste ardita
che mi chiude entro sfere di parole,
di parole d'amore,
che indirizzo agli uccelli, all'acqua, al sole
e che mi rendo tutte assai precise,
premeditata morte di dolcezza.

(*Paura di Dio* in *La presenza di Orfeo*, p.62)

(Man does not suffer from an end all around him,/ but I have a clear outline/ of poverty as a daring garment/ which encloses me in spheres of words,/ words of love,/ I direct them at the birds, the water, the sun / words I render all exact,/ premeditated death of sweetness.)

Nozze romane was also published in 1955 when Alda Merini was no longer a newcomer to the field of poetry and her writing had already been acknowledged. But, by 1962, it was clear that the poet of *Tu sei Pietro* (1962) was suffering from serious psychological problems that would subsequently consign her to silence for almost twenty years. The title, *Tu sei Pietro*, is a watershed between her early poetry and that written at a later stage. The latter is so marked by her experience of life in the asylum that her gift for poetry appears even more remarkable in the poems written later. Her 'follia d'amore' or madness caused by love eventually leads her to the catastrophe represented by the years spent in various asylums.

2 G. Spagnoletti, Introduzione a A. Merini, *La Terra Santa e altre poesie* (Manduria, Bari and Rome, Lacaita, 1984), p.13.

In the early Fifties she was already attending a psychiatrist in Milan but her condition deteriorated to such an extent that from 1965 to 1972 she was interned in a Milanese psychiatric hospital. Although released on a number of occasions, Merini willingly returned there as if that place had become her natural home. Speaking of this part of her life in 1993, Merini revealed that she had been readmitted to mental institutions on several occasions despite numerous efforts to discharge her and to help her reinsert herself in 'normal' life:

In tutto, feci ventiquattro ricoveri perché molti furono i tentativi di dimettermi e di farmi tornare nel mondo dei vivi.[3]

(In all, I was hospitalised on twenty four occasions because several efforts were made to discharge me and help me return to the world of the living.)

Following the death of her second husband, Michele Pierri, who lived in Taranto, Merini once more unable to cope with life, willingly spent part of 1986 in a psychiatric hospital in that city before returning to Milan where she now lives.

Referring to her experiences in Taranto, Merini admitted her willingness to find refuge in mental institutions

So che ci andai spontaneamente, quasi guidata da un destino avverso. Fui trainata là, ricordo, da qualcosa. Come da un'istanza precisa. L'istanza di un capoverso che ti obbliga ad andare a capo mi aveva tradotto in quell'orrenda psichiatria[4]

(I know that I went there willingly, as though guided by a hostile destiny. I remember that I was drawn to it by something. Like a clear need. The need for a new paragraph which makes you return to the start had led me to that terrible area of psychiatry)

although on other occasions Merini was unaware of being there: Sono vissuta nel manicomio a volte volontariamente. Altre volte senza saperlo.[5] (On occasion I willingly lived in the asylum – on other occasions without realising I was there.)

This 'other part' of Merini's life is vividly recalled in this extract written in 1992:

Ricordo il primo giorno che entrai in manicomio. Fin lì non ne avevo mai sentito parlare. Avevo chiesto aiuto a dei neurologi per dei piccoli disturbi,

3 *Il Manifesto*, 27.5.1993: 'Poesie di un'anima indocile' di Luce D'Eramo.
4 *Il Manifesto*, 27.5.1993.
5 Ibid.

ma non conoscevo questi ghetti. Perché, se avessi saputo una cosa simile, mi
sarei certamente uccisa. Ma è incredibile i segni che si avvertono su quelle
facce di reclusi, lo schifo che fanno. E poi tu diventi una di loro e fuori nes-
suno ti riconosce più e tu diventi il protagonista delle metamorfosi kafkiane.
Così la mia bellezza si era inghirlandata di follia, ed ora ero Ofelia, peren-
nemente innamorata del vuoto e del silenzio, Ofelia bella che amava e rifiu-
tava Amleto.   (*L'altra verità*, p.90)

(I can remember the first day I went into the asylum. Until then I had never
heard of it. I had asked some neurologists to help me with some minor dis-
turbances, but I was unfamiliar with these ghettoes. Because, if I had been
aware of something similar, I would certainly have killed myself. The marks
you can see on the faces of those interned are unbelievable and disgusting.
And then you become like one of them and outside no one recognises you
any more and you become the protagonist of a Kafka-like metamorphosis.
This was how my beauty had a wreath of madness and I became Ophelia,
constantly in love with void and silence, the beautiful Ophelia who loved and
rejected Hamlet.)

The often frightening and humiliating experiences endured in these
mental hospitals have left an indelible mark on her poetry. Merini often
speaks of her *male* or illness and of those years when she was deprived
of her freedom and dignity. The poem 'Canto di risposta', written in
the late Eighties makes us acutely aware of the conflicting emotions
that are so much part of her life and verse:

L'essere stata in certi tristi luoghi [. . .]
non dà diritto a credere che dentro
dentro di me continui la follia.
Sono rimasta poeta anche all'inferno
solo che io cercavo di Euridice
la casta ombra e non ho più parole [. . .]
                io sono poeta
e poeta rimasi tra le sbarre
solo che fuori, senza casa e persa
ho continuato mio malgrado il canto
della tristezza . . .   ('Destinati a morire', *Testamento*, p.68)

(Having been in certain sad places [. . .]/ does not give one the right to think
that / inside me madness still exists./ I remained a poet even in hell/ only that
I was searching for the pure/ shadow of Eurydice and I have no more words
[. . .]/ I am a poet/ and remained a poet behind bars/ only that outside, home-
less and lost/ despite myself I have continued/ my song of sadness . . .)

However, for Merini poetry allows her escape from the world of insan-
ity and it also helps her cope with pain. For her the finest poems

si scrivono sopra le pietre
coi ginocchi piagati
e le menti aguzzate dal mistero . . .   (*Vuoto d'amore*, p.104)

(are written on stones/ with injured knees/ and minds sharpened by mystery.)

As she herself acknowledged in 1987, her first serious crisis was over-
come thanks to her talent as a poet. Understandably, poetry then assumed
an ever increasing importance in her life:

La mia poesia mi è cara come la mia stessa
vita, è la mia parola interiore, la mia vita [. . .]
La poesia, semmai, è la liberazione dal male,
come la preghiera è la liberazione dal peccato.
                                          (*Fogli bianchi*, pp.7–8)

(My poetry is as dear to me as my life,/ it is my inner word, my life [. . .]/ If
anything, poetry is a release from evil,/ just as prayer is a release from sin.)

   Alda Merini's psychiatric illness brings to mind images of social and
individual pain but her talent and her work as a poet has a therapeu-
tic function which she clearly states in *L'altra verità* written in 1992:

E gradatamente, giorno per giorno, ricominciarono a fiorirmi i versi nella
memoria, finché ripresi in pieno la mia attività poetica. Questo lavoro di recu-
pero durò circa due anni.   (*L'altra verità*, p.54)

(And slowly, day by day, verses began to spring up once again in my memo-
ry, until I picked up my activity as a poet once more. This work of recovery
lasted approximately two years.)

   For Merini poetry is a sacred gift which allows her express the inde-
finable and the poet a sort of unconscious ascetic who is capable of
escaping from the obsessive rhythm of daily life:

Io, quando scrivo, è come se dormissi ed entrassi nel profondo della mia anima.
Mi fa paura il risveglio, il contatto matematico, aggressivo con la realtà dalla
quale vorrei finalmente slegarmi. Così cominciò anche il mio silenzio.
                                          (*L'altra verità*, p.57)

(When I write, it is as though I were fast asleep immersed in the depths of
my soul. I am afraid of being woken up, of the aggressive mathematical con-
tact with reality from which I would like to finally free myself. That was how
my silence also began.)

   Le più belle poesie were published in 1983 in an effort to meet the
medical expenses incurred by the terminal illness of her first husband,

Ettore Carniti, who died that same year. These poems heightened her awareness both of the afterlife and the fragility of life itself. In 1984 with *Terra dei Santi e altre poesie* Merini ironically comes to terms with the darker moments of her own life because *La Terra Santa* is also the name she uses to describe the asylum. The biblical title has a metaphorical ring to it and it also acts as a mental link between the walls which enclosed the asylum where she was secluded from society and the walls of Jericho which she envisages surrounding her Palestine:

Ho conosciuto Gerico
        ho avuto anch'io la mia Palestina,
le mura del manicomio
        erano le mura di Gerico
    e una pozza di acqua infettata
    ci ha battezzati tutti.   (*Vuoto d'amore*, p.116)

(I have known Jericho,/ I too have had my Palestine,/ the walls of the asylum/ were the walls of Jericho/ and a pool of infected water/ baptised us all.)

For Merini, Jericho here stands for all those years when she was deprived of freedom of mind and movement, when she was separated from the rest of the world and forced to be baptised with her fellow inmates in the water that is infected as opposed to water that is healthy and sane. Fortunately for her there was light at the end of the tunnel from which she emerged 'stupita':

Ma un giorno da dentro l'avello
anch'io mi sono ridestata
e anch'io come Gesù
ho avuto la mia resurrezione,
ma non sono salita ai cieli
sono discesa all'inferno
da dove riguardo stupita
    le mura di Gerico antica.   (*Vuoto d'amore*, p.116)

(But one day from inside the tomb/ I too woke up again/ and like Jesus I too/ have had my resurrection,/ but I did not go up to the skies/ I went down to hell/ from where, astonished, I look again/ at the walls of ancient Jericho.)

Release does not bring instant joy or happiness and the walls of Jericho serve as a reminder of a life spent behind the walls of the asylum in a world foreign to most people.

Poems of this type are a background to the disturbed voice of the poet who is obsessed with her passion for life and yet indelibly marked by her past. At this point Alda Merini's poetry reflects her intention

of highlighting her inner self but this effort causes her bitter disillusion-
ment and grief as she waits for someone capable of understanding her:

Mai donna è stata più perduta
in un mare di tristezza e di angoscia,
mai donna ha sciolto la treccia
dentro un incanto che la rifiuta [. . .]
ma tu che potresti
ascoltare i miei accenti [. . .]
amico di ogni distanza,
perché mi rifiuti?   (*La Terra Santa e altre poesie*, p.66)

(Never has a woman been more lost/ in a sea of sadness and suffering,/ never
has a woman undone her braid/ within a spell which rejects her [. . .]/ but
you who could listen/ to my words [. . .]/ friend of every distance,/ why do
you reject me?)

Merini here measures her wounded pride, considers herself a loser
and hides this painful feeling of love within herself. Already damag-
ing in its own way this reaction makes her analyze herself even more
and makes the futile battle against her *male* or illness more bitter. But
she still has the courage to admit that she is disillusioned while her
grief is expressed in tones that are clear and lucid. She examines her
madness or *follia* with an amazing honesty that is reflected in language
that is both rigid and severe:

il manicomio è il monte Sinai
maledetto, su cui tu ricevi
le tavole di una legge
agli uomini sconosciuta.   (*Vuoto d'amore*, p.92)

(the asylum is the cursed/ Mount Sinai on which you receive/ the tables of a
law/ unknown to man.)

It was Maria Corti who acutely observed that Merini's poetry is dom-
inated most of all by a tragic reality which defeats her in a frightening
way and, yet, she is able to draw on these experiences so that in her
writings she appears to have overcome these disabilities.

Since 1980 Alda Merini's publications in poetry and prose have
been many and varied while affording her the opportunity to go back,
with great candour, honesty and humility, over the path that has made
her a prisoner to her illness. Her writings show that she is coherent
because she is sincere and her words are a true and spontaneous expres-
sion of her spirit that is outside all literary currents or trends in the
field of contemporary Italian poetry. As a woman she voices what she
feels in the few ups and numerous downs which life has dealt her with

the moments of happiness momentarily eclipsing the unhappy ones though she seldom ventures beyond the immediate impact on her of her own experiences in life.

In 1991 Maria Corti's introduction to *Vuoto d'amore* drew public attention once more to Merini's poetry. Much of *Vuoto d'amore* seems to consist of poems written in free non rhyming verse, a sort of rhythmic and measured prose with its own internal music and rhythm. For Maria Corti these are poems written quickly with a liberating intent, 'di getto, spesso a scopo liberatorio', that have become valuable and highly communicative poetic texts – 'testi di alto valore poetico ora di carattere comunicativo' (*Vuoto d'amore*, p.x).

Merini's experience of love, which reappears in *Vuoto d'amore*, ranges from initial enthusiasm to the living experience of love which contains an imponderable dimension that varies from individual to individual. In Merini's case the object of her love changed frequently throughout her life while she fully experienced the rapture of requited love but also the misery of fickleness of rejection. The asylum had sharpened her awareness of the fragility of human relationships while her talent as a poet helped her view her situation with brutal candour.

The poem chosen to open *Vuoto d'amore* is appropriately entitled 'Lo sguardo del poeta' (The poet's gaze). Its brevity, its poetic vigour and its message are emblematic as Merini dispenses her advice to fellow poets:

Se qualcuno cercasse di capire il tuo sguardo
Poeta difenditi con ferocia
il tuo sguardo son cento sguardi che ahimè ti hanno
          guardato tremando.   (*Vuoto d'amore*, p.3)

(If someone tries to understand your gaze/ Poet defend yourself fiercely/ your gaze is a hundred gazes that have alas looked trembling at you.)

The overriding feeling in these poems is one of melancholy enthusiasm as the poet faces the world, examines her often confused perceptions of life and yet is fully aware of her own nature, her art and everything that she is ready to embrace and love:

Il volume del canto mi innamora:
come vorrei io invadere la terra
con i miei carmi e che tremasse tutta
sotto la poesia della canzone.   (*Vuoto d'amore*, p.7)

(The volume of the song makes me fall in love:/ how I would love to invade the earth/ with my poetic songs and that all would tremble/ beneath the poetry of the song.)

In the poem which follows the pendulum swings back once more as
Merini expresses the need for space around her ('Spazio spazio io
voglio') as she feels the need to vent her anguish and craving for free-
dom:

Spazio datemi spazio
ch'io lanci un urlo inumano,
quell'urlo di silenzio negli anni
      che ho toccato con mano.   (*Vuoto d'amore*, p.8)

(Space give me space/ so that I can utter an inhuman cry/ that cry of silence
in the years/ that I have touched with my hand.)

On occasion her longing to be loved seems to be satisfied but noth-
ing, human condition or human relationship, remains stable for her.
When abandoned or deluded in love what grieves her most is the fail-
ure by the loved one to understand the intensity of her tender, pas-
sionate and selfless love:

Io sono folle, folle,
      folle di amore per te.
Io gemo di tenerezza
      perché sono folle, folle,
      perché ti ho perduto.
Stamane il mattino era sí caldo
      che a me dettava questa confusione,
ma io ero malata di tormento
ero malata di tua perdizione.   (*Vuoto d'amore*, p.33)

(I am mad, mad,/ mad with love for you./ I moan with tenderness/ because
I am mad, mad/ because I have lost you./ Today the morning was so hot/ that
it dictated this confusion to me,/ but I was sick with torment/ I was sick with
your perdition.)

The regret she feels for this lost love causes her intense anguish. In
these circumstances life becomes a torment while her existence seems
perpetually directed towards repeated sadness and delusions in love:

Amai teneramente dei dolcissimi amanti
senza che essi sapessero mai nulla.   (*Vuoto d'amore*, p.47)

(Tenderly I loved the sweetest of lovers/ and they never realised it.)

The emptiness and the feeling of rejection in love make her sensitive
to this void which she aptly calls a *vuoto d'amore*. When asked why she
used this title Merini's reply was that the death of her friend and

mentor Giorgio Manganelli had left an irreparable void in her life and so she dedicated these poems to his memory.[6]

With the publication of *Ipotenusa d'amore* in 1992 (a short collection of fifteen poems and a number of prose passages) Merini seems to reach a heightened lyrical vein particularly in the opening poem 'Anima anima ricorda lui' (My soul my soul remember him). Here the central theme is love that is relived, dreamed about, remembered and presented with great spontaneity:

E' dolcezza d'amore è ipotenusa,
donna in amore va raccolta e chiusa.   (*Ipotenusa d'amore*, p.24)

(It is the sweetness of love it is hypotenuse,/ a woman in love needs to be secluded and restrained.)

This woman in love, enclosed in a space that is beyond the norm of daily life, translates this experience into poetry where the pressing need for expression brings us side by side with the poet who is the protagonist and cantor of both her real and imaginative life.

In *La palude di Manganelli o il monarca del re* (1992) Merini, in an imaginary dramatic dialogue and a short number of poems, introduces the reader to the writer Giorgio Manganelli who was the first and perhaps greatest love of her life. While recognising her talent for poetry it was Manganelli who also realised that she was in need of specialised medical treatment as far back as 1947. He was also the first person who attempted to help her cope with the psychiatric problem that ultimately was to leave an indelible mark on her life and work.

The theme of love is present in her most recent work, *Titano amori intorno*. As the title suggests it is dedicated to Titano, one of the recent recipients of her limitless capacity and need for love. Aware of the bright and dark sides of his personality Titano is nevertheless the object of her love and attention in these poems. She is also fully aware of the toll that life has taken on him:

Era una roccia,
ma soprattutto era una roccia spenta.   (*Titano amori intorno*, p.14)

(He was a rock/ but above all a burned out rock.)

6 *La Provincia*, 24.10.1993: 'La donna che canta il bisogno d'amore' di Ugo Lo Rosso: 'La scomparsa del mio amico e maestro Giorgio Manganelli ha creato un "vuoto" incolmabile in me. A lui ho dedicato questa ultima raccolta di liriche.'

Titano too was destined to die and after his death Merini found herself alone and deprived once more of the object of her love. Thus even now, Merini must still endure the pain of loss or even unrequited love whose consequences have had such damaging repercussions for her throughout her life while in a recent interview she acknowledges how much she learned from life in an asylum:

Life has much in common with the asylum because it was in this excommunicated and excommunicating place that I discovered the value of life. For me it was similar to being immersed in the tomb of the Pythagoreans when the disciples of the philosopher must have felt the weight of death beneath the earth before they became acquainted with thought. When I was 'exhumed' I wrote things that were painful and profoundly linked to the earth. It was the profundity of life and the profundity of death but it was not the profundity of peace because the poet will never have peace because he searches desperately for the truth of sorrow.[7]

Alda Merini has never voluntarily opted for that experience. The message of the asylum has been an expedient message for her: had her capacity for love been fulfilled elsewhere, she would have perhaps forsaken the challenge of insanity and no doubt would have drawn on the font of these experiences to produce an exceptional, if a somewhat different type of poetry.

7 Interview between Alda Merini and Catherine O'Brien, Milan, 21 February 1995:

Q. How would you summarise your experience in the asylum?

A. Mi chiedono spesso che cosa è il manicomio ma nessuno mi domanda che cosa è la vita. La vita partecipa del manicomio perché è stato in questo luogo dissacrato e dissacrante che ho scoperto il valore della vita. E' stata per me come l'immersione nel sepolcro di pitagorici quando i discepoli del filosofo dovevano sentire sotto la terra il peso della morte prima di conoscere il pensiero. Una volta 'riesumata' ho scritto cose penose e di una tale profondità della terra, era la profondità della vita, e la profondità della morte ma non quella della pace perché il poeta non avrà mai pace perché cerca disperatamente la verità del dolore.

Il gobbo

Dalla solita sponda del mattino
io mi guadagno palmo a palmo il giorno:
il giorno dalle acque così grigie,
dall'espressione assente.

Il giorno io lo guadagno con fatica
tra le due sponde che non si risolvono,
insoluta io stessa per la vita
. . . e nessuno m'aiuta.

Ma viene a volte un gobbo sfaccendato,
un simbolo presago d'allegrezza
che ha il dono di una strana profezia.

E perché vada incontro alla promessa
lui mi traghetta sulle proprie spalle.

22 dicembre 1948

Confessione

Tu mi domandi per sempre,
ma io non ho vita continua;
ti nutrirei di attimi soltanto.
Sono l'apparizione che dilegua,
e il tempo che intercorre fra due tappe
è una tregua a favore della morte.
Io vivo nello spazio di un amplesso:
tu stesso mi maturi senza accorgerti
sotto il tepore delle tue carezze . . .
Ma ti confesso, e credimi:
non c'è forma di donna che continui,
dentro di me, il rovescio dell'amante.

26 dicembre 1948

The hunchback

From that same morning shore
inch by inch I earn my day:
the day with such grey waters,
and vacant expression.

With difficulty I earn my day
between the two shores which do not change,
I too am unsettled for life
. . . and no one helps me.

But sometimes an idling hunchback comes,
a foreboding symbol of happiness
with the gift of strange prophecy.

And so to go towards the promise
he ferries me about on his shoulders.

22 December 1948

Confession

You always ask me,
but I have not continuous life;
I would nourish you only with moments.
I am the apparition that vanishes,
and the time that passes between two stages
is a truce that favours death.
I live in the space of an embrace:
without realising it you mature me
in the warmth of your caresses . . .
But to you I confess, believe me:
there is no form of woman that may continue,
inside me, the antithesis of the lover.

26 December 1948

Il testamento

Se mai io scomparissi
presa da morte snella,
costruite per me
il più completo canto della pace!

Ché, nel mondo, non seppi
ritrovarmi con lei, serena, un giorno.

Io non fui originata
ma balzai prepotente
dalle trame del buio
per allacciarmi ad ogni confusione.

Se mai io scomparissi
non lasciatemi sola;
blanditemi come folle!

3 novembre 1953

Dies Irae
a mio marito

Tu insegui le mie forme,
segui tu la giustezza del mio corpo
e non mai la bellezza
di cui vado superba.
Sono animale all'infelice coppia
prona su un letto misero d'assalti,
sono la carezzevole rovina
dai fecondi sussulti alle tue mani,
sono il vuoto cresciuto
sino all'altezza esatta del piacere
ma con mille tramonti alle mie spalle:
quante volte, amor mio, tu mi disdegni.

21 settembre 1953

The will

Were I ever to pass away
taken by willowy death,
build for me
the fullest song of peace!

Because, in the world, I was unable
to be calm with it, for a single day.

I was not brought about
but I leaped up overbearing
from the conspiracies of darkness
to latch on to every turmoil.

Were I ever to pass away
do not leave me alone;
soothe me like a mad woman!

3 November 1953

Dies Irae
to my husband

You follow my shape,
you follow the rightness of my body
and never the beauty
of which I am proud.
I am an animal to the unhappy couple
prone on a miserable bed of onslaughts,
I am the caressing ruin
with fertile tremors in your hands,
I am the void grown
to the exact height of pleasure
but with a thousand sunsets behind me:
how many times, my love,
do you despise me?

21 September 1953

Povera è la mia vita

Povera è la mia vita, misurata
e con deboli venti di allegrezza
ma del poco m'allieto come rosa
che prontamente s'alzi se ritorni
prontamente un annuncio di frescura.

Gli altri m'hanno, assai debole, in balìa
e mi possono chiudere, vietare
alla mia conoscenza
e mi possono rendere all'ampiezza.

Poca è la vita e poche le mie cose
ma io sono assai lieta per il giorno
che m'attira dal trepido mattino
e mi vede dal nulla

lievitare siccome un pane buono
e per sé e per ognuno che abbia pace.
Benedico la vita quando sento
ridere nella culla il mio bambino . . .

E piú facile ancora
a Pietro De Paschale

E piú facile ancora mi sarebbe
scendere a te per le piú buie scale,
quelle del desiderio che mi assalta
come lupo infecondo nella notte.

So che tu coglieresti dei miei frutti
con le mani sapienti del perdono . . .

E so anche che mi ami di un amore
casto, infinito, regno di tristezza . . .

Ma io il pianto per te l'ho levigato
giorno per giorno come luce piena

e lo rimando tacita ai miei occhi
che, se ti guardo, vivono di stelle.

Poor is my life

Poor is my life, measured
with weak winds of happiness
but I rejoice in that poverty like a rose
which quickly pricks itself up
with the report of a swift return of coolness.

The others have me, quite weak, at their mercy
and they can close me, prevent
my knowing things
and can restore me to abundance.

Life is not much and few are my possessions
but I am quite happy for the day
that attracts me from the anxious morning
and sees me from nothingness

rise up like a good loaf
both for itself and all who may have peace.
I bless life when I hear
my child laugh in its cradle.

And it would be easier for me
to Pietro De Paschale

And it would be easier for me
to go down to you by the darkest steps,
those of the yearning that attack me
like a barren wolf in the night.

I know that you would gather my harvest
with the wise hands of forgiveness . . .

And I also know that your love for me is
chaste, endless, a realm of sadness . . .

But I have honed down my tears for you
day by day like a full light

and silently send them back to my eyes
which, if I look at you, feast on stars.

Ho conosciuto in te le meraviglie

Ho conosciuto in te le meraviglie
meraviglie d'amore sí scoperte
che parevano a me delle conchiglie
ove odoravo il mare e le deserte
spiagge corrive e lí dentro l'amore
mi sono persa come alla bufera
sempre tenendo fermo questo cuore
che (ben sapevo) amava una chimera.

Resta pur sempre a me

Resta pur sempre a me quella parola
che non ti ho detto e che mi fa soffrire
cosa languente cosa morta e sola
ma come posso amore dirti e dire
che cosa m'aggredisce se son sola
cosa piú che di te mi fa patire
o io mi sento come morta viola
che nessuno raccoglie e fa perire
dentro la terra senza che bellezza
venga mai vista in lei senza che ampiezza
compia sopra 'sto fiore il suo periglio
però a grazia d'amore io mi appiglio.

Io ero un uccello

Io ero un uccello
dal bianco ventre gentile,
qualcuno mi ha tagliato la gola
    per riderci sopra,
    non so.

In you I came to know the marvels

In you I came to know the marvels
marvels of love so open
they seemed like shells to me
where I could smell the sea and the lax
deserted beaches and there enclosed in love
I lost myself as in a storm
always keeping this heart steady
because (I knew well) that it loved a dream.

That word always remains with me

That word always remains with me
which I did not tell you and which makes me suffer
something that languishes dead and alone
but how can I tell you my love
what it is that assails me if I am alone
what it is that makes me suffer more than you
or I feel like a dead violet
that no one picks and leaves to die
in the ground beauty never discerned in it and greatness
never carries out its menace on this flower
despite this I cling to the charm of love.

I was a bird

I was a bird
with a soft white stomach,
someone cut my throat
    for amusement,
    perhaps.

Io ero un albatro grande
e volteggiavo sui mari.
Qualcuno ha fermato il mio viaggio,
senza nessuna carità di suono.
Ma anche distesa per terra
io canto ora per te
le mie canzoni d'amore.

Anima anima ricorda lui

Anima anima ricorda lui,
il mio clavicembalo d'oro,
ricorda come suonava le dolci orchestre
delle passate avventure.
Anima anima ricorda lui,
pietra di paragone preferita,
avida felce tranquilla
rinascente dalle ceneri pura;
ricorda le piume del suo passo,
il suo sandalo pieno di rumore,
ricorda quella comunione di baci,
ricorda il calice di Orfeo.

Sono nata il ventuno a primavera

Sono nata il ventuno a primavera
   ma non sapevo che nascere folle,
   aprire le zolle
   potesse scatenar tempesta.
Cosí Proserpina lieve
   vede piovere sulle erbe,
sui grossi frumenti gentili
e piange sempre la sera.
Forse è la sua preghiera.

I was a big albatross
and circled the seas.
Someone stopped my journey,
with scant regard for sound.
But even laid out on the ground
I now sing for you
my songs of love.

Soul soul remember him

Soul soul remember him,
my harpsichord of gold,
remember how he played the sweet orchestras
of past adventures.
Soul soul remember him,
the favourite touchstone,
eager and restful fern
born again pure from the ashes;
remember his light footstep,
his sandal full of noise,
remember that communion of kisses,
remember the chalice of Orpheus.

I was born on the twenty-first of spring

I was born on the twenty-first of spring
    but I was unaware that to be born mad,
    and to open the clods
    could unleash a storm.
And so the delicate Proserpine
    sees it rain on the grass
over the high gentle wheat
and in the evening she always weeps.
It is perhaps her prayer.

Alda Merini

Amai teneramente dei dolcissimi amanti
senza che essi sapessero mai nulla.
E su questi intessei tele di ragno
e fui preda della mia stessa materia.
In me l'anima c'era della meretrice
della santa della sanguinaria e dell'ipocrita.
Molti diedero al mio modo di vivere un nome
e fui soltanto una isterica.

Le piú belle poesie

Le piú belle poesie
si scrivono sopra le pietre
coi ginocchi piagati
e le menti aguzzate dal mistero.
Le piú belle poesie si scrivono
davanti a un altare vuoto,
accerchiati da agenti
della divina follia.
Cosí, pazzo criminale qual sei
tu detti versi all'umanità,
i versi della riscossa
e le bibliche profezie
e sei fratello a Giona.
Ma nella Terra Promessa
dove germinano i pomi d'oro
e l'albero della conoscenza
Dio non è mai disceso né ti ha mai maledetto.
Ma tu sí, maledici
ora per ora il tuo canto
perché sei sceso nel limbo,
dove aspiri l'assenzio
di una sopravvivenza negata.

Alda Merini

Tenderly I loved the sweetest of lovers
and they never realised it.
And over these I wove spiders' webs
and fell prey to my own web.
In me was the soul of the prostitute
the saint the bloodthirsty and the hypocrite.
Many had a name for my way of life
and I was only hysterical.

The finest poems

The finest poems
are written on stones
with injured knees
and minds sharpened by mystery.
The finest poems are written
before an empty altar,
encircled by delegates
of heavenly madness.
And so, mad criminal that you are
you dictate verses to humanity,
the verses of recovery
and the biblical prophecies
and you are the brother of Jonah.
But in the Promised Land
where golden apples and
the tree of knowledge spring up
the Lord has never come nor has he ever cursed you.
But you yes, you curse
your song hour by hour
because you have descended to Limbo,
where you inhale the wormwood
of revoked survival.

La Terra Santa

Ho conosciuto Gerico,
    ho avuto anch'io la mia Palestina,
le mura del manicomio
    erano le mura di Gerico
e una pozza di acqua infettata
ci ha battezzati tutti.
Lí dentro eravamo ebrei
e i Farisei erano in alto
e c'era anche il Messia
    confuso dentro la folla:
un pazzo che urlava al Cielo
    tutto il suo amore in Dio.

Noi tutti, branco di asceti
eravamo come gli uccelli
    e ogni tanto una rete
oscura ci imprigionava
ma andavamo verso la messe,
la messe di nostro Signore
e Cristo il Salvatore.

Fummo lavati e sepolti,
odoravamo di incenso.
    E dopo, quando amavamo
ci facevano gli elettrochoc
perché, dicevano, un pazzo
non può amare nessuno.

Ma un giorno da dentro l'avello
anch'io mi sono ridestata
e anch'io come Gesú
ho avuto la mia resurrezione,
ma non sono salita ai cieli
sono discesa all'inferno
da dove riguardo stupita
    le mura di Gerico antica.

The Holy Land

I have known Jericho,
    I too have had my Palestine,
the walls of the asylum
    were the walls of Jericho
and a pool of infected water
baptised us all.
Inside there we were Jews
the Pharisees were up high
and the Messiah too was there
    dazed inside the crowd:
a mad man who shouted up to Heaven
    all his love for God.

A flock of ascetics, all,
we were like birds
    and every now and then a dark
net imprisoned us
but we went towards the harvest,
the harvest of our Lord
and Christ the Saviour.

We were washed and buried
we smelled of incense.
    And later, when we loved someone
our treatment was electric shock
because, they said, a mad person
can not love anyone.

But one day from inside the tomb
I too woke up again
and like Jesus I too
have had my resurrection,
    but I did not go up to the skies
I went down to hell
from where, astonished, I look again at
    the walls of ancient Jericho.

A Manganelli

A te, Giorgio,
noto istrione della parola,
mio oscuro disegno,
mio invincibile amore,
sono sfuggita, tuo malgrado,
eppure mi hai ingabbiato
nella salsedine
della tua lingua.
Tu, primissimo amore mio,
hai avuto pudore
del mio atroce destino,
tu mi hai preso un giorno
sull'erba, al calore del sole,
la perla della mia giovinezza.
Com'era bello, amore,
sentirti spergiuro.
E tu che non volevi.
Tu, per cui ero
la sofferta Beatrice delle ombre.
Ma non eri tu ad avermi,
era la psicanalisi.
E in fondo, Giorgio,
ho sempre patito
quel che ti ho fatto patire.

To Manganelli

From you Giorgio,
well known hyberboler of the word,
my dark intention,
my invincible love,
I have escaped, in spite of you,
and yet you have trapped me
in the saltiness
of your language.
You, my very first love,
have shown discretion
for my terrible destiny,
one day on the grass,
in the heat of the sun,
you took the pearl of my youth.
How lovely it was, my love,
to hear you make false promises.
And you did not want to.
You, for whom I was
the suffering Beatrice of the shadows.
But it was not you that possessed me,
it was psychoanalysis.
And in the end, Giorgio,
I have always suffered for
for what I made you suffer.

Jolanda Insana

TEACHER, TRANSLATOR and literary critic, Jolanda Insana was born in Messina in 1937 and has lived and worked in Rome for many years. She first came to the attention of the critics in the early Eighties with the publication of *Fendenti fonici* for which she was awarded the 1982 *Premio Mondello*. Her first poems had appeared five years earlier in 1977 bearing the curious title of *Sciarra amara*. Although few in number, they are a useful indicator of what the reader might expect from Jolanda Insana's poetry in general.[1]

The most striking feature of Insana's work is her manipulation of the language while the main impression is one of a poet locked in mortal combat with the words at her disposal. The title given to her early poems, *Sciarra amara* (Loud and bitter brawl), is highly appropriate as it aptly conveys the idea of a situation where the search for a pretext to cause disturbance, be it verbal or otherwise, is constantly present. Insana's poetry often reflects anger while her dexterous use of language can make it difficult to decipher the various layers of meaning hidden in this poetry.

The simplest and most complete guide to her early poems is provided by the lines themselves where Insana presents herself to the reader:

pupara sono
e faccio teatrino con due soli pupi
lei e lei

1 Jolanda Insana has published five collections of poetry to date including her early poems which first appeared in the 'Quaderni della Fenice 26' and were called, *Sciarra amara*. All references to poems in this chapter are taken from the following editions of her poetry:

Sciarra amara (Milan, Guanda, 1977).
Fendenti fonici (Società di Poesia, Milan, Guanda, 1982).
Il collettame (Società di Poesia, Milan, Guanda, 1985).
La clausura (Milan, Crocetti, 1987).
Medicina carnale (Milan, Mondadori, 1994).

Jolanda Insana has translated several classical authors into Italian, the most notable of which are the *Poems* of Sappho (1985), *Carmina* by Plautus (1991), *De amore* by Andrea Cappellano (1992). She has also edited the poetic version in Italian of Ahmad Shawqi's *Passion of Cleopatra* (1989) and Alexander Tvardovskij's *The right of memory* (1989).

lei si chiama vita
e lei si chiama morte
la prima lei per così dire ha i coglioni
la seconda è una fessicella
e quando avviene che compenetrazione succede
la vita muore addirittura di piacere   (*Sciarra amara*, p.37)

(I am a puppeteer/ and I provide theatrical amusement with just two pup-
pets/ her and her/ one is called life/ and one is called death/ the first one has
balls so to speak/ the second a flighty female opening/ and when penetration
takes place/ life actually dies from pleasure)

From these lines we can deduce a two fold purpose in Insana's poet-
ry. She intends to grapple and battle with the language at her dispos-
al and to push it to the extremes of all types of expression. Language
is something that can be manoeuvred for entertainment or used to
highlight the absurdity of life while Insana herself is convinced that
life is just a battlefield with people constantly in search of conflict and
dissension:

non finiremo mai di fare
sciarra amara
nessun compare* ci metterà
la buona parola
tu stuti² le candele
che io allumo   (*Sciarra amara*, p.46)

(we will never stop/ our bitter conflict/ no godfather will put in/ a good word
for us/ you quench the candles/ that I light)

Insana's poetry immediately catches the reader's eye as the various
compositions are often scattered in an apparently haphazard fashion
across the page. Devoid of capitals or any form of punctuation they
seem to be the remnants of what has survived the poet's assault on
language. Speaking of this verbal delirium Insana says:

Difficile raccontare della febbre che smangia e del delirio che mi disorienta
e però mi fa padrona delle contorsioni. Per riempire altri corpi e tappare buchi
[. . .] mi piego a raccattare torsoli di materia verbale [. . .] annaspando in
depositi fuoriuso [. . .] affilando imprecazioni e bestemmie, le lame della
rissa quotidiana, bagliori dell'evento.³

---

2 *Stutare*, which means to quench in modern Italian, comes from the Sicilian
   verb *astutari*.
* The Sicilian word *compare* (in Latin *compadre*) means godfather, friend, neigh-
   bour. It is also used as a form of address.
3 *Poesia*, anno 1, n.9, settembre 1988, p.20.

(It is difficult to put into words the fever that gnaws away and the delirium that confuses me and which however makes me master of all contortions. To fill up other bodies and to block up holes [. . .] I bend to pick up the stalks of verbal material [. . .] groping through depositories no longer used [. . .] sharpening curses and imprecations, the blades of daily brawls, the flashes of the contest.)

This honesty and frankness highlight the appropriateness of the title, *Fendenti fonici* (Phonic daggers) chosen by Insana for her poems published in 1982. The title deliberately suggests that the words used by the poet are like sabre or dagger blows that swish downwards, wound and leave a mark. These downward blows are also defined as *fonici* and herein lies their real power as it is the sound that strikes the reader as they cut through the air.

Insana makes it clear that she is the one caught in this friction and she makes no apology for her pent up anger:

il referente sono io
e me ne vanto   (*Fendenti fonici*, p.7)

(I am the referent/ and I am proud of that).

Her poetry uses language that is often grotesque, crass and scurrilous and that seems to assault rather than court the ear. This aggressive, sceptical and provocative language seems to come from her impatience with the written word and from her perception that words too can hide or reveal various layers of hatred in all its forms. Why this anger, this brusque form of communication, this rage within? Why is the poet constantly in search of litigation and seldom at peace with herself? Insana rejects the Cinderella role which publishing houses reserve for poetry and is also aware that those who read poetry are few while the fortune of poets is often in the hands of critics, some of whom are scrupulously honest, others less so. It is not possible, however, to find a precise answer to these questions. The hurried and anxious rhythm which persists throughout leaves the reader with the precise impression that something seems to be hot on the poet's heels causing her to react angrily and to express these emotions in her radical use of language:

io voglio essere e sono con crudelezza
quello che segno
non voglio simboleggiare

via la sacralità
è un modo antico per tapparmi la bocca e fottermi ancora
                                        (*Fendenti fonici*, p.19)

(I want to be and mercilessly I am/ that which I mark down/ I do not want
to be a symbol/ away with sacredness/ it is an old way of blocking my mouth
and fucking me again)

Although Jolanda Insana does not say what it is specifically that
causes her to react in this way, the reader is left with the impression
that she has suffered some hurt in the past from which she may be
unable to free herself. The reader is unable to locate what it is that
pursues and torments the poet while her enemy could be a man, a
poet, or a god to mention a few plausible possibilities. The obsession
of this hurt – which also reflects the way in which poetry is poorly treat-
ed – and the desire to seek revenge resound throughout her work and
it is almost as though the poet decided to satisfy this pent-up anger by
relentlessly battering the language at her disposal. She sees no other
alternative to poetry as a form of resistance:

[. . .] il poeta sfortunato
o s'impicca o è martoriato   (*Fendenti fonici*, p.56)

([. . .] the unlucky poet/ either hangs himself or is martyred)

while, at the same time, Insana challenges those whom she considers
threatening:

e a chi mi vuole spogliare svergognare
e spubblicare
io dico
ti do la lana non la pecora   (*Fendenti fonici*, p.12)

(and to those who want to strip, disgrace/ and shame me in public/ I say/ I
will sacrifice the wool not the sheep)

Litigious and ironic, Insana creates a division between herself and
life that the written word is unable to bridge. The only thing that exists
for the poet is the *sciarra amara* and this fracas accounts for the con-
stant, variable, and angry register of the words she uses. Fully con-
scious of her own attitude, she also knows, however, that her situation
will not change:

potessi essere reale
legittima con una madre e un padre regolari
non scambiabile con nessuna parafrasi o perifrasi

ma il fatto è che non sono un'altra cosa   (*Fendenti fonici*, p.19)

(if only I could be real/ legitimate with a regular mother and father/ unex-
changeable with any paraphrase or periphrasis/ but the fact is that I am not
another thing).

This fracas is used by the poet both to search for and imprison the truth while the variety of registers indicate not only the power but also the inadequacies of the written word. The poet and critic Giovanni Raboni draws attention to the combination of contrasting registers representing the tragic and also the comic and burlesque in Insana's poetry. He refers to her *plurilinguismo*[4] and considers her verbal substance to be something innate and solid which she works on with considerable competence and skill. This multilinguism is also strongly influenced not only by the Sicilian dialect with which she is familiar but particularly by Latin which she uses in her work as teacher and translator of classical Latin authors. In her poetry she often uses Latin (and also Greek) to play on a range of meanings, some direct, others indirect, that vary between Latin and Italian:

scialate-scialate[5]
rattoppatori di cenci raccattonati
prima o poi arriva il giubileo mengaldo
che depone croce de profundis et de sanctis

(Fendenti fonici, p.13)

(enjoy yourselves, enjoy yourselves/ menders of picked up rags/ sooner or later the mengaldo[6] jubilee will arrive/ for the deposition of croce[7] de profundis and de sanctis[8])

Il collettame (The consignment) bridges the gap between *Fendenti fonici* (1982) and *La clausura* (1987). The title refers to the collective

4 G. Raboni, *Poeti del secondo Novecento*, Storia della Letteratura Italiana (Milan, Garzanti, 1987), p.241.
5 The verb *scialare* comes from the Latin *exhalare* and means to enjoy oneself.
6 Pier Vincenzo Mengaldo (1936–), philologist and contemporary Italian literary critic. Here Insana plays on the names of three outstanding literary critics and historians whose opinions have carried much weight in Italian literature since the middle of the nineteenth century. The 'mengaldo jubilee' refers both to the emergence of Mengaldo as a literary critic and also to his anthology on Italian poets in the twentieth century (*Poeti italiani del Novecento*, Milan, Mondadori) first published in 1981.
    A jubilee is usually preceded by a period of penance and then final pronouncements are made. There was much controversy when Mengaldo's anthology appeared in 1981 with some disputing his choice of poets while others who were not included voiced their disappointment and anger. Mengaldo replied to all these accusations and justified his selection. His work sets aside Croce's approach to literary criticism and presents poetry for what it is. He particularly values the link between the word, life and reality.
7 Benedetto Croce (1866–1952), philosopher, historian and literary critic.
8 Francesco De Sanctis (1817–1883), critic and literary historian.

consignment of words and poems which the poet commits to the writ-
ten page. Language remains the poet's mask while the truth of her
poetry can be found in the epigraph selected for the introduction where
she defines herself as a poet, both chosen and branded for sentence:

mi hai scelto e il marchio è una condanna
                                        (*Il collettame*, p.5)

This phrase is addressed by the poet to poetry itself which she con-
siders both a vocation and an inferno. The tragicomic figure of the
poet emerges from these poems and Insana maintains an ironic dis-
tance from it all:

– hai detto poeta?
– sì, poeta, poietés,[9] che fa, che crea, fattore insomma
– e tu che fai? io per conto mio mi costruisco scaffali
   d'abete o pino russo per le più prestigiose collane di
   poesia, ma tu che fai?   (*Il collettame*, p.25)

(– did you say poet?/ – yes, poet, poietés, who makes, who creates, in short,
a maker/ – and what do you do? for my part I make myself bookshelves/ from
deal or Russian pine for the most prestigious collections/ of poetry, but you
what do you do?)

When asked what it is the poet creates the answer is simply 'versetti/
gli uni agli altri simiglianti,' (*Il collettame*, p.26), little verses/ all simi-
lar to each other. Elsewhere she calls her creations 'fantasie burbesche'[10]
(haughty goliard fantasies) and she finds herself threatened and trapped
within a circle that is on fire:

è infuocato il cerchio da cui non esco e rischio
                                        (*Il collettame*, p.26)

The poet, more than others, comes face to face with a 'sorte ladra' or
thieving destiny and the only defence becomes the way in which ideas,
thoughts and emotions are articulated in poetry. Faced with this sit-
uation Insana uses her mask of irony and so we see the two sides to
the poet, the two extremes. Her predilection is for the word that risks
most, the one that willingly jumps on the high tension wire, the 'filo
dell'alta tensione' (*Il collettame*, p.8). The mask allows her create two

9 Taken from the Greek word which means 'to do'.
10 A neologism formed from *burbanza* (arrogance) and *furbesco* (cunning). Insana
   has further adjusted the latter part to include the Medieval idea of the live-
   liness of student life.

poets, the real and the false, while this ironical stance allows her distance herself from the word, especially when poetry is defined as the

[. . .] alchimia d'incantamenti e d'ironia
senza pretesa di alloppiare[11] la gente   (*Il collettame*, p.35)

([. . .] the alchemy of enchantments and irony/ with no pretension to sedate people)

The publication of *La clausura* (Cloistered life) in 1987 introduces the reader to another aspect of Insana's poetry which makes her unique in the Italy of the closing decades of this century. She is acutely aware of the contrast that exists between dialect and language and many of the words or invented words in her earlier works reflect her own Sicilian dialect. Her awareness of the force and attraction of dialect forms is, in the opinion of Giacinto Spagnoletti, one of the best arguments in defence of dialect poetry that has been published in Italy in the last half of this century.[12]

For Insana, the dilemma that exists between the use of Italian vis à vis dialect is even more acute:

La lingua letteraria ha di fronte a sé la storia del disagio o addirittura del dramma per la dissociazione dal dialetto [. . .] Anche quando cerchiamo di recuperarlo nella scrittura, siamo costretti a reinventarlo per dargli una dignità letteraria'.[13]

(The language of literature comes face to face with the history of the discomfort or indeed the drama caused by its disassociation from dialect [. . .] And when we attempt to retrieve dialect in writing, we are obliged to reinvent it in order to give it literary dignity.)

One of the distinguishing features of *La clausura* is the variety and richness of the poems and the language used in them. In this work Giovanni Raboni values her linguistic ingenuity ('ingegnosità linguistica')[14] while the poet, Antonio Porta, in his analysis of one of the sections entitled, 'La colica passione', finds that the attraction of her

---

11 The verb *alloppiare* is typical of the many old, unusual or even invented verbs and words which Insana uses in her poetry. The meaning of *alloppiare* is defined as: 'Acconciar bevande con alloppio, ovvero oppio, a fine di fare addormentare' in the *Vocabolario Italiano della lingua parlata*, novamente compilato da Giuseppe Rigutini (Florence, Barbèra, 1871), p.48. Its meaning here is to anaesthetize or sedate.
12 G. Spagnoletti, in *Il Messaggero*, 30.4.1988.
13 *Il Messaggero*, 30.4.1988.
14 Giovanni Raboni, 'Per il verso giusto' in *L'Europeo*, 17.4.1988.

poetry lies precisely in the manner in which she challenges opposites and apparent contradictions. How, for example, can a passion be described as colic but this is exactly what Insana does in one of the poems. In Antonio Porta's opinion she also finds a balance in language that recalls the propensity for the use of opposites often apparent in baroque poetry.[15]

The opening lines of La clausura make us aware of the poet's intent when she says:

m'infrastocchio in angiporti e non mi smielo [. . .]
e intorno tanti scippi e scempi e mi lascio sfaldare e
    sfiocchettare
                        [. . .] e in uno scoppio sfregio
    e sfrotto
le sbarre della clausura   (La clausura, p.9)

(I hide around in blind alleys and I do not cast good aside [. . .]/ so much stealing and destruction all around I let myself crumble and unravel/ [. . .] and in an outburst I disfigure and deface/ the bars of the cloister)

The initial impression is one of formal linguistic creative exploration that is particularly apparent in the invention of verbs such as 'm'in-frastocchio'[16] and the striking use of alliteration, assonance and rhyme. The title, La clausura (Cloistered life) is ironic and the poet, instead of searching for the quiet of the cloister, intends to chose the opposite by fleeing from the bars which mark its confines and give herself over to the reality that is all around. On the one hand, there is the world with all its highs and lows which the poet is fully aware of. On the other there is the person, representing the individual, the mask and the soul and, through them, there is the poet who looks for and attempts to reach the extremes offered by word and language alike.

La clausura is divided into five sequences and one of them recounts a trip to the northern parts of Africa which allows the poet bring colour and excitement to her diary-like account of this journey. What follows is a firm conviction of the power of poetry and the word itself. The poet retraces the lost road, so to speak, while her voice rises and falls with landscapes which reflect her varying states of mind:

15 Antonio Porta in 'Almanacco dello specchio', n.12 (Milan, Mondadori, 1986), p.368.
16 M'infrastocchio comes from the Sicilian frastocchia which means the creation of things with words. Insana has forced its meaning here to create a verb of movement.

il tutto che mi abita è un niente
se lo estrapolo dai suoi contorni certi
e lo scorporo dal fianco che frange il fragile momento
e posso pensare quanto voglio ma non riuscirò a pesare
quanto ardo e sento il male del corpo talieggiato

(La clausura, p.20)

(everything that lives in me is nothing/ if I take it from its sure surroundings/ and strip it from the side that breaks the fragile moment/ and I can think as much as I like but I will not succeed in calculating/ how much I burn within and I feel the evil of the blackmailed body)

Expressions such as 'ardo e sento' recall similar ones used by the poet Gaspara Stampa and also make us aware of Insana's sensual ability in the lyrical sphere. In this collection Insana seems to have acquired a certain form of tranquillity that was absent in her earlier poetry. Despite her awareness of the lonely destiny of the poet in general, midway through *La clausura*, she states that poetry can provide significant consolation for those who are prepared to devote themselves to it:

e credo che la parola molto assista chi per lei molto
rischia   *(La clausura, p.31)*

(and I believe that the word is of great assistance to those who/ risk a lot for it)

Insana's efforts to immerse herself in the surrounding reality are reflected in some of the closing lines of *La clausura*:

troppo cauta cerco il varco nella strettoia del momento
e sembra che tutto avvenga lentamente perché di
    scatto mi levo
e metto mano al fuoco volendo risentire la storia
delle due pietre e della scintilla che apre la pupilla
al seduttore di fantasmi canforati e lo rianima
e lo seduce alla vita   *(La clausura, p.52)*

(too cautiously I look for the opening in the tightness of the moment/ and all seems to happen slowly because suddenly I get up/ and start the fire wishing to hear again the story/ of the two stones and the spark which opens wide/ the eye of the seducer of camphor lined ghosts/ reanimates him and seduces him towards life).

Here Insana would seem to be pointing towards a new direction which implies an effort, on the part of the poet, of being involved with life itself.

Jolanda Insana published *Medicina carnale* (Carnal medicine) in 1994 and there she presents life where everything has reached a crucial stage – the body of the world is ill, it stutters, mumbles and totters about. She does not oppose this world but lets it be and voices her distress in verse:

come sistemarlo in vita
questo che non è un ingombro e vacilla
quando fa la fila davanti agli sportelli e ha freddo
e suda
e scende dalle gambe e a perturbato infiammamento
schizza via che è un incanto
nel canto più sicuro
questo corpo incauto e previdente
che ama l'alta temperatura e gela
male patendo il malo uso   (*Medicina carnale*, pp.12–13)

(how can you sort it out in life/ it is not in the way and staggers/ when it queues at the window counters and is cold/ and sweats/ and collapses and with disturbing inflammation/ darts off magnificently/ to the safest corner/ this careless and circumspect body/ which loves high temperature and freezes/ poorly suffering the evil use)

In *Medicina carnale* the poetry reaches out towards all than can be seen or touched in a reality that is caught in a feverish grasp. In a sympathetic way the words seem to try and defend the body as though they possess curative and restorative powers. Insana's medicine does not prescribe moderation and her emotions oscillate constantly between violence and restriction:

Non posso evitare il veleno
amando io il pungiglione della vita
e in dosi quotidiane lo prendo
antidoto contro il grande veleno amaro
e così pur avendo ferite aperte sulle mani
tocco le cose e punto i piedi
per spostare la parete . . .   (*Medicina carnale*, p.17)

(I can not avoid the poison/ as I love the sting of life/ and I take it in daily doses/ as an antidote against the great bitter poison/ and so despite the open wounds on my hands/ firmly I plant my feet/ to move the wall . . .)

The poems of *Medicina carnale* try to provide verbal responses and reactions to pain or attempt to explore the seriousness of the wounds caused by that same pain or despair:

poiché la vista stava variando ho svuotato le tasche
e deposta la sacca ho scagliato elci e bastone
all'imbocco dell'erto passo
per lasciare lì il peso dicendo e non dicendo
qui resta la stanchezza
e volendo essere leggera m'inerpico alleggerita
contando di lasciare alla prossima salita l'altro
peso

in cima si arriva prima con la mente   (*Medicina carnale*, p.17)

(since the view was changing I emptied my pockets/ put aside my knapsack
threw far away oak branches and stick/ at the entrance to the steep pass/ to
leave the burden there saying and not saying/ weariness stays here/ and want-
ing to be nimble I climb up unburdened/ planning to leave the other burden
on the next climb/ first to arrive at the summit is our mind)

Poetry here has a decidedly therapeutic role as it offers a definitive
escape from anguish and pain:

e dunque mitigare le molestie della mente
rifiutando l'eccesso di ripienezza
per non preparare il corpo a stupore
e febbre di paralisi
ma temperarlo biada buona al sole
nei luoghi più alti e più ventosi
dove gli odori aprono i pori e i vapori buoni
vanno alla testa   (*Medicina carnale*, p.41)

(and therefore to mitigate the troubles of the mind/ by refusing the excess of
padding/ so as not to prepare the body for torpor/ and the fever of paralysis/
but to strengthen it like good corn in the sun/ in the highest and most windswept
places/ where herbs open the pores and good vapours/ go to the head.)

Medicina carnale seems to have brought Insana a certain form of
tranquillity while the restorative power of the poems would appear,
temporarily, to have brought her some degree of serenity. The clarity
of these lines sets them apart from others because the poet, like a good
doctor, realises that in order to recover from illness, the body often
needs to be given both physical and mental respite from the demands
of daily living.

The language used by Insana reflects the varying states of emotion
which she experiences from poem to poem. She moves from the parox-
ysm of new turmoil, 'convulsione di nuovi fermenti,' (*Medicina carnale*,
p.13) to the sharpness and fury of blood, 'acutezza e furia di sangue',
(*Medicina carnale*, p.42) all of which are curiously accompanied by a

longing to call out in names the months and days, 'smania di dire i mesi e i giorni' (*Medicina carnale*, p.23). Any attempts at communication offer little outcome of success:

traviando in mille andirivieni perviene
dove la vertigine è più fonda   (*Medicina carnale*, p.33)

(straying through a thousand comings and goings leads/ to the dizziest vertigo)

Contradictions continue to play their part here and the word, which still thirsts to be heard, 'assetata ancora è la voce di parlare' (*Medicina carnale*, p.12), can still be a source of darkness too:

che strano questo nunzio che arriva
e porta l'alba e mi acceca e oscura la forma
                                        (*Medicina carnale*, p.57)

(how strange this messenger who comes/ and brings the dawn blinds me and darkens form)

In these poems Insana also presents the freshness of the countryside and the sea in a sun drenched light against a background of the warmth and fertility of the Sicilian countryside. This abundance of the earth with its terrestrial beauties is neither a prize nor comfort but something that keeps us away from the insane water, 'acqua insana', (*Medicina carnale*, p.53) to become a force that prevents destruction of self. The play of meaning on her surname allows the poet suggest too that all is not well with her but she is determined to overcome whatever it is that troubles her. There is a suggestion of a new beginning in the following lines:

e scendemmo al porticciolo di san Paolo
chiostrato dalla muraglia marina [. . .]
bello avere un mantello di cielo
andando con i piedi a terra   (*Medicina carnale*, p.54)

(and we went down to the tiny port of St. Paul/ cloistered by the sea barrier [. . .]/ nice to have an azure mantle/ walking with your feet on the ground)

This communication with the surrounding world allows these poems to reach a conclusion. The departure now marks the return, the medicine points to the illness while the illness shows the various stages of recovery that finally heal the wounds. For Insana the period in between, however, can be both tortured and tormented.

The distinguishing feature of Insana's poetry therefore is its linguistic adeptness which can, on occasion, make the real meaning of her verse difficult to comprehend. Her creation of new words together with her complete rejection of punctuation is indicative of her dissatisfaction with the language at her disposal as she reduces all to the bare essentials. The combination of references to Sicilian, Latin and Greek together with her own rendition of the Italian language make this poetry challenging from a linguistic point of view, different yet stimulating on the cultural level.

Niente dissi

1
di referenze ne ho assai
più di quanto basta

2
il referente sono io
e me ne vanto

3
mi specchio e sgravo con dolore
figliando famiglie di parole
immagini pargolette e sorelline maggiori

lo specchio sono io
sono io il mio stesso io
e tu ci sformi

Un' altra afasia

6
io voglio essere e sono con crudelezza
quello che segno
non voglio simboleggiare

via la sacralità
è un modo antico per tapparmi la bocca e fottermi ancora

7
non spunta giunco dove non c'è acqua
e sono oggetto di religione di beffa o d'ironia
perché senza soggetto e senza padri
piccolo o audace gioco di fantasia
e chissàcosasia

8
potessi essere reale
legittima con una madre e un padre regolari
non scambiabile con nessuna parafrasi o perifrasi

ma il fatto è che non sono un'altra cosa

I said nothing

1
I have enough references
more than is necessary

2
I am the one referred to
and I am proud of that

3
In the mirror I see myself and deliver with pain
giving birth to families of words
infant images and tiny older sisters

I am the mirror
I am my very self
and this disappoints you

Another aphasia

6
I want to be and mercilessly I am
that which I mark down
I do not want to be a symbol

away with sacredness
it is an old way of blocking my mouth and fucking me again

7
where there is no water reeds do not grow
and I am the butt of religion jest or irony
because I am devoid of subject and of fathers
small or daring game of fantasy I am
and who knows what it is

8
if only I could be real
legitimate with a regular mother and father
unexchangeable with any paraphrase or periphrasis

but the fact is that I am not an other thing

E venga un nuovo scorticatore

1
non potendo salire muri lisci
per punto de honor – puntiglio
portare al trotto le rumorose batterie
per le vie auguste di nostra terra

2
in faccia a stragi e contumelie
non ci servono nonne speranze
che sbrodettano

3
e venga un nuovo scorticatore
a trarre Marsia di sua pelle
piripacchio spockiano e spocchioso
che succhia con la bocca a cuore

4
come il padrone è padrone
perché ha torto e vuole ragione
così tu sei poeta
(Petrarca Petrarca
quanti guai

5
e se indovini 'io travaglio e lei suda'
ti do quattro versi senza metronomo

6
tu ce l'hai
io ce l'ho
non nominare il mio invano

7
eppure il poeta sfortunato
o s'impicca o è martoriato

8
solo la seppia ha i figli in testa
e il padreterno fa figli crocifissi

May a new flayer come

1
unable to climb smooth walls
as a point of honour – punctilio
to trot out the noisy assaults
through the hallowed streets of our land

2
faced with massacres and humiliating insults
we have no need for granny hopes
that dribble along

3
may a new flayer come
to drag Marsia from his skin
spockish and dogmatic caricature
who sucks with his heart-shaped mouth

4
as the boss is the boss
because he is wrong and wants to be right
in the same way you are a poet
(Petrarch Petrarch
how much trouble

5
and if you guess 'I labour and she sweats'
I will give you four verses that have no metronome

6
you have it
I have it
do not name mine in vain

7
and yet the unlucky poet
either hangs himself or is martyred

8
only the cuttlefish has its offspring in its head
and God Almighty makes crucified children

9
carne venduta merce in ribasso
vuoi diventare come il santo del quadro
appeso al muro
e quattro di pappa cinque di nappa
metti o soqquadro comparati e baronie
e fai il soldo con la carta
nascondendo l'asso nella manica

Hai detto poeta?

- hai detto poeta?
- sì, poeta, poietés, che fa, che crea, fattore insomma
- e tu che fai? io per conto mio mi costruisco scaffali
    d'abete o pino russo per le più prestigiose collane di
    poesia, ma tu che fai?

ordinatore di pena e di penna
il libro stempra il mio barbarico ondamento
ma la fantasia del cuore non è buona
e mi trae a caso per figure d'ornamento

Non c'è tempo

troppo cauta cerco il varco nella strettoia del momento
e sembra che tutto avvenga lentamente perché di
    scatto mi levo
e metto mano al fuoco volendo risentire la storia
delle due pietre e della scintilla che apre la pupilla
al seduttore di fantasmi canforati e lo rianima
e lo seduce alla vita

9
exploited flesh reduced goods
do you want to become like the saint in the picture
hanging on the wall
and four of this and five of that
you cause trouble among friends and baronies
and you make money with cards
by hiding the ace in your sleeve

Did you say poet?

– did you say poet?
– yes, poet, poietés, who makes, who creates, in short, a maker
– and what do you do? for my part I make myself bookshelves
    from deal or Russian pine for the very best collections
    of poetry, but you what do you do?

organiser of pain and pen
the book brakes my savage interior swell
but the fantasy of my heart is not good
and by chance it drags me through figures of adornment

There is no time

too cautiously I look for the opening in the tightness of the moment
and all seems to happen slowly because
    suddenly I get up
and start the fire wishing to hear again the story
of the two stones and the spark which opens wide the eye
of the seducer of camphor-lined ghosts reanimates him
and seduces him towards life

a calda forza precipita la ripida assenza

a calda forza precipita la ripida assenza
e poiché mi costringo a riceverla come dono
ho deciso di mettermi a tavola prima del suo ritorno
e scontando al meglio la mia parte
racconto dell'inferno come un angelo per
      riconquistarmi
la quotidiana porzione di sete

poiché la vista stava variando ho svuotato le tasche

poiché la vista stava variando ho svuotato le tasche
e deposta la sacca ho scagliato elci e bastone
all'imbocco dell'erto passo
per lasciare lì il peso dicendo e non dicendo
qui resta la stanchezza
e volendo essere leggera m'inerpico alleggerita
contando di lasciare alla prossima salita l'altro
peso

in cima si arriva prima con la mente

la vita si mantiene a cielo aperto

la vita si mantiene a cielo aperto
e più gagliardo esercizio si conviene al mattino
quando più liberamente svaporano le fumosità
per i meati del corpo aperti
e più schietti piaceri tirano il sangue

la linea viene al mondo per errarvi liberamente
nella slegatura delle trame
senza sciupare il fiore né il colore

the steep absence falls headlong with sheer strength

the steep absence falls headlong with sheer strength
and since I force myself to accept it as a gift
I have decided to sit down to table before it returns
and paying as best I can for my portion
like an angel I tell of hell so as to
   recover
the daily share of thirst

since the view was changing I emptied my pockets

since the view was changing I emptied my pockets
put aside my knapsack cast far away oak branches and stick
at the entrance to the steep pass
to leave the burden there saying and not saying
weariness stays here
and wanting to be nimble I climb up unburdened
planning to leave the other burden on the next
climb

first to scale the summit is our mind

life takes strength in the open air

life takes strength in the open air
and more robust exercise is suited for the morning
when smoky shades evaporate more freely
through the openings of the body
more genuine pleasures excite the blood

the line is born to wander freely
in the unloosening of the wefts
spoiling neither flower nor colour

decisa a partire senza libro

decisa a partire senza libro
medicina carnale
della mente e del corpo bellissima mai
mai a nessuno donata
la prenotazione era cancellata e ricciuto
capitano occhiverdi imbarcava acqua insana
mentre Citera mandava lampi

non era il caso
di nuotare nel tormentamento per devoti

non siamo osservanti in nulla stando sulla porta

non siamo osservanti in nulla stando sulla porta
della moschea nella città murata
e qui c'è l'agrume desto in frutti e zagara
nato in terreno grasso da caldo vento ventilato

in che senso la doppia immagine fotografata
nello specchio sopra la fontanella per i piedi

l'acqua ha profumo di limone e ne usiamo la bellezza
pure sapendo che le promesse finiscono in pioggia

e ci fermiamo sotto linde finestre

e ci fermiamo sotto linde finestre
davanti a portoncini ad ante cordate
e non fu necessario riprendere i fili
avendo capito che perisce ogni cosa creata
pure davanti alla trireme cicladica
incisa sulla roccia di Lindos

l'assenza è devotamente donata in bocca al lupo

determined to leave without the book

determined to leave without the book
carnal medicine
of the mind and of the body
beautiful never given to anyone
the booking was cancelled and the curly
green-eyed captain took aboard insane water
while Cythera sent out lightening flashes

out of the question
to swim in the stormy waters for devotees

we are not observers as we stand by the door

we are not observers as we stand by the door
of the mosque in the walled in city
and here is the live citrus scent in fruit and orange blossoms
born in fertile ground caressed by warm winds

the meaning of the double image reflected
in the mirror above the fountain for the feet

the water smells of lemon and we use its beauty
even if we know that promises end in rain

and we stop beneath spruce windows

and we stop beneath spruce windows
in front of small entrances with roped shutters
and it was not necessary to pick up the threads again
having realised that all created things perish
even in front of the Cycladic trireme
carved on the rock at Lindos

absence is devotedly donated to the wolf

e scendemmo al porticciolo di san Paolo

e scendemmo al porticciolo di san Paolo
chiostrato dalla muraglia marina
e si fece da sé e da sé si diede nuovo nome
la schiena contornata d'azzurro
e vidi che bisognava pensare dentro e in proprio
impugnando la torcia

bello avere un mantello di cielo
andando con i piedi a terra

mai viste olive concave con l'osso piegato

mai viste olive concave con l'osso piegato
e la pelle piagata
cremìdi è la parola dell'estate
la cipolla e l'insalata
e ripresi il flauto e la spada e rimasi esitante
di fronte al pane appaiato sulla tovaglia

passando poi per la via dei cavalieri
odòs ippodòn
tornai all'agorà di tutti i giorni

così per la prima volta fotografai mulini a vento

mi stringo addosso il giorno

mi stringo addosso il giorno
e m'inviluppo nella sua luce ricca di cortesia
e sento che mi guazza dentro come un'ape nel suo fiore
e ho paura di gesti sconsiderati
perché ho paura che si sfasci per troppa frenesia
e mi lasci al buio
accucciata in un nome di città

and we went down to the tiny port of St. Paul

and we went down to the tiny port of St. Paul
cloistered by the sea barrier
its back surrounded by blueness
it came from itself and of itself took a new name
and I saw one had to think deep and for oneself
holding the torch

nice to have an azure mantle
walking with your feet on the ground

never seen concave olives with curled stone

never seen concave olives with curled stone
and wrinkled skin
cremìdi[1] is the word of the summer
the onion and the lettuce
and I picked up the flute again and the sword and hesitated
in front of the bread paired out on the tablecloth

then passing through the horsemen's street
odòs ippodòn[2]
I went back to the agorà[3] of every day

so I took a picture of windmills for the first time

I cling to the day

I cling to the day
wrap myself in its light full of kindness
it wallows within like a bee in its flower
and I dread thoughtless gestures
because I dread too much frenzy will break it up
and leave me in the dark
huddled up in the name of that city

1 *Cremìdi* is the Greek word for onion.
2 *Odòs ippodòn* is Greek for horseman's street.
3 *Agorà* is Greek for market place.

Biancamaria Frabotta

WHEN BIANCAMARIA FRABOTTA published *Donne in Poesia*[1] in 1978, this new anthology drew attention to the work of Italian women poets whose formation had been determined by the social, political, cultural, economic and ideological changes that had taken place after the war. The anthology opens with a quotation taken from the French poet and writer Marceline Desbordes-Valmore who says that she writes precisely because she wants to counteract the then prevalent opinion that women should not write.[2]

Frabotta attempts likewise to justify her presentation of an anthology of women poets by showing that their poetry is worthwhile and deserving of greater critical attention than the token gesture paid to it in the many anthologies of modern Italian poetry. At the same time she emphasises not only the apprehensions of these women in life but also those divergencies which make them different as writers of poetry. She is careful, however, not to ghettoise this poetry or to separate it from mainstream literature. Her objective is to show that women's poetry can be as valid and warrant the same attention as much of the poetry written by men though at the same time reflecting the varying and divergent interests of women. Frabotta puts the record straight once and for all and uses the poem *Floridano*, written by the sixteenth century Venetian poet, Modesta Pozzo, in 1581 to make her point. In so doing Frabotta shows that the obstacles faced by women poets now are not peculiar to the twentieth century:

Le Donne in ogni età fur da Natura
Di gran giudicio, e d'animo dotate,
Ne men atte à mostrar con studio, e cura
Senno, e valor de gli huomini son nate,
E perché, se commune è la figura,
Se non son le sostanze variate,
S'hanno simile un cibo, e un parlar denno
Diferente haver poi l'ardire, e 'l senno?   (*Donne in Poesia*, p.8)

(In all ages women were by Nature gifted/ With great wisdom and spirit./ Nor are they born less gifted than men,/ To display wisdom, care, learning

1 *Donne in Poesia* (Rome, Savelli, 1976).
2 *Ibid.*, p.9: 'Les femmes, je le sais, ne doivent pas écrire; j'écris pourtant.'

229

and valour/ And why, if they have the same character,/ If substance does not vary,/ If they share similar food and speech,/ Why should their passion and wisdom be different?)

Born in Rome in 1946 Frabotta is now professor of modern and contemporary Italian literature at the Sapienza University in Rome and throughout her life she has combined an academic career with an active involvement in women's issues. Her first collection of poetry, *Il rumore bianco*, was published by Feltrinelli in 1982 though many of the poems it contains were written from the early Seventies onwards and had first appeared in various journals and anthologies.[3] *Il rumore bianco* (The white noise) represents the niche Frabotta creates for herself and her world of poetry, a sort of exile that is beyond the reaches of life, language and daily living. It is a fluctuating space which she sought out for herself during the turbulent 1970s and which allowed her face its ideals and contradictions without being overwhelmed by these experiences. The title, *Il rumore bianco* (which also symbolically recalls the poet's name Biancamaria)[4] is explained in the introduction to the poems. From the outset, therefore, the poet's space is clearly delineated:

Per esempio consideriamo il moto casuale di una piccola particella immersa in un fluido e la fluttazione del numero di collisioni che le molecule del fluido hanno con la particella. Questa fluttazione la chiamiamo 'rumore bianco'.

(*Il rumore bianco*, p.15)

(For example, let us consider the random movement of a small particle immersed in a fluid and the fluctuation of the number of collisions that the molecules in the fluid have with that particle. This fluctuation is known as the 'white noise'.)

3 The journals are 'Tam Tam', 'Nuovi Argomenti', 'Salvo Imprevisti', 'Tabula' and 'Prato pagano' while the anthologies are *Poesia italiana degli anni settanta* (Milan 1979), *Le printemps italien. Poésies des années 70*, 'Action poétique' Paris 1977), *Poesia femminista italiana* (Rome, 1978) and *Dal fondo. La poesia dei marginali* (Rome, 1978). In 1989 she published the novel *Velocità di fuga* (Trent, Reverdito).
   The following are Frabotta's poetry collections to date:
   Il rumore bianco (Milan, Feltrinelli, 1982).
   Appunti di volo (Rome, Edizioni del Cometa, 1985).
   La viandanza (Milan, Mondadori, 1995).
   In this chapter all references to her poems are taken from these texts.

4 *I Quaderni del Battello Ebbro*, Anno IV, n.8, Aprile 1991, p.7. In this article the poet Roberto Carifi considers the white in the title of these poems and in the poet's name to be a symbol of the poetic power of language: 'Anche il nome del bianco, il bianco del nome [. . .] rappresenta la potenzialità poetica del linguaggio'.

Frabotta's propensity for metaphor is striking and the titles of later
works reflect this predilection which singles her out among the poets
of her generation. Tomaso Kemeny and Cesare Viviani, in their defi-
nition of metaphor in recent Italian poetry, give us a sharp insight into
the linguistic possibilities which it can offer and which Frabotta reg-
ularly uses in her poetry:

La metafora nasce dalla considerazione che il linguaggio non dice soltanto
quello che è ma dice anche quello che non è. La metafora nasce da una cod-
ificazione di usi e spazi del linguaggio [. . .] La metafora nasce da una rego-
lazione di spazi e di percorsi di lettura. O si potrebbe dire il linguaggio è il
luogo dove il soggetto si perde e si ritrova continuamente. La metafora diven-
ta una misura di controllo di questo perdersi.[5]

(Metaphor arises from the consideration that language does not just say that
which is but it also defines that which is not. Metaphor arises from a cate-
gorisation of use and space in language [. . .] Metaphor is born from a reg-
ulation of space and paths within the written text. Or one could say that
language is that place where the subject loses and finds itself continually.
Metaphor becomes a controlling measure of this loss of self.)

This need to express herself in poetry is alluded to by Antonio Porta
in his Introduction to *Il rumore bianco*. He remarks on her need for
poetry, her 'bisogno di poesia' (*Il rumore bianco*, p.7) that is both per-
sonal and linguistic and which became apparent to Frabotta during
the period of student and social strife in 1968. For Porta, this unrest
created the urgency in Frabotta to suspend herself in a realm of absence
so that silence and reflection might bring her closer to linguistic rigour
and poetic inspiration. Poetry therefore is synonymous with this absence
and, through the metaphor of silence which poetry relies on, it para-
doxically becomes a live presence in the language used by the poet.
White, which marks the absence of all other colours, is, in the realm
of physics, the absolute concentration of all colours. Like the poet's
name, Biancamaria, the colour white is also a metaphor for absence
and presence in the written word just as the white page may be the
indicator of the presence or absence of the written message:

O è colpa del mio nome se annullo nell'assenza
ogni colore e il tuo calore guidatore di stelle
io disfo nel biancore? E' che mi chiamo bianca . . .
                                        (*Il rumore bianco*, p.134)

5 *I percorsi della nuova poesia italiana* edited by Tomaso Kemeny and Cesare
   Viviani (Naples, Guida, 1980), p.1.

(Or is it the fault of my name if I cancel out every colour/ in this nothingness and in the whiteness I undo your warmth/ guide to the stars? It is because I am called Bianca . . .)

In order to fully appreciate the meaning of these words it is helpful to consider what Frabotta tells us about her first introduction to poetry:

non dimentico che io stessa ho cominciato a scrivere poesie perché un piccolo gruppo di poeti e di lettori si riuniva in uno scantinato dove liberamente cominciava a esprimersi il bisogno di poesia di una generazione. Eppure attorno imperversava il '68 . . . [6]

(I cannot forget that I began to write poetry simply because a small group of poets and readers used to gather in a cellar and in great freedom began to express the need for poetry of an entire generation. And yet 1968 was milling all around . . .)

For Frabotta, therefore, poetry is a need which allows her express urgent ideas and thoughts. It also represents a moment of recollective calm while elsewhere chaos and confusion may dominate.

In the poetry of *Il rumore bianco*, which covers a creative period of approximately ten years, the reader is struck by the recurrence of the themes of division and reversal. The opening poem speaks of the *simile* and the *dissimile*, what is similar and what is different, while the closing lines accentuate the play of opposites, the dialectic of Hegel:

Su altra pioggia cade la pioggia di ieri
ciò che sta sopra a ciò che sta sotto
chi scacciato torna dorme con noi
semina insieme panico e sonno.   (*Il rumore bianco*, p.19)

(Yesterday's rain falls on another rain/ what is on top of what is underneath/ he who is chased away comes back sleeps with us/ creating both panic and sleep.)

This idea of psychological division is heightened in the poems which follow where the images evoked are that dusk splits the wood into two distinct verses, 'la penombra spacca il bosco in due distinti versi,' (*Il rumore bianco*, p.20). Elsewhere Frabotta describes the mirror which doubles the head of good hope, the head split in two by a fog which walks by, 'lo specchio che doppia il capo di buona speranza/ la testa sdoppiata da una nebbia passeggiatrice,' (*Il rumore bianco*, p.22) or, rather disturbingly, she states that the one who comes intact goes away divided, 'chi viene intera se ne va divisa'. (*Il rumore bianco*, p.24)

6 *Il Manifesto*, 27.2.1981.

The reality which emerges from the dialogue of these and other poems is full of contradictions and changes, excesses and omissions. This uninterrupted dialogue where the participants are both male and female allows the poet keep her distance and yet her link with others allows her adopt various patterns of irony which she uses as a form of defence in her poetry. It is a feature which makes her aware of the virtues of poetry and the risks which it can entail. Conscious of its instability she says that often the answer can be legible to all and illegible to her, 'leggibili per tutti e per me indecifrabile,' (*Il rumore bianco*, p.31) while it also induces her to comment ironically:

Da queste parole nascono altre parole
onesta ve le affido
con un parto lieve ed elegante . . .   (*Il rumore bianco*, p.28)

(Other words are born from these words/ honestly I entrust them to you/ with a light and elegant delivery . . .)

This ironic tone sets Frabotta apart from other poets and allows her say of herself:

Ho un buco nel mezzo della testa
che non basta la bussola
per il vento che ci fischia.   (*Il rumore bianco*, p.79)

(There is a hole in the middle of my head/ and the compass is not strong enough/ to recognise the wind that whistles through it.)

Elsewhere the tone is both mischievous and serious:

e io mi compro gli stivaletti
neri come la notte e con alti tacchi
per mettere la testa fuori dalle nuvole. (*Il rumore bianco*, p.96)

(and I buy boots for myself/ that are black as night and with high heels/ so that my head may emerge from above the clouds.)

This idea of withdrawal above the clouds is further emphasised when she ironically admits that she is different from others:

E' vero. Non come te poeta io sono
io sono poetessa e intera non appartengo a nessuno.
                                         (*Il rumore bianco*, p.101)

(It is true. I am not a poet like you/ I am a woman poet and in no way do I belong to anyone.)

Frabotta here asserts her independence as a poet: she will not conform to a particular view of what poetry is or should be (according to others) but asserts her right to be herself even if this means having to pay a certain price for such emancipation. Her frankness and directness as a poet makes her confess:

vivo di giorno disperdendo la mia ombra
e di notte mi confondo ombra nell'ombra.

(*Il rumore bianco*, p.129)

(I live by day dispersing my shadow/ and at night I disappear a shadow in the shadows.)

In the introduction to these poems Antonio Porta suggests that the silent world, filled with absences and presences in Frabotta's poetry, could well be a metaphor for the female body with the words of this woman poet interpreted as the products or fragments of internal interactions. Referring to herself as a 'poetessa' or woman poet, Frabotta tells us about her world, often not fully recognising perhaps but giving us a reflection of herself. Her poetry is self reflective and gathers together objects and events from life so that the image she wants to present may have a reality or an objective appearance of its own. Unlike Julia Kristeva who insists that language is asexual, Porta also makes a number of other suggestions: that poetry for a woman poet may be created within that silence rather than outside of it, that the language of poetry may be both male and female or that it may be bisexual because it participates in each of the processes associated with silence or submission, represented by the female, and reproduction represented by the male. (*Il rumore bianco*, pp.9–12)

The titles chosen by Frabotta for her poetry reflect a constant interchange between action and immobility that has increased with time. These variations move from *Affeminata* (1977)[7] to *Rumore Bianco* (1982), *Appunti di volo* (1985) and *La Viandanza* (1995). This interchange is further accentuated by the title chosen for her novel *Velocità di fuga* (1989)[8] which contrasts sharply with the poems of *La vita sedentaria* (a subsection of *La Viandanza*) that are dedicated to different types of fish whose appearance and habits Frabotta describes from the sedentary position of one who watches, observes, and annotates.

The novel *Velocità di fuga* (Speed of flight) presents two protagonists, mother and daughter, Elvira and Olga, whose relationship is

7 First published in 1977 (Rome, Geiger), it was later included in *Il rumore bianco* (1982).
8 *Velocità di fuga* (Trent, Reverdito), 1989.

fraught with tension. The silence of the city at night acts as a back-drop to the claustrophobic atmosphere in the house where the daughter feels suffocated and trapped. In order to break free from this situation and escape in a flight that seems to offer some perception of freedom, the daughter needs to confront both her mother and that inner self she has inherited from her mother. It is this last feature that presents her most difficult obstacle as she attempts to break free, because, as Frabotta noted perceptively in *Donne in poesia*:

[. . .] quasi sempre una donna che comincia a scrivere trova in sé la prima nemica, il primo ostacolo da superare. (*Donne in Poesia*, p.11)

([. . .] A woman who begins to write almost always finds the first enemy within herself, the first obstacle she has to overcome.)

The final chapter of this novel is called *Appunti di volo* (Flight notes), which recalls the title given to a poetry subsection in 1985, and here it shows a certain determination by the protagonist to achieve her goal. At the start of the novel she declared her intention to become a writer but this novel does not allow for reconciliation nor does it reach any definitive conclusions. It does however intimate certain possibilities of escape or 'fuga'. All else is left suspended and the reader may consider a variety of outcomes which seem plausible in the circumstances.

It is possible that the path of many female lives are similar to that of Olga who anxiously searches for a way to escape but who is devoid of any clear awareness of pitfalls and who lacks comforting objectives at the point of arrival. This novel does not provide any reassuring balance sheets for the older generation or the younger one, for the student disturbances of 1968, feminism, nor the disturbing political developments of the previous decade. All pass under the scrutiny of the writer's gaze that is both disillusioned and severe and Frabotta neither identifies with nor redeems any of these elements. In like manner her poetry does not offer any certainties either to the author or the reader.

Frabotta's most recent work *La Viandanza* (1995) contains a number of sequences with subtitles that once more accentuate the fluctuation between movement and stillness, action and recollection. The sequences are entitled *Appunti di volo*,[9] *I giorni della sosta, La vita sedentaria, La Viandanza, Le spezie morali*, and *Spiragli sull'equivoco* (Flight notes, Rest days, Sedentary life, Travel path, Moral spices and Glimmers over the equivocal.) Frabotta has long been drawn to the figure of the traveller and the melancholy image associated with wandering. The

9 Some of these poems are taken from the collection *Appunti di volo*, 1985.

title chosen for this work, *La viandanza* or travel path, is both myste-
rious and archaic but it is at the heart of the subject matter in this
work. Setting out on a path or journey has long been associated with
the figure of the male traveller while here, the traveller is female as she
attempts to find and understand her past through the quagmire that
represents the present time. While the actual journey may be imbued
with an air of excitement it can also bring the poet face to face with
facts that are often impenetrable and evasive. It is at this point then
that the real journey is shown to be the one that brings the poet close
to those who are dearest to her. The two longest poems in this col-
lection are 'La viandanza', dedicated to her mother, and 'Vento a Bures'
where the tomb of an unknown man buried near Paris brings to mind
her recently deceased father. Elsewhere in these poems the journey
across different paths continues but with a greater degree of calm and
recollection. It is less punctuated by the desire to escape and accord-
ingly, more aware of the fanciful nature of every effort to escape real-
ity.

Space and time play a significant part in this journeying as the poet
tells us in the opening poem 'Appunti di volo':

E' l'ora dell'imbarco [. . .]
Alzai gli occhi dal libro sulla via
e mi vidi, Partenza, irta di tornanti.   (*La Viandanza*, p.9)

(It is boarding time [. . .]/ On the way I looked up from the book/ and saw
myself, Departure, bristling with sharp turns.)

Once the journey has started there is no return. The twists and turns
referred to are not just geographical but also sentimental. The poems
'La viandanza' and 'Il vento a Bures' are ones where the journey through
memory brings the poet back to her parents. 'Vento a Bures' (Wind
in Bures) begins with a visit to the tomb of an unknown person in a
cemetery in the Parisian suburb of Bures. As she contemplates this
tomb Frabotta's journey of the mind brings her back to the life and
death of her father buried some months earlier in a cemetery near
Rome. This tomb in Bures kindles a lyrical vein in the poet's imagi-
nation and memory. Her imaginary conversation with this dead man
allows Frabotta bring her father back momentarily to life and it allows
her see him again.[10] This posthumous dialogue is similar to the musi-
cal artifice of the diminished fifths which allows each note to be repeat-
ed on the musical scale but always one octave higher so that in due
course the scale returns to the sharp of the initial note. The image of

10 *La Viandanza*, p.43: 'Di nuovo come si vedono le cose già viste'.

her father is recalled but enriched with several seemingly trite mem-
ories which find a new lyrical vein that is full of musical resonances,
rhymes, assonances and alliteration. Frabotta's propensity for irony
appears once more towards the end of the poem:

> E se gli ultimi
> saranno i primi venga presto la primula
> a ultimare le dimenticanze dello scalpellino.
> Domani avrò anch'io l'impareggiabile lucentezza del marmo.
> (*La Viandanza*, p.45)

(And if the last/ shall be the first may the primrose come quickly/ to finish
the forgetfulness of the stone-cutter./ Tomorrow I too will have the incom-
parable lustre of marble.)

By drawing on the evangelical saying that the last shall be the first
Frabotta ironically suggests that it gives her the opportunity to create
a new poetic colouring, the primula or spring primrose that will soon
cover over the imperfect work of the stone mason on the tomb of her
loved one.

By contrast, 'La Viandanza', is written for Frabotta's mother, a
native of Civitavecchia, the Roman Centum Cellae, one of the Italian
towns worst hit during the Second World War, now heavily polluted
by industrial development. In this long poem a palpable sense of par-
ody prevails: the ancient Roman necropolis is now side by side with
the thermo-electrical plant of Fiumaratta. Frabotta brings places and
time together to condemn the deterioration that has taken place in
recent years:

> e se nell'afa sfuma
> la ciminiera più alta d'Europa
> neppure tu le cerchi più le lapidi lambite
> dal liquame della Fiumaretta
> necropoli di vivi incrementi
> al fabbisogno di Roma . . .   (*La Viandanza*, p.80)

(and if the highest chimney stack in Europe/ disappears in the sultry weather/
you too will no longer search for the tomb stones licked/ by the sewage of
Fiumaretta electricity station/ a necropolis of live progress/ for the needs of
Rome.)

There is much flexibility in the language used by Frabotta. She is
always ready to change, adapt, expand or reduce it as she moves from
moments of meditation to ones that ponder on the harsh reality of
industrial development that is often accompanied by pollution and

wanton destruction of the environment. The language, which is controlled and intense, responds well to the effects sought by the poet. The verbal game becomes darker, deeper and sharper as the poet lists those things once prized in Civitavecchia and now destroyed by the pungent and malodorous fumes of the thermoelectric plant at Fiumaratta:

. . . spirava lo jodio sull'indomito
falò amico ai naviganti
che un vezzoso odio eclissò e ora lo smog
amico ai benestanti?   (*La Viandanza*, p.80)

(. . . iodine blew over the indomitable/ bonfire friend of travellers/ which an engaging hatred eclipsed and now smog/ is a friend to the wealthy?)

In this case, the path of progress, followed eagerly by so many travellers, has become one of pollution and destruction. This travelling or *viandanza* forces Frabotta to realise that this apparent development has a decidedly negative side to it that almost obliterates the memories of childhood.

Such progress brings with it the longing to be subversive but that too has been catered for elsewhere in the normal level of interdiction that exists and is understood in several languages:

Il paranoico estro di disastri all'attesa
comparti e defense
custodi e silence
it's forbidden, non leggi?
de stationner sur la passerelle . . . [11]   (*La Viandanza*, p.79)

(The paranoid whim of waiting disasters/ divisions and defence/ custodians and silence/ it's forbidden, can you not read? de stationner sur la passerelle . . .)

Acutely aware of the risks this journeying may entail, Frabotta balances it with moments of quiet and reflection. In the section entitled *La vita sedentaria*, the poet, from a motionless vantage point, reflects on life and movement in the marine world of shellfish and other fish who live deep down in the sea and whose habitat is called the vita sedentaria or sedentary life. This section is in stark contrast to the first section of *La Viandanza* where the emphasis is on action and movement particularly mechanical movement while the second section is more contemplative. The poem 'La sogliola' belongs to the second

11 'Défense de stationner sur la passerelle' = Forbidden to dally on the bridge. Here Frabotta deliberately uses some of the most common phrases found in English and French to indicate things that are forbidden.

part and in it Frabotta associates herself with animal life, specifically with the sole, a humble fish relegated by nature to the depths of the sea bed, a creature whose shape has also been sharply defined by the rigours of sea life:

Greve asimmetria che mostri all'alto
un solo fianco a la portentosa migrazione
entrambi gli occhi sulla stessa banda schiaccia
e con ardua compressione
il mare ti lavora ai fianchi [. . .]
l'onda ti costringe
a strisciare adulta lungo il fondo
ricordi le ore beate della larva
la perfetta simmetria di un tempo
e la grazia del nuoto, vuoto
affiorante in superficie?　　　　　(*La Viandanza*, p.51)

(Austere asymmetry, up high you show/ a single side and the prodigious migra-tion/ flattens both eyes on that one side/ and with hard pressure/ the sea wears away your sides [. . .] the wave makes you/ an adult crawl along the sea bed,/ do you remember the happy hours of the larva/ the once perfect symmetry/ and the graceful swim emptiness/ floating on the surface?)

These lines suggest that the fate of the sole may not be very different from that of humans who are often buffeted and battered by the vagaries and vicissitudes that can afflict them on the journey through life.

That same stillness can also make us contemplate the destruction caused by man and which often becomes apparent to the trained eye several centuries later. In the penultimate section of *La Viandanza* the poem 'Archeologia involontaria' (Unintentional archaeology) makes us aware of the way archaeological excavations can reveal the harsh-ness of previous centuries while also highlighting the cruelty of cer-tain aspects of life on this planet:

Fu forse troppa audacia nel disegno
malasorte, una frana nel terriccio
un capriccio della luna ingolfata
nelle secche di un secolo tomba
e torto il peso d'ossa sfatte
da uno scudo esorbitante [. . .]
e oggi la scienza dello scavo onora
il tuo cranio schiacciato dalla pietra . . .　　(*La Viandanza*, p.98)

(There was perhaps too much daring in the plan/ bad luck, a land slide in the soil/ a whim of the moon immersed/ in the shallows of a dead century/ and the twisted weight of bones undone/ by an outrageous shield [. . .]/ and today the science of excavation honours/ your skull crushed by stone . . .)

Frabotta's poetry challenges her readers to delve deep into the meaning of her poems and to reflect on what she has to say. In the poem 'Il tributo', Frabotta tells us how the creation of a poem is an attempt to give the reader an idea of what the poet is and what she thinks. Such efforts are often more likely to provide intimations rather than furnish reassuring certainties:

E allora mi sconsolo: suvvia
madrigali o acuti puntali
non è una sindrome la mia
che possa lasciare un ricordo
qualunque di sé una trapunta
a maglie grosse e larghe tanto basta
per specchiarsi nella propria Sindone.   (*La Viandanza*, p.23)

(And then I become disheartened: away with/ madrigals or sharp ferrules/ mine is not a syndrome/ that could leave any/ memory of itself a quilt/ with large wide stitches is sufficient/ to mirror oneself in one's own Sindon.)

The blank page which initially faces the writer is not like the sheet which miraculously records an image of our grieving face. What we leave behind is a flimsy rather than a stable image of ourselves on which others may base their conjectures of what we looked like. There is nothing new about this because in *Il rumore bianco* Frabotta had already challenged her readers to become live participants in her discussions:

Orsù dunque lettori, prima che la valvola cilecchi
fatevi tutti orecchi, finestre
slarghi imprevisti nell'etere
non occhi, ma versi, voi stessi
e vegliate, vegliate, vegliate!   (*Il rumore bianco*, p.30)

(Come on then readers, before the fuse fails/ be all ears, windows/ unexpected widening in the ether/ not eyes, but verses, you yourselves/ and be on guard, be on guard, be on guard!)

What then is the ultimate objective of Frabotta's poetry? She provides an explanation of the dilemma encountered whenever she attempts to write:

Scrivo per non fumare ma se non fumo non scrivo
scrivo per non aspettare il sanguinoso squillo del telefono
ma se non telefoni non scrivo
scrivo per non scappare dalla abbondanza della tua vena
ma se non scappo non scrivo [. . .]

scrivo per non darvela vinta moschettieri del vento e del falso
ma se più non vivo e scrivo ahimè
vinta voi sempre l'avrete su di me.   (*Il rumore bianco*, p.83)

(I write not to smoke but if I do not smoke I do not write/ I write not to wait for the bloody shrill of the phone/ but if you do not phone I do not write/ I write not to escape from the profusion of your talent/ but if I do not escape I cannot write [. . .]/ I write not to give in to you musketeers of wind and fraud/ but alas if I no longer live nor write/ you will always have the upper hand on me.)

These negative inverted lines are followed by Frabotta's affirmation of intent and they present a poet whose writing centres on the theme of speed and flight and whose search for a personal identity is projected against the exterior world. It is an autobiographical journey of discovery that starts with the fleeting motion which gives life, 'il moto fugace che ti dà la vita' (*Il rumore bianco*, p.32) while the poet then journeys on alone and contemplates this life with all its snares and pitfalls.

There is indeed a cynical dimension to Frabotta's poetry: she invokes the dialectic which provides an interesting intellectual dimension to her poetry, but in reality, it conceals a certain mischievousness that is revealing in certain respects but which also must be quite amusing for the poet. On the surface, her poetry is more objective than that of many modern Italian women poets but on closer scrutiny, the feminist dimension is still ticking quite loudly beneath the surface. This of course need not in any way compromise her objectivity but it does however cast doubts on her global protestations, especially in the case of her sensitive response to the pollution now rampant in her mother's home town in the poem 'La Viandanza' and then to her father's demise in 'Vento a Bures'. Obviously, the laudable human dimension apparent in these poems adds to their emotional perceptiveness but in terms of the universality which she obviously espouses in her poetry, this recent work introduces an element of parochialism, not dissimilar from many of her female contemporaries. This is an irresolvable dilemma: the deep empathy experienced from close personal involvement is difficult to translate to more universal encounters so that the range of satisfaction for the poet can be variegated. Frabotta has made the choice of sacrificing the personal satisfaction of indulging in her deep responses to idiosyncratic occurrences, for the sake of a more objective response to events which, while having a more general appeal, can limit somewhat the human dimension.

La mela m'insegni è doppiare la metà di sé.

La mela m'insegni è doppiare la metà di sé.
La vita mi insegni è gli spicchi della mela
la meta dell'incresciosa circostanza
lo specchio che doppia il capo della buona speranza
la testa sdoppiata da una nebbia passeggiatrice
due metà in una, la mela intera, una copula di cattivo gusto.

Erosione dell'utopia o rigore della pazienza?

Erosione dell'utopia o rigore della pazienza?
Rispondere è sostituire il bianco al nero.
Prova tu che ami il disordine
delle tinte, le onde morte dell'etere
lèccane il nero di grassa dolce colla
e sulla lingua spergiura ti resterà neo nata
l'altra metà della domanda, l'inesprimibile bianco
(non la domanda ma la risposta è il nostro nobile privilegio)
essere leggibile per tutti e per me indecifrabile.

Spegnamo la luce per fare la conta.

Spegnamo laluce per fare la conta.
Cosí fa il pastore di notte con le pecore non sue.
La notte è risaputa di improduttività.
Non sedimenta. È un furto di sonno, di sogni.
Non si dorme esposti all'antico ordine delle stoviglie.
Inventiamo vertenze contro il compromesso.
Auspichiamo il silenzio dei posteri.
Se tu sei ancora sveglio,
scrivimi ti prego una poesia
che vinca la vita che si ostina
che mi affretti l'alba
un inizio di non vita.
Una poesia che non mi si chiuda addosso come una tenaglia.

The apple you teach me is to double the half of self.

The apple you teach me is to double the half of self.
Life you teach me is the slices of the apple
the ambition of the regrettable circumstance
the mirror which doubles the head of good hope
the head split in two by a fog walking by
two halves in one, the complete apple, copulation of poor taste.

Erosion of Utopia or severity of patience?

Erosion of Utopia or severity of patience?
To reply is to substitute white with black.
Let you try you who like the disorder
of colours, the dead waves of ether
lick its blackness of sweet fat glue
and over your perjured tongue will remain new born
the other half of the question, the unspeakable white
(not the question but the reply is our noble privilege)
to be legible for all and illegible for me.

Let us put off the light and count out our numbers.

Let us put off the light and count out our numbers.
The shepherd does this at night with sheep that are not his.
Night is well known for unproductiveness.
It does not settle. It thieves sleep, dreams.
We do not sleep imperiled by the old arranging of crockery.
Against compromise we invent disputes.
We long for the silence of posterity.
If you are still awake,
write a poem for me I beg you
that may defeat obdurate life
and hurry on dawn for me
a beginning of non life.
A poem like pliers may not close in on me.

Ho un buco nel mezzo della testa

Ho un buco nel mezzo della testa
che non basta la bussola
per il vento che ci fischia.
Ieri avrei detto: è la croce dei venti
il nido cilestrino dei monsoni.

Oggi certo me l'ha sparato un amico
un cecchino che pratica l'arte del rattoppo.
Chi ha aperto questa falla nello scafo?
Aria e acqua fanno a gara.
Piú cedevole agnella non c'è per la tua pasqua.

Scrivo per non fumare ma se non fumo non scrivo

scrivo per non fumare ma se non fumo non scrivo
scrivo per non aspettare il sanguinoso squillo del telefono
ma se non telefoni non scrivo
scrivo per non scappare dalla abbondanza della tua vena
ma se non scappo non scrivo
scrivo per non tornare sulla cattiva strada
ma se non torno non scrivo
scrivo per non darvela vinta moschettieri del vento e del falso
ma se piú non vivo e scrivo ahimè
vinta voi sempre l'avrete su di me.

È vero. Non come te poeta io sono

E' vero. Non come te poeta io sono
io sono poetessa e intera non appartengo a nessuno.
Da me, come da te la pura stella dell'inizio del mondo
è lontana la menzogna primaria, vestita di nero e
        maschile nella voce.

There is a hole in the middle of my head

There is a hole in the middle of my head
and the compass is not strong enough
to recognise the wind that whistles through.
Yesterday I would have said: it is the wind-cross
the pale blue nest of monsoons.

Today certainly a friend opened it up
a sniper who practises the art of patching.
Who opened up this breach in the hull?
Air and water are competing.
There is no more pliable lamb for your Easter.

I write not to smoke but if I do not smoke I do not write

I write not to smoke but if I do not smoke I do not write
I write not to wait for the bloody shrill of the phone
but if you do not phone I do not write
I write not to escape from the abundance of your talent
but if I do not escape I cannot write
I write not to return to the evil path
but if I do not return I cannot write
I write not to give in to you musketeers of wind and fraud
but alas if I neither live nor write
you will always have the upper hand on me.

It is true. I am not a poet like you

It is true. I am not a poet like you
I am a woman poet and in no way do I belong to anyone.
The primeval lie, dressed in black and male in voice
    is far from me
just as the pure star of the earth's beginning is far from you.

Con mia madre io ho altri problemi
anche se oggi ti rendo l'onore delle armi
il fuoco sacro dell'imitazione.
Vicino alla morte e a morire è la
corolla spampanata di questa coppa di veleni
la verità si fa piú semplice e facile da ricordare.
Chi di noi dunque per primo ha perso la memoria?

Appunti di volo

È l'ora dell'imbarco. L'altoparlante
ci invita per l'ultima svolta della notte
a risalire il crinale del passato
ardore diurno
a permutare ciò che non è ancora stato
utopia, primizia
o rosa del deserto
questo salto nel vuoto improvviso
di ore che sembravano gremite e ora
nel loro lento sfarsi sulla pista
che appare fumigante e nebbiosa
dietro i vetri
si fanno rade e disperse mentre
si accalcano gli angeli in coda alla lista
d'attesa, l'alfiere biondo del nord
che sbandiera una sua penna iridata
per fuggire la sua pena segreta
l'araldo obliquo del sud che se ride
risplende color Libano di cedro
e s'imbosca al suo desiderio proibito.
Tutti l'altoparlante vinse.
Alzai gli occhi dal libro sulla via
e mi vidi, Partenza, irta di tornanti.

With my mother I have other problems
even if today I pay you military honours
the sacred fire of imitation.
Close to death and to dying
is the overblown corolla of this cup of poison
truth becomes simpler and easier to remember.
Which of us therefore lost our memory first?

Flight notes

It is boarding time. The loudspeaker
invites us for that final turning point of night
to climb back over the ridge of the past
daytime fervour
to change what has not yet been
utopia, first fruit
or desert rose
this unexpected jump in the void
of hours which seemed so crowded and now
with their slow dissolving on the track
which looks steaming and misty
behind the glass panes
they become sparse and dispersed while
the angels crowd in the queue for the waiting
list, the blond standard-bearer from the North
who unfurls a rainbow feather
to escape from his secret pain
the sloping herald from the south who if he laughs
glows like the colour of the cedar of Lebanon
and hides away from his forbidden wish.
All defeated by the loudspeaker.
On the way I looked up from the book
and saw myself, Departure, bristling with sharp turns.

Svuotando il guscio

Svuotando il guscio a ritroso della volta
come un agnél che succhia la via lattea
dalla notte di quell'età scontrosa
risorse l'alba dell'ora locale
e fu una pallida eco dell'altra
sommersa nei tempi morti di un tutto pieno
blu acqua e salino.
Ora è perfino vano cercarti o Siderea!
Di notte rimbombi ma di giorno
il sonno mi assale e nulla prosciuga
come il sale del sogno diurno.
Gli immortali come te lo sanno
dove spira il réfolo del volo cieco
e non chiesti ci ridonano
il colpo di coda dell'ora legale.

L'ultima corsa

Una volta è già capitato
e non fu né la prima né l'ultima
ma fu una delle tante nostre
luminose lunazioni
sopra il fiume che s'insabbiava
in mezzo alle sterpaglie, le fumanti immondizie
che la Magliana spreca
per chi ha dentro un bastante
lembo di azzurro e le stoppie
bruciate sulla franosa pianura
che giace sotto al livello del Tevere.
Poi tornammo al centro per bere
ancora un sorso del giorno
che smoriva con l'ultima corsa
prima del tramonto
rosso di piacere e di angustia
in forse davanti al finestrino già estivo
se fosse colpa dei nostri vent'anni.
Così ci avventammo contro il nostro destino.

Emptying in reverse

Emptying in reverse the shell of the sky vault
like a lamb that sucks on the Milky Way
from the night of that sullen age
the dawn of the local hour rose once more
and was a pale echo of that other one
submerged in the dead times of fullness
deep blue and saline water.
To look for you now, oh Siderea, is even futile!
You ring out at night but by day
sleep assails me and it dries out nothing
like the salt of the daytime dream.
The immortal ones like you know
where the wind gust of the instrument flight blows
and unasked they give us back
the tail flick of the legal hour.

The last run

It happened once already
and it was neither the first not last run
but it was one of our many
shining lunations
over the river which silted up
among the brushwood, the steaming rubbish
which the Magliana wastes
for one who possesses within a sufficient
hem of blue and the burned
stubble on the landslide prone plain
which lies beneath the level of the Tiber.
We returned then to the centre to savour
once again a drop of the day
which was paling with the last run
before the sunset that was
red with pleasure and with want
wondering in front of the already summery window
if it were the fault of our twenty years.
And so we hurled ourselves against our destiny.

La sogliola

Greve asimmetria che mostri all'alto
un solo fianco e la portentosa migrazione
entrambi gli occhi sulla stessa banda schiaccia
e con ardua compressione
il mare ti lavora ai fianchi
la coda ti si accorcia e il muso
maestro agli interminabili agguati
alle sinistre ore del riposo
e alle stente nuotate, ora che
l'onda ti costringe
a strisciare adulta lungo il fondo
ricordi le ore beate della larva
la perfetta simmetria di un tempo
e la grazia del nuoto, vuoto
affiorante in superficie?

Archeologia involontaria

Fu forse troppa audacia nel disegno
malasorte, una frana nel terriccio
un capriccio della luna ingolfata
nelle secche di un secolo tomba
e torto il peso d'ossa sfatte
da uno scudo esorbitante
per pur sì grande eroe o fu
forse il pudore del Macedone
l'oro massiccio di una Menade
cui certo per l'oblio e non per tanto
furto l'artista smemorato si ritrovò
nello sbalzo estremo di un amore per sempre
ma viva guida fece il morto al morto
e oggi la scienza dello scavo onora
il tuo cranio schiacciato dalla pietra
inviolabile ladroncello di Vérgina
secolare agonia in cambio di un tesoro.

Salonicco, 1990

The sole

Austere asymmetry, on high you show
a single side and the prodigious migration
flattens both eyes on that one side
and with hard pressure
the sea wears away your sides
your tail shortens itself and your head
guides through the endless snares
the ominous hours of rest
and the difficult swims, now that
the wave makes you,
an adult, crawl along the sea bed,
do you remember the happy hours of the larva
the once perfect symmetry
and the graceful swim, emptiness
floating on the surface?

Unintentional archaeology

There was perhaps too much daring in the plan
bad luck, a land slide in the soil
a whim of the moon immersed
in the shallows of a dead century
and the twisted weight of bones undone
by an outrageous shield
for so great a hero or was it
perhaps the constraint of the Macedonian
the massive gold of a Maenad
whom through forgetfulness and not for so clamorous
a theft the forgetful artist found himself
in the final sudden change of a lasting love
but the dead one was a live guide for the dead
and today the science of excavation honours
your skull crushed by stone
inviolable pilferer of Vérgina
centuries-old agony in place of treasure.

                                          Salonika, 1990

Vivian Lamarque

ONE OF THE MOST striking features of Vivian Lamarque's poetry is its apparent simplicity. This feature of uncomplicated directness was recognised by Vittorio Sereni when he reviewed her first work, *Teresino*, and pointed out that apparently simple lines could have an unexpected and devastating effect.[1] Although born in Tesero in the province of Trent in 1946 Lamarque has lived all her life in Milan where she alternates the teaching of Italian at secondary school level with the writing of poetry and other related activities. She is also one of Italy's most successful creators of children's stories and there is a direct link between the suffering related in these fables with Lamarque's own life.[2]

Vivian Lamarque has produced five collections of poetry to date.[3] The first, *Teresino*, which appeared in 1981, was awarded the 1981 Viareggio prize for a first poetry collection. It opens with a quotation from Charles Perrault, author of the fable, *Babes in the Wood*. The quotation refers of the exact moment when the children realise they have been abandoned by their parents and they immediately vent their terror by crying and calling out for help as loud as possible.[4] At first sight such a quotation might seem irrelevant and out of place were it not immediately followed by the opening poem, 'Aprile dal bel nome' which describes the fate of the infant who was curiously christened Vivian Daisy Donata:

1 Vittorio Sereni, 'Cuore fa rima con intelligenza' in *Europeo*, 19.10.1981.
2 Lamarque considers her work in this sphere to be as important as her commitment to poetry. There is a striking and deliberate symmetry between the number of poetry collections (5) and children's fables (5) that she has published to date. These are *Il libro delle ninne-nanne* (Milan, Paoline, 1989); *La bambina che mangiava i lupi* (Milan, Mursia, 1992); *La bambina di ghiaccio* (Trieste, E.Elle, 1992); *La bambina senza nome* (Milan, Mursia, 1993); *Il sogno di Sara: Arte della libertà* (Milan, Mazzotta, 1995).
3 Vivian Lamarque has published the following collections of poetry:
   Teresino (Milan, Società di Poesia e Guanda), 1981.
   Il signore d'oro (Milan, Crocetti), 1986.
   Poesie dando del Lei (Milan, Garzanti), 1989.
   Il signore degli spaventati (Rovigo, Pegaso), 1992.
   Questa quieta polvere (Milan, Mondadori), 1996.

   All references to Lamarque's work in this chapter are taken from these texts.
4 *Teresino*, p.7: 'Le Père et la Mère les menèrent dans l'endroit de la Forêt le plus épais et le plus obscur . . . Lorsque ces enfants se virent seuls, ils se mirent à crier et à pleurer de toute leur force.'

Aprile dal bel nome
quando sono nata
io stessa con nomi curiosi
di bei significati
per dire che ero pratolina . . .
e che dovevo vivere
(da una parte o dall'altra)
per dire donata
(o donanda) (4)[5]   (*Teresino*, p.9)

(Lovely name of April/ when I was born/ with strange names/ and fine meanings/ to say I was a daisy . . . / and that I had to live/ (in one place or the other)/ given as a gift/ (or to be donated.)

The poem which follows tells us of the event which has marked Lamarque's life since infancy:

A nove mesi la frattura
la sostituzione il cambio di madre.
Oggi ogni volto ogni affetto
le sembrano copie cerca l'originale
in ogni cassetto affannosamente. (456)   (*Teresino*, p.9)

(At nine months came the break/ the substitution the change of mother./ Today every face every affection/ look like imitations./ She searches frantically for the original in every drawer.)

The child's reaction to the trauma of abandonment and to the loss of her mother is one of silent bewilderment while the apparent simplicity of the poetry reaches deep down into the reader's reserves of sympathy and anguish:

Valdesina trascinata per una mano
giù fino a Milano
appena appena finito Natale
zitta guardava attorno
il nuovo presepe
la nuova mamma. (586)   (*Teresino*, p.10)

---

5 Vivian Larmarque has written over 2000 poems each bearing a number that refers to the chronological order in which they were written while a selected number have appeared in print. The bracketed numbers which follow each poem refer to the sequence in which they were written and not to the order in which they appear in printed form.

(Tiny Waldensian[6] dragged down by hand/ to Milan/ Christmas just over/ silently she looked around/ at the new crib/ the new mother.)

The reader is brought fully into the situation and the poignancy of this child's experience is totally encapsulated in the lone adjective 'zitta' mentioned above and in the silence which marks these traumatic changes in her life:

Senza piangere mentre una madre la passava a un'altra
mentre i padri sparivano ad uno ad uno . . .
in silenzio ad osservare come volano
mosche piume foglie sguardi affetti figli via. (525)

(Teresino, p.11)

(No tears as she was passed from one mother to another/ while the fathers disappeared one by one . . . / silently watching how /flies feathers leaves glances affection children all fly away.)

It is at a point like this that we can fully appreciate Sereni's acute observation that certain lines by Lamarque are unexpected, stark and overwhelming. Once again we are reminded of the line from the fable that relates how the parents bring the children to the darkest point of the forest. Those same people who should epitomise love, protection, security, responsibility and parental affection are the very ones who relinquish all responsibility and abandon their children to the darkness and confusion of the wood. The break with her own family, its substitution of another one that is duly accompanied by a change of mother are the dominant themes of these early poems. The original mother is similar to a lost and precious object and she becomes the focus of the child's frantic search for her missing identity.

There are times too in these poems when Lamarque deliberately brings us face to face with confused identity as in 'Andai in chiesa' where it initially seems that the poet is playing a game of hide and seek with the reader. It is almost like a game of split personality where the reader must work out who is who and what their respective relationship may be:

Andavi in chiesa per sposarti un'altra volta.
Con la stessa persona di prima.

---

6 Adjective which refers to Waldo and the religious movement founded in the twelfth century AD which was based on poverty and preaching. Following various upheavals and persecutions down through the centuries it is now part of the Italian Evangelical Federation of Churches. Lamarque's maternal grandfather was a minister of this church in Tesero.

Io stavo in mezzo agli invitati
ma anch'io ero vestita da sposa.
Certi si confondevano e fotografavano me
ma tu chiarivi immediatamente l'equivoco. (132)

                                        (*Teresino*, p.32)

(You were going to church to marry once more./ To marry the same person
as before./ I was among the guests/ but I too was dressed as a bride./ Some
were becoming confused and they photographed me/ but you quickly clari-
fied any ambiguity.)

Teresino is interspersed with quotations which keep the reader abreast
with the experience and progress of both the *Babes in the Wood* and
the poet herself. At a certain point she wonders how she might warn
her daughter and her young friends of the pitfalls ahead:

In mezzo a indiani
e piccoli cani
mia figlia e i suoi amici
hanno in corso l'infanzia
e come avvertirli?   (40)   (*Teresino*, p.46)

(Between Indians/ and little dogs/ my daughter and her friends/ are going
through childhood/ and how can I warn them?)

The final section of *Teresino* is preceded by a further quotation from
Perrault's fable which tells how the children ran through the night,
terrified and lost in their surroundings.[7] These poems then are organ-
ised around a story which tells of children being abandoned and then
forced to flee from a house which instead of welcoming them was a
source of great danger. Fable and reality are a source of live inspira-
tion for Lamarque in this early work while the structure of the children's
story allows her use and suggest a parallel with her own experience
as a frightened and confused child.

Traumatised by separation and deprived of the love of her natural
mother, Lamarque's situation recalls, albeit at a distance of some sixty
years or so, the trauma experienced and recorded by Umberto Saba
when forcibly separated from his wet nurse, the beloved maternal fig-
ure of his youth. Saba's lines poignantly record his grief while the adult
Saba is immersed in melancholy reflections. His poem, 'Il piccolo
Berto', allows Saba cope with his own heartache and it also puts
Lamarque's poems into a new perspective:

7 *Teresino*, p.83: 'Ils coururent presque toute la nuit, toujours en tremblant et
   sans savoir où ils allaient.'

> . . . Un grido
> s'alza di bimbo sulle scale. E piange
> anche la donna che va via. Si frange
> per sempre un cuore in quel momento.
> Adesso
> sono passati quarant'anni.
> Il bimbo
> è un uomo adesso, quasi un vecchio, esperto
> di molti beni e di molti mali. E' Umberto
> Saba quel bimbo. E va, di pace in cerca,
> a conversare con la sua nutrice
> che anch'ella fu di lasciarlo infelice
> non volontaria lo lasciava. Il mondo
> fu a lui sospetto d'allora fu sempre
> (o tale almeno gli parve) nemico.[8]

(. . . A child's cry/ rings out from the stairs./ The lady leaving weeps too./ A heart breaks at that moment./ Since then/ forty years have passed./ The child/ is now a man, almost an old man/, acquainted with much good and evil. That child/ is Umberto Saba. In search of quiet/ he goes to talk with his wet nurse/ who was also sad to leave him/ unwillingly she gave him up. Since then/ suspicious of the world it always/ (or so it seemed) was hostile to him.)

Umberto Saba sought the assistance of the analyst, Edoardo Weiss, a friend of Freud's, to help him cope with and understand this event in later years. Lamarque too has sought the help of a psychoanalyst, who uses Jung's theory of psychological analysis, to help her cope with the pain of these childhood memories and she dedicated the poems of *Il signore d'oro*, *Poesie dando del Lei* and *Il signore degli spaventati* to this person. Determined to communicate with the world around her she has decided to relate her feelings both to and for her analyst and does so in the above named trilogy that contains a selection of the numerous poems written between 1984 and 1992.

For the critic Alida Airaghi the poems of *Il signore d'oro* should be regarded as prose poems and SOS type messages directed both at the reader and the protagonist, the *signore d'oro*.[9] About him we are told little: he wears a grey overcoat and exudes a radiant and golden aura. He may well be the doctor mentioned in the dedication or the gentleman who meets a lady (whom he presumably directs through the various stages of analytical therapy) in the final poem, 'Il signore e la signora':

8 Umberto Saba, *Canzoniere* (Turin, Einaudi) 1978, p.389.
9 A. Airaghi, *La collina*, 1987, p.53.

Erano un signore e una signora che si erano cono-
    sciuti lo stesso giorno.
Che ore erano?
Le dieci e trenta.
E dove erano?
Erano sotto il livello stradale di 4 o 5 gradini.
E come avvenne?
La signora suonò alla porta e il signore aprì.
E dopo?   (*Il signore d'oro*, p.87)

(A man and woman met that same day./ What time was it?/ Half past ten./
And where were they?/ 4 or 5 steps below street level./ How did it happen?/
The lady rang the bell and the gentleman opened./ And then?)

The reason we are given little information about the doctor may
also be attributable to the fact that the patient herself knows little about
her analyst. It is a basic premise for successful analytical therapy as it
offers ample space to patient and doctor in which to successfully inter-
pret and analyze the patient's deepest feelings.

From this point onwards Lamarque attempts to express through
poetry this experience of transfer therapy in which the protagonist (the
doctor) helps the patient (Lamarque) come to terms with episodes
and ordeals that are deep in the past. In psychological terms 'trans-
fer' indicates the special rapport created between the analyst and the
patient who tends to transfer unconsciously to the analyst feelings and
emotions previously experienced for an important figure in his or her
childhood. This characteristic makes it one of the key factors in ther-
apy as it helps the analyst interpret and explain previously unresolved
mental traumas.

Lamarque dedicates *Il signore d'oro* to a doctor identified only with
the initials *B.M.* The importance of the relationship with her analyst
is apparent in the title *signore d'oro* (The gentleman of gold) both of
this work and the one which follows which refers to him as *Lei*, the
polite form of address which is also indicative of the distance required
between patient and analyst in a therapeutic setting. There are eighty
poems in *Il signore d'oro* and it is divided into three parts: the longest
one, comprising fifty eight poems, is dedicated to the protagonist, the
signore. The second part, with twenty poems, has another protagonist,
the *signora* while the final section has just two poems entitled 'Il sig-
nore e la signora' and 'Il bambino delle cantine'.

The poem which describes this 'signore d'oro' comes towards the
end of the first section:

Era un signore d'oro. Un signore d'oro fino, zec-
    chino.
Per il suo carattere duttile e malleabile, per il suo
    caldo dorato colore, per il luccichio dei suoi
    occhi, era un signore molto ricercato.
I corsi dei fiumi venivano deviati, i fondali scan-
    dagliati e setacciati, ma i signori che affiorava-
    no brillavano poco poco, erano signori pallidi,
    opachi, non erano d'oro vero, erano signori
    falsi . . .   (*Il signore d'oro*, p.63)

(He was a gentleman of gold. A gentleman of pure gold./ He was a most sought
after gentleman/ because of his flexible and pliable character,/ his warm gold
colour, the glittering of his eyes./ The course of rivers was diverted,/ the depths
sifted and combed,/ but the gentlemen who surfaced barely shone,/ wan, dull
gentlemen,/ they were not of real gold, they were false gentlemen . . .)

What we are told of this 'signore' emphasises his golden splendour
and when confronted with him all others are mere 'signori falsi'. The
combing of the depths fails to bring the desired object to the surface
and the personal situation now moves to a more symbolic one. The
diverted river symbolises a move away from the natural flow of things
and an inability to fall in with the various aspects of life which such
things might represent.

These poems are often punctuated by questions and answers which
show the poet's need to establish a dialogue that is vital for her. It is
not clear who asks such questions but their pseudo interrogative nature
would seem to suggest that their purpose is not to elicit an answer but
rather to keep the dialogue alive. Typical in this respect is 'Il signore
che non arrivava':

Alla finestra di una casa una signora aspettava
    sempre un signore che non arrivava.
E allora perché lo aspettava?
Perché la signora non lo sapeva che il signore non
    arrivava.
Questo lo sappiamo noi, non lei.   (*Il signore d'oro*, p.31)

(At the window of a house a lady was waiting for a gentleman who was not
coming./ So why was she waiting for him?/ Because the lady did not know he
was not coming./ We know this, she does not.)

The waiting referred to recalls the waiting and hopeful expectation
that is typical of children and children's stories and here it is no less
effective when transposed to the world of adults. There is however

another dimension implied in the repetition of the negative form *non*, particularly when it is left in isolation at the end of the third line. A poem, like a child's story, can reduce a dramatic situation to a simple event like the lady who is waiting for the gentleman in the poem. However, it can also be full of tension if, as here, the waiting is accompanied by the anguish of desertion.

In many ways *Il signore d'oro* sets the style and tone for the work which followed in 1989, *Poesie dando del Lei* (Poems using the polite form of address) dedicated by the poet to both 'Dottor B.M.' and her mother. It consists of seventy four short poems written by Lamarque for the person referred to as 'Lei' and they recount the story of her falling in love with the doctor who, through successful therapy, should help her recover her own person and grow to love herself once more. The language used by Lamarque is disarmingly straightforward because thanks to successful analysis she has learned to be honest about her feelings and to reveal them in verse:

Desiderio improvviso
di vedere il Suo viso
e poi di fuggire adagino
con negli occhi felici il bottino. (1159)   (*Poesie dando del Lei*, p.47)

(A sudden longing/ to see Your face/ and then to fly away quietly/ with the spoils in my happy eyes.)

When asked about herself and her poems Lamarque admitted that she prefers synthesis and brevity in poetry, she dislikes talking about herself but is happy to read her own work.[10] The reader is struck most of all by the playful and often infantile side to her poetry and it is only at a later stage that the 'amore sempre irraggiungibile'[11] or constantly inaccessible love becomes apparent as the real subject of her poetry. That same tormented sentiment is almost a paraphrase of a further poem:

La mia superficie è felice,
ma venga venga a vedere
sotto la vernice.   (1100)   (*Poesie dando del Lei*, p.19)

(My surface is happy,/ but come come and look/ beneath the varnish.)

These are lines that refer both to the surface of her poems and to her inner self. Here, as elsewhere, we become more familiar with Lamarque's

10 *Corriere della sera*, 19.3.1989, p.19.
11 *Corriere della sera*, 19.3.1989, p.19.

dilemma and she is perfectly frank about her longing and desire when, in apparent dialogue with her doctor, she asks the mischievous question:

Mi sono innamorata tanto?
Oh sì!
La prego faccia altrettanto!   (1189)   (*Poesie dando del Lei*, p.22)

(Am I so much in love?/ Oh yes!/ I beg you, do the same!)

She admits the love she feels for her doctor and although she encourages him to do likewise her use of the polite form of the imperative, 'faccia altrettanto', makes us acutely aware of the distance that separates them. This same feeling makes her say:

Con tutte le ali della mia vita
da Lei volerei se si potesse
invece a fatica resto
da uccello terrestre mi travesto.   (1106)   (*Poesie dando del Lei*, p.48)

(With all the wings of my life/ were it possible I would fly to you/ instead with difficulty I stay here/ in the disguise of a terrestrial bird.)

Here, as already happened in *Il signore d'oro*, the dialogue consists of statements, questions and answers without any direct intervention from the analyst. The use of the hypothetical clause, 'volerei se si potesse' together with the concrete immediacy of the verb 'resto' and the adjective 'terrestre' confirm the impossibility of the situation becoming reality. Lamarque is duly forced to come to terms with the distinct possibility of unreciprocated love:

Credevo non mi amasse
perché è vietato
forse invece non mi ama
perché non è innamorato.   (1192)   (*Poesie dando del Lei*, p.54)

(I thought you did not love me/ because it is forbidden/ instead perhaps you do not love me/ because you are not in love.)

The analyst has kept a perfectly professional approach to his patient who instead transfers to him the feelings and emotions of love that she had experienced as a child for her 'lost' mother. The poet speaks to herself and her imagined interlocutor is ever present. The dialogue tells us that:

Il mio Dottore è gentile,
ma io vorrei morire. (1171)   (*Poesie dando del Lei*, p.65)

(My doctor is kind,/ but I would like to die.)

We now know what it is that makes her long for death while the sympathetic reader can fully appreciate the depths which inspire the lines:

Questa follia così leggera
pesa come una montagna
verso sera. (1165)   (*Poesie dando del Lei*, p.72)

(This madness so light/ weighs like a mountain/ towards evening.)

Lamarque fully recognises the limits of this madness when she says:

Con un filo d'oro
La vorrei a me legare
poi, come prova d'amore,
La vorrei per sempre liberare. (1149) (*Poesie dando del Lei*, p.50)

(I would like to bind you to me/ with a golden thread/ then, as a test of love,/ I would like to free you forever.)

   One of the final poems reiterates the unique role the analyst has played in the patient's life while Lamarque comments ironically:

Libereranno i cassetti
dalle mie ingombranti parole
ma resteranno le Sue più discrete più lievi
mai scritte mai dette
per le orecchiette del mio cuore
le predilette.   (1163)   (*Poesie dando del Lei*, p.82)

(They will empty the drawers/ of my intrusive words/ but yours lighter more discreet never written/ never uttered my favourite ones/ will live on/ for the tiny ears of my heart.)

   This must surely be one of the first occasions in Italian poetry where the poet introduces the reader to the subtle implications of psychological analysis. One of the fears of those who seek out analysis is the possibility that their anguish may be reduced to the level of the routine and the mundane. The opposite happens here because it is precisely through analysis that Lamarque's anguish avoids the sphere of the prosaic and finds its own singular dimension in her poetry.
   In 1992 Vivian Lamarque published *Il signore degli spaventati* with an introduction by the poet Giovanni Giudici who observed, as Sereni

had already done in 1982, that there is more to Lamarque and her poetry than first meets the eye.[12] The value of Lamarque's contribution to modern Italian poetry was recognised the following year when she was awarded the Premio Montale for this work.

This collection of forty poems is dedicated to the same Dottor B.M. while the addition of the word 'ancora' ironically underlines the inescapable fact that Lamarque is still in love with her doctor. We can correctly imagine that the analyst may not have appreciated the dedication of these poems and that he would also have been opposed to their publication.

In the final part of the trilogy Lamarque reveals the depths of her love for her analyst together with the frustrating realisation that such love was doomed to failure. It was, as she recounts, a gigantic transfer of love towards this same person and of it she says:

Sono all'ottavo anno di analisi, sto per concluderla [. . .] Il mio Dottore ha rappresentato tutte le madri e tutti i padri che avevo perso per strada. Una catena di separazioni, di lutti, che mi rendeva la vita insopportabile. All'inizio lui, il mio analista, era la mamma e io – proprio come una bambina che vuole disperatamente essere amata – gli portavo di tutto: fiori, rami, sassolini, pane, latte, disegni, piantine, giocattoli dell'infanzia. E soprattutto lettere e poesie . . . [13]

(This is my eighth year of analysis and I am about to end it [. . .] My doctor stands for all the mothers and fathers I lost along the way. A chain of separation and mourning that made my life impossible. In the beginning, my analyst was the mother figure while I myself – just like a child who wants desperately to be loved – brought him everything: flowers, branches, pebbles, bread, milk, drawings, little plants, children's toys. And most of all letters and poems . . .)

The above was an earlier phase of the therapy and then the relationship of patient to therapist changed. The doctor, B.M. became the object of the patient's erotic desire, a fact alluded to in an earlier poem:

– Non si spaventi immediatamente
  se ora Le dico
  Vivian La desidera fisicamente

12 V. Lamarque, *Il signore degli spaventati*, p.14: 'La "signora spaventata" che qui si contempla [. . .] è un personaggio drammatico di questo secolo d'angoscia ormai alla fine (il secolo, però, non l'angoscia).' (The 'frightened lady' considered here [. . .] is a dramatic character who belongs to this anguished century that is now near its end (the century, however, not the anguish).
13 *La Repubblica*, 30.1.1993.

– Fisicamente?
– Sì, il sangue mi è entrato nella mente. (1166)

(Poesie dando del Lei, p.52)

(Be not suddenly frightened/ if I now tell you/ that Vivian physically desires you/ Physically?/ Yes, My blood has gone to my head.)

and confirmed here in another poem entitled 'Il signore nel cuore':

Le era entrato nel cuore.
Passando dalla strada degli occhi e delle
orecchie le era entrato nel cuore.
E lì cosa faceva?
Stava.
Abitava il suo cuore come una casa.   (Il signore degli spaventati, p.18)

(He had entered her heart./ Passing through the eyes and ears/ he had entered her heart./ And what did he do there?/ He stayed there./ Her heart was like a home to him.)

What this doctor restored to his patient was the ability to distinguish the confines between fantasy and reality, a debt duly recognised by Lamarque:

Un confine che, prima dell'analisi, avevo completamente smarrito. Dover accettare la realtà mi è servito moltissimo, e molto gradualmente l'innamoramento per il mio analista si è trasformato in un sentimento di affetto, in un'infinita gratitudine. Un po' alla volta, ho recuperato energia per me stessa, per il mio lavoro, per la mia vita. Oggi mi chiedo cosa sarebbe accaduto se non avessi avuto la fortuna di essere capitata nelle mani di un professionista serio e capace . . . [14]

(Confines that I had completely lost before (starting) the analysis. Having to come to terms with reality was very helpful and gradually the love for my analyst became a feeling of affection and one of endless gratitude. I slowly recovered the energy for myself, my work and my life. Now I wonder what would have happened had I not had the good fortune to end up treated by a professional who was both serious and capable.)

The figure of the doctor, described as 'l'uomomamma' or 'man-mother' (Poesie dando del Lei, p.23) is the key figure of the psychoanalyst who frees the poet from the tyranny of the past and releases her into the present. A calm acceptance of reality is apparent in the final poem 'Il signore e la signora stelle':

14 *La Repubblica*, 30.1.1993.

Vivevano fra loro lontani come stelle
lontane fra loro.
Per tutta la lunga eternità divisi come
stelle divise, solitariamente nei loro singoli
cieli, divisi, luccicavano.   (*Il signore degli spaventati*, p.54)

(They lived distant from each other like far flung stars./ For all the long eternity separated like/ separated stars, alone in their single skies,/ separated, they sparkled.)

Here Lamarque has acquired a clearer conception of life and reality and this is even most apparent in her most recent work *Questa quieta polvere* (This still dust). Divided into seven sections it reviews the major events in Lamarque's life while the title suggests a temporary setting aside of past themes and the introduction of new ones that show an interest in urgent civil themes. It is possible that this may be the direction her poetry will now follow at the close of this millennium and the start of a new one.

In the subsection entitled *Fine millennio* there is a poem called 'Testamento' that she dedicates 'ai milanesi di colore'. These are the new immigrants in Italian society, many of whom come from the African continent and here they represent all those who are now marginalised and often exploited in Italian society. She calls this poem her 'testamento' or will but it is also her way of bearing witness to the wretched plight of these people. The curious postscript added to this poem for her daughter suggests a spiral of hope for all caught in this plight and poverty trap not just in Italy but throughout the world:

. . . ma fammi figlia mia due finestrelle
per qualche volta salire a riveder le stelle.[15]   (*Questa quieta polvere*, p. 115)

(. . . but daughter, make two tiny windows for me/ so that sometime I can climb up to see the stars again.)

The final poem of the trilogy dedicated to the 'signore' closed with the image of separated yet sparkling stars while these lines show us a poet who has reacquired a certain zest for life and living but who is also concerned with the plight of others who are less fortunate in society.

It is therefore clear that Lamarque's loss of her mother was quite traumatic and has been a major, even an all absorbing factor in her poetry. Her long association with her therapist, where her longing for

---

15 First published in the *Corriere della sera*, 17.4.1992, it is now part of *Questa quieta polvere*.

her mother was transferred to her doctor, extended that obsessive rela-
tionship and has dominated her poetry. While in her early years these
experiences may have deepened her poetic perceptions, because of her
continued fixation with these aspects of her life, the repetition which
has ensued has been somewhat corrosive and consequently an imped-
iment to the full flowering of her talent – a talent that has become more
obvious in recent times, especially in a poem such as 'Testamento',
where her focus has been more widely dispersed.

Aprile dal bel nome

Aprile dal bel nome
quando sono nata
io stessa con nomi curiosi
di bei significati
per dire che ero pratolina
e questo e quest'altro
e che dovevo vivere
(da una parte o dall'altra)
per dire donata
(o donanda)

insomma sono nata d'aprile
in montagna. (4)

A nove mesi

A nove mesi la frattura
la sostituzione il cambio di madre.
Oggi ogni volto ogni affetto
le sembrano copie cerca l'originale
in ogni cassetto affannosamente. (456)

Il primo mio amore

Il primo mio amore il primo mio amore
erano due.
Perché lui aveva un gemello
e io amavo anche quello.
Il primo mio amore erano due uguali
ma uno più allegro dell'altro
e l'altro più serio a guardarmi
vicina al fratello.
Alla finestra di sera stavo sempre con quello
ma il primo mio amore erano due
lui e suo fratello gemello. (111)

Lovely name of April

Lovely name of April
when I was born
with strange names
and fine meanings
to say I was a daisy
with this and that
and that I had to live
(in one place or the other)
given as a gift
(or to be donated)

in short
I was born in April in the mountains.

At nine months

At nine months came the break
the substitution the change of mother.
Today every face every affection
look like imitations.
She searches frantically for the original in every drawer.

My first love

My first love my first love
were two.
Because he had a twin brother
and I loved him too.
My first love was for two who were equal
but one happier than the other
and the other more serious looking at me
who was near his brother.
Always with that one in the evening by the window
but my first love were two
him and his twin brother.

Sempre più mi sembri

Sempre più mi sembri una persona innamorata
e so che con me questo non ha a che vedere
e so che con me questo non ha a che vedere.
Ecco perché questo dopocena se ne va a rotoli
e non la smetto più
stasera
di lavare i bicchieri. (248)

Precipizio

Come in un film da ridere
mi stai facendo la fotografia
e mi dici di fare un passo indietro
ancora uno ancora uno uno
mentre mi spingi verso il precipizio
ti sorrido fiduciosamente
(forse hai agito innocentemente). (659)

Tumore

Lentamente silenziosamente
mi sta crescendo dentro un amore
come un tumore.
È nato a forma di puntino invisibile
poi a poco a poco è cresciuto mi ha preso tutto il cuore
lo sento che avanza e avanza
con paziente furore. (660)

19 aprile

È il giorno del suo compleanno
in un angolo al sole si lecca le ferite
certe fanno tanto male
e certe sono un po' guarite. (652)

Increasingly you seem

Increasingly you seem like one in love
and I know this has nothing to do with me
and I know this has nothing to do with me.
That is why this evening is a shambles
and this evening
I never stop
washing glasses. (248)

Precipice

Like in a film comedy
you are taking my photograph
and you tell me take a step backwards
another one, yet another and another
as you push me towards the precipice
with trust I smile at you
(perhaps you acted innocently). (659)

Tumour

Slowly silently
a love is growing inside me
like a tumour.
It began in the shape of an invisible dot
then slowly it grew and took over my heart
I can feel it progress steadily
with patient fury. (660)

19 April

It is her birthday:
from a corner in the sunshine she licks her wounds
some really hurt
and others are slightly healed. (652)

Il signore che partiva

Era un signore che partiva ma dopo ritornava.
Comunque partiva.
Comunque ritornava.
Stava via tanto tempo quel signore?
Sí, ma il tempo passa e dopo le partenze delle per-
    sone amate vengono i ritorni delle persone
    amate, le braccia si abbracciano tanto come
    per non lasciarsi piú.

La signora di quarant'anni

Era una signora che aveva quarant'anni, come
    mai?
Va bene era nata quarant'anni fa. Però gli anni
    non erano durati veramente un anno e i mesi
    non erano durati veramente un mese.
Cosí i quarant'anni erano arrivati in due tre minu-
    ti, non era giusto, protestò la signora.

Il mio Dottore è sparito
tra Ponente e Levante
io mi affaccio e lo cerco e lo chiamo
come un amante. (856)

Con Lei camminerei
tra l'erica del mio vaso
millimetri e millimetri di cammino
microscopico bosco
io a Lei vicino. (1133)

The gentleman who left

He was a gentleman who left but afterwards returned.
Anyhow he left.
Anyhow he returned.
Did that gentleman stay away for long?
Yes, but time goes by
    and after the departures of the loved ones
    there are the returns of the loved ones,
    arms embrace each other so strongly
    as if never to let go again.

The lady who was forty

She was a lady and was forty, how
    come?
Well she was born forty years ago. However the years
    had not really lasted for a year and the months
    had not really lasted for a month.
And so the forty years had passed in two three
    minutes, it was not fair, the lady protested.

My Doctor has disappeared
between East and West
I come out and look for him and call him
like a lover. (856)

With You I would walk
among the heather in my vase
millimetres and millimetres of path
microscopic wood
with me near You. (1133)

Assente il ragno dalla nostra tela
intatti restiamo nessuno ci divora
sospesi a un filo ci guardiamo attorno
moschina che sorride
io La guardo tanto. (1085)

Lontanissime vacanze
erano incominciate.
In opposti luoghi ubicati
vedevano i bellissimi mari
e le alte montagne
separati. (1092)

Con un filo d'oro
La vorrei a me legare
poi, come prova d'amore,
La vorrei per sempre liberare. (1149)

Questa convivenza
con la Sua assenza
sta diventando una prova troppo dura
la natura va contro la natura. (1120)

Il signore del bastimento

Abitava su un bastimento fermo in mez-
zo al mare.
Gli dicevano sempre torna a casa ma lui
non ci pensava affatto.
Si spostava con calma da poppa a prua,
guardava le onde, le stelle quando c'erano,
l'altezza del sole.

With no spider in our web
we remain intact no one devours us
suspended by a thread we look around
a smiling midge
I look at you intently. (1085)

Far flung holidays
had begun.
Located in opposite places
separated
they could gaze at the handsome seas
and the tall mountains. (1092)

I would love to bind you to me
with a golden thread
then, as a test of love,
I would like to free you forever. (1149)

This living
with your absence
is becoming too difficult a test
nature against nature. (1120)

The man on the ship

   He lived on a ship that was motionless in the
middle of the sea.
   They always told him return home but he would not
even consider it.
   Calmly he walked from stern to prow,
looked at the waves, the stars whenever they appeared,
the height of the sun.

I pesci ormai lo conoscevano.

Un ippocampo tutte le notti, verso mez-
zanotte, mezzanotte e un quarto, usciva dal
mare, lo guardava fisso come per chiedergli
chi sei?

La signora della paura

La paura era così grande, che la voce
non le usciva più.

Come negli spaventati sogni della notte,
come inseguita da adirati Dei dentro adira-
te fiere, fuggiva e fuggiva, dalle ombre.

Ma nel fuggire e fuggire, infine si ar-
restò. La paura era diventata così grande
che bisognava ormai risponderle, esserci,
prepararsi fermamente al disperato raduno
delle forze.

Il signore e la signora stelle

Vivevano fra loro lontani come stelle
lontane fra loro.

Per tutta la lunga eternità divisi come
stelle divise, solitariamente nei loro singoli
cieli, divisi, luccicavano.

Testamento – ai nuovi milanesi di colore

A certi che so io
lascio tutto e agli altri niente.
E le poesie belle agli amici
e ai nemici le brutte.
E le cose di valore? Le cose di valore

By then the fish knew him.
Every night, towards midnight or a quarter
past, a seahorse emerged from the sea, stared
at him, as if to ask
who are you?

The lady who feared

Her fear was so great, that her voice
no longer sounded.
As in terrifying dreams at night,
as if pursued by angry gods inside angry
wild beasts, she fled and fled, from the shadows.
But after all the fleeing, she stopped
at last. Her fear had grown so great
that she had to answer to it, be there,
firmly prepare herself for the gloomy gathering
of the forces.

Mr and Mrs Star

They lived distant from each other like
far flung stars.
For all the long eternity separated like
separated stars, alone in their single skies.
Separated, they sparkled.

Last will and testament – for the new Milanese who are coloured

To some whom only I know
I leave all and to others nothing.
All the fine poems to my friends
and the ugly ones to my enemies.
And the valuable items? The valuable items to

ai nuovi milanesi di colore
che per due lire ci fanno i vetri luccicanti
(oh nostri innocentissimi emigranti
per due lire venuti da lontano
con i vostri negozietti in una mano).
E lascio i miei fiori al mio giardino
e alla terra gentile che mi starà vicino
ci faremo senza voce compagnia
e buongiorno morte e così sia.

P.S. ma fammi figlia mia due finestrelle
        per qualche volta salire a riveder le stelle

Ruanda

Fine millennio con un fiume infernale?
Con noi che cambiamo canale?
Si vergogna l'erba che guarda
gli alberi arrossiscono
se ne vorrebbero andare.

Dall'acqua (dai forni)
come da finestrini
salutano il millennio
braccia e braccia
di bambini.

the new Milanese who are coloured
who make our car windows sparkle for tuppence
(oh our most innocent emigrants
who have come from afar for tuppence
with your tiny shops in one hand).
I bequeath my flowers to my garden
and to the kind earth which will be near me
voiceless we will keep each other company
and hello death and so be it.

P.S. but daughter make two tiny windows for me
      so that sometime I can climb up to see the stars again.

Ruanda

A hellish river to close the millennium?
With us who are changing channel?
The grass witnesses and is ashamed
the trees blush
and would like to move away.

From the water (from the incinerators)
as if through tiny windows
arms upon arms
of children
greet the millennium.

Patrizia Valduga

ONE OF THE LEADING poets of her generation, Patrizia Valduga was born in Castelfranco Veneto in 1953 but has lived and worked in Milan for a number of years. Her first collection of poetry, *Medicamenta e altri medicamenta*, published in 1982, earned her a much discussed Premio Viareggio. Since then she has published four other collections of poetry[1] and is also active in the field of translation and theatre.[2]

Patrizia Valduga's poetry deals with the border between life and death where life, with all its medicaments, potions and temptations, has led the poet dangerously close to the point where the borderline between life and its dissolution is frighteningly immediate. Her poetry reveals an interior crisis and she speaks from inside the crisis identified as her own. The language used by contemporary poets is insufficient for Valduga and therefore she digs deep into the reserves of Italian poetry and uses those metric forms that give structure and voice to her sense of suffering and oppression. The impact of those she has translated has left it mark too: Donne's obsession with death, Beckett's conviction of man's limited space in life and Mallarmé's sensual predilection for the sonnet are all reflected in her work.

The title of her first poetry collection, *Medicamenta e altri medicamenta* (Palliatives and other palliatives), is highly significant as it draws

---

1 Valduga's poetry collections to date are:

Medicamenta e altri medicamenta (Turin, Einaudi, 1982).
La Tentazione (Milan, Crocetti, 1985).
Donna di dolori (Milan, Mondadori, 1991).
Requiem (Venice, Marsilio, 1994).
Corsia degli incurabili (Milan, Garzanti, 1996).

In this chapter all references to her poetry are taken from these texts. *Medicamenta e altri medicamenta* is abbreviated to *Medicamenta*.

2 Valduga has translated work by the following authors into Italian: John Donne, Stéphane Mallarmé, Paul Valéry. In the field of theatre she has translated Molière's *L'Avare* and *Le Misantrope*, Céline's *Féerie* and Cocteau's *Voix humaine*. She is currently working on a new Italian translation of Shakespeare's *Richard III*. A one woman show, based on *Donna di dolori*, featuring the actress Franca Nuti and produced by Luca Ronconi has been widely performed in Italy since 1992. Patrizia Valduga also founded the journal *Poesia* in 1983 and was its editor for that year.

attention to the medicaments, remedies or treatment that are a nec-
essary part of life for Valduga. In his introduction to these poems Luigi
Baldacci called such medicaments 'farmaci, veleni, filtri d'amore'
(drugs, poison, love potions) (*Medicamenta*, p.v) that should in theo-
ry act as a protection for the creator of these poems but instead they
rebel against her and become the source of her torment.

Medicamenta e altri medicamenta opens with the tortured cry of the
poet who has fallen victim to her own potions while her cry for help
and comprehension from her fellow travellers: 'In nome di Dio, aiu-
tami!' (*Medicamenta*, p.11) rings out loud and clear. These medica-
ments have brought destruction rather than remedies in their trail and
the final poem bears a tone of strange resignation as the poet surveys
her changed condition where life and death are both curiously and
frighteningly close to each other:

Signore caro, tu vedi il mio stato,
vedi che ho l'avvenire nel passato,
e questo rotto scoppiato e crepato.
Vita non sono mia, ma del peccato [. . .]

O ombra del morire, se in agguato
alla memoria chiami il tempo andato,
lo chiami come un sogno già sognato,

su un amore che zoppo è sempre andato,
né medica la morte, se è malato,
se vive come un morto sotterrato.   (*Medicamenta*, p.81)

(Dear Lord, you see my condition,/ you see that my future lies in the past,/
that is itself shattered, cracked and ruptured./ I belong not to my life but to
one of sin./ [. . .] Oh shade of death, if you call/ on the past to ambush mem-
ory/ you call it as a dream already dreamt,/ over a love that has always stum-
bled,/ nor can it cure death, if it is ill,/ if it lives like a dead one in the ground.)

The world she presents is a hellish one that is enmeshed in life while
its Beckett-like figures are stuck forever in a limited space. The poet
herself is acutely aware of this condition when she says:

O gran dio, nell'inferno son per certo!   (*Medicamenta*, p.40)

(Oh great Lord, I am certainly here in Hell!)

The urgency to express the abyss that is within her together with the
need to reveal her innermost self to the reader is a constant aspect of
Valduga's poetry:

O datemi qualcuno che mi ascolti,
ché di parole straripo . . .   (*Medicamenta*, p.36)

(Oh give me someone to listen to me,/ because I overflow with words . . .)

Her poetry is one where joy or happiness seldom appear while her personal torment causes her to lacerate all words at her disposal:

Stanca di stomaco, stanca di cuore,
alba dopo alba io mangio per dolore.   (*Medicamenta*, p.74)

(Weary of stomach, weary of heart,/ dawn after dawn I eat through grief.)

   Two of the outstanding features that strike the reader who approaches Valduga's poetry for the first time are her scintillating use of language and the variety of poetry structures that she uses to communicate her innermost thoughts and feelings. Words are chosen carefully to show the poet's resistance to the world in which she finds herself:

Sa sedurre la carne la parola,
prepara il gesto, produce destini . . .
E martirio è il verso,
è emergenza di sangue che cola
e s'aggruma ai confini
del suo inverso sessuato, controverso. (*Medicamenta*, p.24)

(The word can seduce the flesh,/ it prepares the gesture, produces destinies . . . / And the verse is tortured,/ like a surge of blood that flows/ and clots on the edge/ of its sexual, controversial opposite.)

Her words are chosen with care while the rhythm of the hendecasyllabic line is often effective in its reproduction of the poet's physical and existential exhaustion. Her torment is also accentuated by the apparent unwillingness or inability of words to come to her assistance:

Mi dispero perché
non ho che poche erose scrofolose
parole, a darsi all'ozio solo intente,
che non sanno far niente.   (*Medicamenta*, p.47)

(I am distraught because/ all I have are a few worn out scruffy/ words interested only in idleness,/ incapable of doing anything.)

   She has fully understood the problem of attempting to express oneself and one's dilemma by using those tools of language that are available to the poet in the twentieth century. In many ways, more than any other poet of her time, she can identify closely with the sentiment expressed by Montale:

Codesto solo oggi possiamo dirti,
ciò che *non* siamo, ciò che *non* vogliamo.[3]

(This alone is what we can tell you today,/ that which we are not, that which we do not want.)

Valduga grapples with the language at her disposal and almost always returns to the poetic forms most favoured by Italian poets in the past such as the hendecasyllabic line, the sestina, the octave and the sonnet. These rigid forms allow her fuse the rhetorical and existential dilemma of her own existence.

When queried about her predilection for these classic metrical forms, so often used by poets in the past, Valduga justifies her use of them by saying that she is a sensual person who initially found gratification in her efforts to express herself within their rigid strictures. Later she achieved a heightened awareness of the fundamental role played by language and the use of individual words in poetry, all of which have served to sharpen her perception of life. For Valduga the deepest emotions can be reached through the manipulation of language while the poet must never be ashamed of revealing such emotions. A work of art, in her opinion, is like a prison and poetic forms too are prisons that compress the poet's thoughts and make the poetic word irreplaceable.[4]

---

3   E. Montale, *Ossi di seppia*, in *Poesie Scelte*, a cura di Marco Forti (Milan, Oscar Mondadori), 1987, p.10.
4   Paper given by Patrizia Valduga at a Conference on Literature and Religion held at the Catholic University, Milan, 30 September 1995. The proceedings will be published in the review *Testo*, nos. 32/33 (Rome, Bulzoni) 1996. On that occasion Valduga made the following statement when queried about the language of her poetry: 'Perché questa mia ossessione della forma, degli endecasillabi, delle terzine? Mi avessero fatto questa domanda dieci anni fa avrei risposto che sono una persona sensuale e che l'uso di queste forme dà un piacere sensuale. Ora direi che sono una persona religiosa e che si arriva al pensiero emoziante attraverso il lavoro sulla lingua [. . .] Non bisogna mai vergognarsi dei propri sentimenti, bisogna esprimerli. L'opera d'arte è una prigione e la forma poetica è una prigione che comprime il linguaggio, è proprio la forma a rendere la parola insostituibile [. . .] scrivo, dunque, per non ammattire.' (Why my obsession with form, the hendecasyllables, the terzine? Had I been asked this question ten years ago I would have said that I am a sensual person and that the use of these forms gives a sensual pleasure. Now I would say that I am a religious person and that one reaches emotional

The epigraph chosen by Valduga for this work is a curious one, a terzina from Dante's *Inferno*, from the canto of the thieves, which highlights the linguistic agility which permits Dante to switch from the sublime to the ridiculous from one line to another:

Co' piè di mezzo gli avvinse la pancia,
  E con li anterior le braccia prese;
  Poi li addentò e l'una e l'altra guancia.[5]   (Inferno XXV, vv.52–54)

(Clasping his middle with its middle paws,/ Along his arms it made its forepaws reach,/ And clenched its teeth tightly in both his jaws.)[6]

Valduga uses her often poisonous medicaments against the devils that she perceives in the world around her and many of the poems relate how these medicaments rebel against her and almost become the cause of her perdition:

 . . . in questi giorni persi neri e duri
se qualcosa mi resti non ho prove,
se qualcosa qui o altrove per me duri,

e non so se la sera ora congiuri
contro di me, o sui druidi miei dall'ovest
induri, sui passati e sui futuri.   (*Medicamenta*, p.21)

(. . . in these dark forlorn and harsh days/ I have no proof of anything that still is mine,/ or if anything here or elsewhere lasts for me,/ neither do I know if evening now plots against me,/ or hardens against my lovers from the West, the past and future.)

The metaphor of the scorpion that kills itself with its own sting when imprisoned by fire is used by the critic Luigi Baldacci to describe the manner in which Valduga's remedies prove futile when confronted with the agony of life (*Medicamenta*, p.vii). Valduga carries with her a sense of persecution that confirms the existence of a hell among the living while the action of certain fellow humans often recalls the cruelty,

thoughts through the work on language [. . .] You must never be ashamed of your feelings, you must express them. The work of art is a prison and the poetic form is a prison that compresses language, it is the form that makes the word irreplaceable [. . .] therefore, I write to retain my sanity.)

5 Dante Alighieri, *La Divina Commedia*, ed. S. Barbi (Florence, Sansoni, 1921), Vol.I, p.231.
6 Translation by Dorothy L. Sayers in Dante, *The Divine Comedy. Hell* (Penguin Classics), 1949, p.228.

harshness and sheer vulgarity of those devils who tried to block the progress of Dante and Virgil in Inferno XXV:

E dicono: 'Se ne vada all'inferno
a star coi morti!' e fanno segni osceni.
Nella cena mi mettono veleni.
'Sia dannata in eterno!' Io che l'eterno

proprio non curo, io qui per vuoto alterno
tenagliata in tanta strettura, leni
declini discerno, buio, baleni . . .   (*Medicamenta*, p.69)

(And they say: 'Go to Hell/ and stay with the dead!' and make vulgar ges-tures./ They put poison in my supper./ 'May you be damned for all eternity!' I, who care not a whittle/ for eternity, here in a void I fluctuate/ squashed in such stricture, and/ pick out gentle slopes, darkness, thunderbolts . . .)

An overriding feeling of affliction, suffering and oppression is now constant and it offers no respite to Valduga:

Tristemente il mio giorno tempra il tempo,
scarica tenebra al farsi dell'ora,
volge in veleno, mi vieta il piacere,
mentre guardo come argine alla sera
le lune tonde e quelle in falce, a sorte,
e ne misuro i moti tristemente.   (*Medicamenta*, p.79)

(Sadly my day tempers time,/ unloads shadows as the hour approaches,/ turns into poison, forbids me pleasure,/ as I look like a barrier to evening/ the round and crescent moons, randomly,/ sadly I measure their movements.)

In many ways, *Medicamenta e altri medicamenta*, with its accent on grief and torment, life and death, prepared the way for Valduga's sec-ond collection of poetry *La Tentazione* (The Temptation) which was published in 1985. The similarities with the poetic forms used by Dante in the *Divine Comedy* are remarkable. Not only does Valduga use the linked *terza rima* and the hendecasyllabic line throughout but her poem is also divided into ten sections or cantos, each of which has thirty three tercets followed by a single concluding line. The total number of lines in each canto is therefore one hundred while the use of numbers such as three, ten and one hundred deliberately recall the symbolism of perfection associated with such numbers and multiples thereof in early Italian literature. The objective of Dante's poem was to help Dante and all men find perfection and happiness in the Creator while the rigour of his poetic form reflects the severity of the effort

284 ITALIAN WOMEN POETS

required to find the *dritta via* or the right path to human and eternal happiness.

For Valduga instead, the rigidity of the poetic form provides a sensual satisfaction in its attainment and, most importantly, a vehicle where the poet initiates a lengthy dialogue on love, wonders what it is that constitutes temptation and attempts to identify those elements that are a source of real beguilement on earth. Her verses vibrate with life despite the striking recurrence of images of death and darkness throughout. Human love may bring with it a certain fleeting joy but it also brings a sense of futility and shame:

In questa maledetta notte oscura
con una tentazione fui assalita
che ancora in cuore la vergogna dura.   (*La Tentazione*, p.13)

(In this cursed dark night/ I was set upon by temptation/ and the shame still lingers in my heart.)

Life and living have accentuated the poet's feeling of doom and disaster:

Amore mio, che disastro è nell'aria!
che fantasmi, che larve vedo e sento,
che strana processione sanguinaria!   (*La Tentazione*, p.31)

(My love, there is so much disaster in the air!/ what ghosts, what shades I see and feel,/ what strange and bloody procession!)

This nightmare continues and Valduga sees that the life of the living is further threatened by the attempts of the dead to eat the living: 'E i morti uscivano a mangiare i vivi' (*La Tentazione*, p.45). These verses contain an almost manic pathological use of words by the poet as a means of revealing her conscience and her grief-stricken yet combative soul:

In nome di Dio, apri quella porta!
la notte fissa in me il suo occhio nero;
apri per tempo, la mia vita è corta,

è un vomito d'inferno il mio pensiero
e l'anima mi giace pietra al fondo
e invischia di spropositi ogni vero.   (*La Tentazione*, p.63)

(For God's sake, open that door!/ night stares at me with its dark eye;/ open up in time, my life is short,/ my thoughts are a hellish vomit/ and my soul is a sunken stone/ that entangles every truth in errors.)

For Valduga then, life is permeated by death and these cantos are dedicated to death which is a siren that helps recreate the resurrection of the past and in some way guarantees the continuity of the future. Alone, beset by all sorts of temptation, the poetic form is the one thing that remains most faithful to the poet and through it Valduga bares both her soul and spirit to the reader:

Prima che mi rinchiuda in una fossa
a farmi sugo della terra nera
non darmi a quelle mani, fa' che possa

dei miei sensi non esser prigioniera,
apri tanto di me quanto nascondo,
oh salvami, poi che tutto s'annera! (*La Tentazione*, p.70)

(Before I am enclosed in a grave/ to turn into sauce for the dark soil/ do not hand me over to those hands, help me/ not to be prisoner to my feelings,/ open up as much of me as I hide,/ oh save me, because all is turning black.)

When Patrizia Valduga published *Donna di dolori* in 1991, again a logical progression from her previous work, she could not have chosen a more apt title to describe her delicate psychological state. Its various poems function as an extended monologue where the protagonist, a woman who is already dead, speaks from beyond the grave. It is the monologue of a corpse who wants to establish contact with a live interlocutor. With macabre tones she discusses her betrayal in love, the complete indifference of those around her, she highlights the deceptions suffered in life and the humiliating illusions of life itself. Her body is now putrefied by death and she herself is reduced literally to tears and slush, 'lacrime e poltiglia' (*Donna di dolori*, p.35). The horror experienced when she realises that her body is actually flowing away aptly captures the nightmarish situation in which she now finds herself:

Non vedi che ho ripreso a sgocciolare?
Annego in me senza poter gridare.   (*Donna di dolori*, p.21)

(Can you not see that I have begun to drip once more?/ I am drowning inside myself and am unable to call out.)

The feeling of isolation and impotence is chillingly presented by the determined stress of the hendecasyllabic lines:

Mia gioventù, epoca mia di fede,
decifrarti torturandomi gli occhi . . .
oh luce dei miei occhi che trabocchi

tutto d'un colpo di tutto il mio cuore . . .
Sta' zitto, sta' più calmo, mio dolore,
perché non c'è nessuno che ti ascolta.   (*Donna di dolori*, p.20)

(My youth, my time of faith,/ trying to decipher you by torturing my eyes . . .
/ oh light of my eyes which overflows/ suddenly with all my heart . . . / My
grief, stay silent, stay quiet,/ because no one is listening to you.)

As an epitaph for this book, Valduga chose a curious quotation from
Gerard Manley Hopkins where the transient nature of the body is pre-
sented as one long passage towards death which marks the tragedy of
our human voyage:

But man – we scaffold of score brittle bones;
Who breathe, from groundlong babyhood to hoary
Age gasp; whose breath is our *memento mori* –
What bass is our viol for tragic tones?   (*Donna di dolori*, p.9)

The protagonist gives us a clear and stark description of the condition
in which she finds herself and once again Valduga uses the rhyming
couplet and hendecasyllables to express her thoughts and ideas. The
choice of these metric forms places Valduga well outside the conven-
tions of contemporary Italian poetry where traditional metric or rhyming
forms are seldom found. It is also a further indication of the manner
in which such forms correspond to her innermost needs and desires.
In order to prevent herself from becoming completely insane with grief
and terror the protagonist of these poems tries to find a way to tell
others of her condition. There is a strong parallel here between the
poet and the 'donna di dolore' as Valduga, when discussing the ther-
apeutic value of writing says it helps her keep her sanity: 'Scrivo per
non ammattire'.[7]
   The rhythm of these hendecasyllabic lines gives a powerful evoca-
tion of this *donna di dolore* together with the excruciating and intense
awareness of her present situation:

Poi goccia a goccia misuro le ore.
Nel tutto buio, sotto il mio dolore,
Più giù del buio della notte affondo [. . .]
             viva di un cuore
che mi sgocciola via senza rumore,
in me ringorgo sotto il mio dolore.
Dolore della mente è il mio dolore . . .
per il mio mondo . . . e per l'altro maggiore . . . (*Donna di dolori*, pp.15–16)

7 See note 4.

(Then drop by drop I measure out the hours./ In the total darkness, beneath my grief,/ I sink down deeper than the dark of night [. . .]/ . . . alive with a heart/ that flows away silently from me,/ my grief blocked up again beneath me/ My grief is the grief of the mind . . . / for my world . . . and for the other greater one.)

Surrounded by the shades of darkness and total silence she remembers things and people that were dear to her in life and calls out in desperation:

Ma ancora solo un po' lascia che guardi
quell'estate lontana col suo fiore.
Lascia che guardi più addentro al mio cuore,
lasciami vivere del mio passato,
lascia che cerchi quel bacio mai dato;
in questo buco buio e senza uscita
lasciami piangere sulla mia vita.   (*Donna di dolori*, p.27)

(Let me still just for a while look at/ that distant summer with its flower./ Let me look deeper inside my heart,/ let me live on my past,/ let me search for that kiss never given;/ let me weep for my life/ in this dark hole that has no exit.)

The existential agony of this woman is accentuated by the ghostly silence that surrounds her and by her palpable fear of loneliness:

Ma c'è qualcuno lì sopra, Dio buono?
Nessuno mi risponde.   (*Donna di dolori*, p.28)

(Is there anyone up there, good Lord?/ No one answers me.)

The stages of this *Via Crucis* are long and protracted and the agony is drawn and extended through the decomposition of mind and body. Memories of the past bring little comfort and often are an acute source of torment:

Sei lì? mi senti? Oh mondo ammutinato,
chiedo soltanto un poco di conforto!
Nel primo anniversario del mio aborto
io prendo la frequenza d'agonia:
per il mio mondo che mi cola via,
per quello tuo, fatto di pranzi e cene,
per tutto il sangue che va e che viene,
per la muta di iene che mi preme . . .   (*Donna di dolori*, p.37)

(Are you there? Do you hear me? Oh rebellious world,/ I just ask for a little comfort!/ On the first anniversary of my abortion/ I am racked with torment:/ for my world that ebbs away from me,/ for your one, packed with lunches, dinners,/ for all the blood that comes and goes,/ for the pack of hyaenas that bears down on me . . .)

Valduga's ability to express the harshest feelings through the hendeca-syllabic line is remarkably efficient. So too is her ability to evoke the sensations of terror experienced when hounded by this 'muta di iene', a horror similar to that experienced when confronted with death and with a void of Dantesque proportions which opens up in front of her:

Oh notte solo mia! Niente più aurora
adesso [. . .]
e niente sangue e niente più domani,
come se il sogno fosse cosa vera,
e come se l'aurora fosse sera,
e come se una nera notte. Nera.   (*Donna di dolori*, p.44)

(Oh night just mine! No more dawn/ now . . . / and no more blood and no more tomorrow,/ as if the dream were really true,/ as if the dawn were evening,/ as if a night were black. Black.)

A dark, unnerving and disturbing tone on which to end were it not for the curious line from St. Augustine which she uses to conclude this volume of poetry: 'Amate quod eritis' (p.45) which incites the reader to love what he will become in the future. Despite the disintegration of the body and the torment of the mind, there is the intimation of a hereafter where the body may be resplendent once more.

Valduga published *Requiem* in 1994 to commemorate her father who had died some years earlier. In Valduga's life and poetry the images evoked are of supreme importance. Here, the title deliberately recalls a musical *Requiem* normally used to mark the life and death of some-one considered deserving of such an honour by the composer. The parallel here is deliberate. Presented in a way that recalls the urgency of a musical composition these poems recall the final agonizing stages of her father's terminal illness. The sentiments expressed therein are the daughter's testament or *Requiem* that articulate the deep-rooted filial emotion that is particularly poignant given the time limit of her father's life.

Unlike *Donna di dolori* where the discourse of the protagonist takes place after death, *Requiem* presents a conversation with a loved one who is close to death, and, when the latter becomes reality, it then become a hymn of praise for that person's life and gift of love.

The long mortal agony of the father and the anguish experienced by his daughter are deliberately expressed in the concentrated form and metre of the octave which lends itself admirably to the poet's design. There is perfect fusion between word and intent and all is reduced to the essence of a tortured yet natural occurrence, viz. the death of a father. In Valduga's poetry this event then assumes the dimension of an epic poem. The words used are straightforward and both the rhythm and rhyme give an almost obsessive repetition of the theme to hand:

Anima, perduta anima, cara,
io non so come chiederti perdono,
perché la mente è muta e tanto chiara
e vede tanto chiaro cosa sono,
che non sa più parole, anima cara,
la mente che non merita perdono,
e sto muta sull'orlo della vita
per darla a te, per mantenerti in vita.   (*Requiem*, p.7)

(Beloved soul, lost soul,/ I know not how to ask your forgiveness,/ because my mind is dumb and yet so clear/ and clearly sees what I am,/ who knows no more words, beloved soul,/ the mind which deserves no pardon,/ and I remain silent on the edge of life/ to give it to you, to keep you alive.)

The words and sentiments used here and elsewhere are simple, direct and effective as when Valduga intercedes and offers her life in place of that of her father:

Oh no, non lui, Signore, prendi me,
che sto morendo più di lui, Signore,
liberalo dal male e prendi me!   (*Requiem*, p.31)

(Oh no, not him, Lord, take me,/ who am dying more that he, Lord,/ free him from pain and take me!).

For the critic, Luigi Baldacci, Valduga's poetry is a 'lessico famigliare'[8] (familiar lexicon) where the structure and vocabulary used are straightforward, and immediate:

Padre nostro liberalo dal male,
oh, fa' presto, liberalo dal male!   (*Requiem*, p.33)

(Our Father free him from pain,/ oh! quickly, free him from pain!)

These intercessions are followed by an increased awareness of the isolation of the individual when confronted with an impossible situation:

Non si piange dagli occhi, il pianto vero
è invisibile, qui, dentro il pensiero.   (*Requiem*, p.35)

(You do not weep from the eyes, real tears are invisible, here, inside your mind.)

8 L. Baldacci, *Corriere della Sera*, 30.9.1994.

The intercessions continue to call out for our attention:

Dio, ti scongiuro, prendigli la mente,
non torturare un cuore torturato,
oh, fa' presto, fa' che non senta niente . . .   (*Requiem*, p.45)

(Lord, I beg you, take his mind,/ do not torture a tortured heart,/ oh! hurry,
let him not feel anything . . .)

but the bareness of the lines underlines this human agony and tragedy:

Invece Dio ti ha preso la parola:
e volevi parlarci e non riuscivi
e sentivi la morte anche alla gola
e non potevi dirci che morivi . . .   (*Requiem*, p.47)

(Instead the Lord has taken your voice:/ and you wanted to speak to us and
could not/ and you felt death also in your throat/ and could not tell us you
were dying . . .)

The inexorable progress of the illness finally makes the poet ask that
the end might come quickly:

Patrizia, da quanti giorni son qui? [. . .]
Oh padre padre come mi hai guardata . . .
Sì, venti giorni e eri inchiodato al letto:
Dio, per pietà, affretta il tuo verdetto!   (*Requiem*, p.41)

(Patrizia, how long have I been here? [. . .]/ Oh father, father, how you looked
at me . . . / Yes, twenty days and you were nailed to the bed:/ God, for pity's
sake, hurry up your verdict!)

All that remains now for the daughter is to ask for forgiveness:

Oh padre padre, patria del perdono,
mi hai dato questa vita e questo cuore,
mi hai dato tutto quello che ho di buono,
e io a te non ho dato che dolore . . .   (*Requiem*, p.59)

(Oh father father, homeland of forgiveness,/ you gave me this life and heart,/ all
that I have that is good you gave me,/ and I have only caused you sorrow . . .)

This *Requiem* helps Valduga commemorate her father and also allows
her expiate publicly the anguish she feels she may have caused him in
life. Her plea to be taken in his place has not been granted and she,
who considers herself worthless, a 'donna da niente' (*Requiem*, p.31)
now places her hope for the future in the treasure of paternal love that
she came to appreciate, perhaps, too late in life:

Padre mio, benedicimi ti prego,
benedicimi ora come allora [. . .]
Stammi vicino, aiutami ti prego,
per i giorni che mi restano ancora,
i giorni del dolore e dell'amore
che il cuore non ti ha detto per pudore.   (*Requiem*, p.61)

(Father, bless me I beg you,/ bless now as you once did [. . .]/ Stay near me,
help me I beg you,/ through these days that I still have,/ days of grief and of
love/ that my prudish heart did not tell you.)

   Valduga's most recent work, *Corsia degli incurabili* (Ward for incur-
ables) is presented in a dramatised poetic form that has shares certain
features with *Donna di dolori*. Here, however, the protagonist is not a
dead woman but someone who is still alive and who rages against the
vulgarity and banality she sees in Italian society today. The poet adopts
the unusual metrical form of the classical sirvente for these poems in
an attempt to give back some meaning and dignity to poetry which is
often and incorrectly considered unworthy of mention or reflection.
Although depressed and pessimistic about what she sees wrong in Italy
– her main objection regards the impoverishment of language by tele-
vision – this work is characterised by a febrile irony and humour that
plays everything down.
   Despite the fact that Valduga still considers the content and the
motivation for *Corsia degli incurabili* a release from her recurring health
problems,[9] the substance of these poems reveals a broader canvas and
wider concerns than in her early works; they are less obsessive and,
accordingly, more objective and are quite removed from the fatalism
of *Donna di dolori*. It would therefore appear that in her moving out-
pourings of filial affection, so evident in *Requiem*, that she has suc-
ceeded, at least in part, even if unintentionally, of purging much of
the self pity so characteristic of her earlier work. While she still retains
that acute sensitivity which these emotional experiences have sharp-
ened, it now looks as if she can apply that to a wider range of objects,
with poetry still serving the liberating purpose for which she has always
acclaimed it.

9 See *La Repubblica*, 8.3.1996 where she states: 'E' il motivo per cui ho scritto
   Corsia degli incurabili. Avevo problemi di salute, non riuscivo a uscirne, mi
   sono detta: o mi ammazzo o mi sfogo. E ho messo in scena tutta la mia dis-
   perazione.' (This is the reason why I wrote *Corsia degli incurabili*. I had health
   problems I was unable to get rid of and so I said: either I kill myself or give
   vent to my feelings. And so I have depicted all my despair.)

In nome di Dio, aiutami!

In nome di Dio, aiutami! Ché tanto
amor non muta e muta mi trascino.
Ancora sete ho di te . . . soltanto
sola a te solo e col sole declino.

O marea d'amore viverti accanto
e arresto del cuore, amor mio divino,
che eterni della vita luce e canto.
La mia ne muore . . . dal ricordo sino

al qui ancora verso il cuore in cammino,
verso te, mio dissorte eppur destino . . .
se non di morte . . . ora di te rimpianto . . .

e il mare discolora il mio mattino.
Ma tu incatenami all'amato incanto,
resta, è giorno, vieni piú vicino.

In me cogli anni crescono

In me cogli anni crescono, a mio merito
o demerito, quei danni d'ascrivere
interi a plurime carnali sterili
dilettazioni in cui involta o proclive

m'affatico . . . a diletti semiseri
e periferici . . . alle loro derive . . .
cosí che non mi viene dal preterito
il come e tanto meno il cosa vivere,

che in questi giorni persi neri e duri
se qualcosa mi resti non ho prove,
se qualcosa qui o altrove per me duri,

e non so se la sera ora congiuri
contro di me, o sui drudi miei dall'ovest
induri, sui passati e sui futuri.

In the name of the Lord, help me!

In the name of the Lord, help me! Because so much
love does not change and silent I drag myself along.
I still thirst for you . . . alone
alone you alone and I set with the sun.

Oh tide of love to live beside you
and the heart stops, my divine love,
you immortalise the light and song of life.
Mine dies from it . . . from the memory

to this moment towards the heart in movement,
towards you, not my spouse and yet my destiny . . .
if not of death . . . now the regret for you . . .

and the sea discolours my morning.
But chain me to the beloved enchantment,
stay here, it is day, come closer.

For my honour or dishonour

For my honour or dishonour, as the years
go by, there is an increase in damage,
wholly out of repeated pleasures,
carnal, sterile, in which bundled up or prone

I tire myself . . . in half serious marginal
delights . . . that drift along . . .
and so time past offers me no reason
of how and even less what to live,

and in these dark forlorn harsh days
I have no proof of anything that still is mine,
or if anything here or elsewhere lasts for me,

neither do I know if evening now plots
against me, or hardens against my
lovers from the West, past and future.

A me creduta esangue, non veduta

A me creduta esangue, non veduta,
un'oncia di coraggio, una manciata
di ragione scovata e già perduta,
lo dica qui dei vati la brigata,

di astrologi e indovini, il ciel li aiuta,
a che punto, lo dica di volata,
io sono con la vita (a mia insaputa)
e con la morte . . . a che punto agguantata

e goduta, di che godente . . . O notte,
che su di me t'inarchi e mi tormenti,
mi sono inutili i pensieri . . . Notte

sifone del mio sangue e alba di lenti
lenti piaceri, disperdi le rotte
d'amore sveleniscile ai tuoi venti.

Di vacuità, vacazioni di sé

Di vacuità, vacazioni di sé
in assenze . . . e il futuro che sta là
e non si fa presente . . . né si sa
se rinnegarlo o prevenirlo in sé . . .

Darsi uno scopo che ancora non è
vita . . . se il vacuo invita o addita . . . Ma
certo a mancare il tempo poi verrà,
con vuoto di piaceri pianti o che,

e tempo di dar sale, d'assalire
l'altrove, il non per me, l'altro avvenire . . .
o perlomeno il perché d'altri giorni

d'altri, come dormire . . . di ritorni
del non ancora, di chi sia a morire . . .
e del rifar notte . . . infine capire.

Considered lifeless, already lost

A handful of reason unearthed –
an ounce of courage: not noticed,
considered lifeless, already lost –
let the company of bards, astrologers and prophets

say it here, the heaven helps them,
at which point, then say it hurriedly,
I am with life (without knowing it)
and with death . . . grabbed at what point

and enjoyed, and enjoying what . . . Oh night,
that bends over and torments me,
thoughts are useless to me . . . Night

syphon of my blood and dawn of slow
slow delights, you scatter the routs
of love, unpoison them with your winds.

Of vacuities, vacancies of self

Of vacuities, vacancies of self
in absences . . . and the future ever close
yet never present . . . hard to know
whether to deny it or prepare for it . . .

To give oneself a purpose that is yet
not life . . . if the vacuum beckons or points out . . . But
time surely will then fall short,
with a void of pleasure, tears, whatever,

and time for wisdom, to assault
the elsewhere, what is not for me, the other future . . .
or at least the reason of further days

of others, like sleeping . . . of returns
of what is not yet, of those about to die . . .
of night again . . . at last to understand.

In verità, in verità ti dico

In verità, in verità ti dico,
nulla variando qui nel greve esilio,
se ne uscirà l'amor dall'ombelico,
con doloroso assalto al pube e all'ilio.

E dopo i giorni tutti in un intrico,
tentata in corpo e in anima mi umilio,
mia croce, mio sacramentale amico,
collettore di voglie e solo ausilio.

Mentre il tuo dio ti mangi e bevi vino,
lasci la pace a produrmi un destino,
e predichi che cristo di martiri

contro gli accanimenti del mattino,
che la ruota dei giorni giri giri
muta di baci e muta di sospiri.

Signore caro, tu vedi il mio stato

Signore caro, tu vedi il mio stato,
vedi che ho l'avvenire nel passato,
e questo rotto scoppiato e crepato.
Vita non sono mia, ma del peccato.

O notte senza oggetti, dal tuo lato,
dove non corre tempo, io ho cercato
una gioia lontana dal mercato
del giorno che m'imbara, disensato.

O ombra del morire, se in agguato
alla memoria chiami il tempo andato,
lo chiami come un sogno già sognato,

su un amore che zoppo è sempre andato,
né medica la morte, se è malato,
se vive come un morto sotterrato.

In truth, in truth I say to you

In truth, in truth I say to you,
nothing changing here in this heavy exile,
love will emerge through the navel,
painfully assaulting pubis and ilium.

And after all these jumbled days,
tempted in flesh and soul I humble myself,
my cross, my sacramental friend,
collector of yearnings and sole support.

While you eat your god and drink wine,
let peace make my destiny,
while you preach what kind of torment

against the frenzies of the morning,
may the wheel of days turn round and round
bared of kisses and bared of sighs.

Not my life, but one of sin

Not my life, but one of sin:
dear Lord, you see my condition,
you see that my future lies in the past,
that is itself shattered, cracked and ruptured.

Oh night, forgetful of objects,
where time stands still, I have looked
for happiness far from the market
of the senseless day which coffins me.

Oh shade of death, if you call on
past time to ambush memory
you call it a dream already dreamt,

over a love that always stumbled,
nor can it medicate death, if it is ill,
if it lives like a dead one in the ground.

Fior tra i fiori al saluto del sole

Fior tra i fiori al saluto del sole
maledici in catene il tuo dio . . .
ed io sposa segreta al tuo cuore
penso solo alle mosche e al ronzio.

Padre mio, benedicimi ti prego

Padre mio, benedicimi ti prego,
benedicimi ora come allora,
non ho tregua, in una morsa mi piego,
una morsa che l'anima perfora . . .
Stammi vicino, aiutami ti prego,
per i giorni che mi restano ancora,
i giorni del dolore e dell'amore
che il cuore non ti ha detto per pudore.

Anima, perduta anima, cara

Anima, perduta anima, cara,
io non so come chiederti perdono,
perché la mente è muta e tanto chiara
e vede tanto chiaro cosa sono,
che non sa piú parole, anima cara,
la mente che non merita perdono,
e sto muta sull'orlo della vita
per darla a te, per mantenerti in vita.

Oh no, non lui, Signore, prendi me

Oh no, non lui, Signore, prendi me,
che sto morendo piú di lui, Signore,
liberalo dal male e prendi me!

Flower among flowers at the greeting of the sun

Flower among flowers at the greeting of the sun
chained down you curse your god . . .
and I secret spouse of your heart
only think of buzzing and of flies.

Father, bless me I beg you

Father, bless me I beg you,
bless me now as you once did,
I have no respite, in a vice I bend myself
a vice that perforates the soul . . .
Stay near me, help me I beg you,
through those days that I still have,
days of grief and of love
not revealed by a prudish heart.

Beloved soul, lost soul

Beloved soul, lost soul,
I know not how to ask your pardon,
because my mind is dumb and so clear
and clearly sees what I am,
who knows no more words, beloved soul,
that mind which deserves no pardon,
and I remain silent on the edge of life
to give it to you, to keep you alive.

Oh no, not him, Lord, take me

Oh no, not him, Lord, take me,
who am dying more than he, Lord,
free him from pain and take me!

prendi me, per giustizia, me, Signore,
per la vita morente dentro me,
per la vita che vive in lui . . . Signore,
sii giusto, prendi me, donna da niente,
e vissuta cosí, morentemente . . .

Oh padre padre, patria del perdono

Oh padre padre, patria del perdono,
mi hai dato questa vita e questo cuore,
mi hai dato tutto quello che ho di buono,
e io a te non ho dato che dolore,
e il non volermi ancora come sono . . .
Oh padre padre, anche come si muore
tu mi hai insegnato, il senso della vita
dentro la morte, a prezzo della vita . . .

Poi goccia a goccia misuro le ore

Poi goccia a goccia misuro le ore.
Nel tutto buio, sotto il mio dolore,
Più giù del buio della notte affondo.
Scena muta di sogno, ombra di mondo,
un niente di due tutti e di due vite,
piccola eternità, e ore infinite,
pienissima di me, viva di un cuore
che mi sgocciola via senza rumore,
in me ringorgo sotto il mio dolore.
Dolore della mente è il mio dolore . . .
per il mio mondo . . . e per l'altro maggiore . . .

Ammetti, non può esser che così

Ammetti, non può esser che così.
Ancora io, eccomi ancora qui,
nella mia abituale eterna attesa

take me, Lord, in justice, me,
for that life dying inside me,
for the life that lives in him . . . Lord,
be just, take me, a worthless woman,
having lived, like one about to die . . .

Oh father father, home of forgiveness

Oh father father, home of forgiveness,
you gave me this life and this heart,
all that I have that is good you gave me,
and I have only caused you sorrow,
and not wanting me still as I am . . .
Oh father father, you have also taught me
how to die, the meaning of life
in death, at the expense of life . . .

Then drop by drop I measure out the hours

Then drop by drop I measure out the hours.
In the total darkness, beneath my grief,
I sink down deeper than the dark of night.
Scene bereft of dreams, shadow of the world,
a nothing of two entireties and two lives,
tiny eternity, and endless hours,
full of myself, alive with a heart
that flows away silently from me,
my grief blocked up beneath me.
My grief is the grief of the mind . . .
for my world . . . and the other greater one . . .

Admit it, it can only be like this

Admit it, it can only be like this.
It is still me, I am still here,
in my typical eternal waiting

e tenuta in tremore ancora, stesa
lungo un inconcepibile passato . . .
Sei lì? mi senti? Oh mondo ammutinato,
chiedo soltanto un poco di conforto!
Nel primo anniversario del mio aborto
io prendo la frequenza d'agonia:
per il mio mondo che mi cola via,
per quello tuo, fatto di pranzi e cene,
per tutto il sangue che va e che viene,
per la muta di iene che mi preme,
per le mie mute pene tutte insieme,
per tutte le ragioni e tutti i torti,
e per tutti i miei morti, cari morti
gli uni sugli altri, aringhe sottoterra,
per quest'amore qui al chiaro di terra
o per le vie dell'universo intero,
per il bello che è splendore del vero,
e per amarmi ancora come sono
e per essere ancora come sono
chiedo perdono perdono perdono . . .

Gli occhi sono i cancelli della mente

Gli occhi sono i cancelli della mente;
meglio chiuderli, adesso, per prudenza,
che il giorno adesso avanza indifferente . . .

E le porte dell'anima . . . gli orecchi;
chiudiamo pure loro per prudenza.
Preghiamo per i morti e per i vecchi,

perché abbiano qualcuno che li ami . . .
un po' d'amore, garanzia di vita,
senza bisogno di leggi e proclami . . .

Meglio un frammento minimo di vita
che idiozia viva e vegeta e ammattita.

and still in mortal fear, laid out
against an inconceivable past . . .
Are you there? Can you hear me? Oh rebellious world,
I just ask for a little comfort!
On the first anniversary of my abortion
I am racked with torment:
for my world that ebbs away from me,
for your one, packed with lunches, dinners,
for all the blood that comes and goes,
for the pack of hyaenas that bears down on me,
for my silent pain all together,
for all the reasons and all the wrongs,
and for all my dead ones, beloved dead
one on top of one another, sardines underground,
for this love here in the paleness of earth
or for the roads of the entire world,
for the beauty that is the splendour of truth,
and to love me again as I am
and to be again as I am
I ask for pardon, pardon, pardon . . .

The eyes are the gates of the mind

The eyes are the gates of the mind;
best to close them, now, as a precaution,
as day advances now indifferent . . .

And the ears . . . the doors of the soul;
let us close them too as a precaution.
Let us pray for the dead and for the old,

that they may have someone to love them . . .
a little love, guarantor of life,
without need for laws and proclamations . . .

Better a tiny fragment of life
than live, thriving and mad idiocy.

Mi è venuta anche la tachicardia

Mi è venuta anche la tachicardia:
ora bisogna correre ai ripari . . .
su . . . prima che si svegli la corsia,

che la morfina finisca il suo effetto,
che arrivino coi loro armamentari . . .
Cerco dentro la mente . . . mi trasmetto . . .

una romanza . . . potrebbe servire?
Canta a voce bassa e flebile   'L'alba separa dalla luce l'ombra
e la mia voluttà dal mio desire.

O dolci stelle, è l'ora di morire.
Un più divino amor dal ciel vi sgombra.'
Sì, anche per me è l'ora di morire . . .

'Pupille ardenti, o voi senza ritorno
stelle tristi, spegnetevi incorrotte!
Morir debbo. Veder non voglio il giorno . . . '

Come vorrei vederlo, invece, il giorno!
' . . . per amor del mio sogno e della notte.'
Tutto l'oro . . . l'azzurro tutto intorno . . .

sento che è l'ora . . . tutto trascolora . . .
'Chiudimi, o Notte, nel tuo sen materno,
mentre la terra pallida s'irrora.

Ma che dal sangue mio nasce l'aurora
e dal sogno mio breve il sole eterno!'
I miei sogni . . . poter sognare ancora . . .

Ho perduto i miei sogni ad uno ad uno . . .
e senza sogni non si è più nessuno . . .

I have had tachycardia too

I have had tachycardia too:
now it is time to do something . . .
come on . . . before the ward wakes up,

before the morphine wears off,
and they come with their instruments . . .
I look inside my mind . . . to myself I pass on

a romance . . . could it be of use?

She sings with
a weak low
voice

with 'Dawn separates darkness from light
and my voluptuousness from my desire.

Oh sweet stars, it is time to die.
A more divine love clears you from the sky.'
Yes, for me too it is the hour to die . . .

'Blazing pupils, oh you without return
sad stars, switch yourselves off untainted!
I must die. I do not want to see the day . . . '

How I would love, instead, to see the day!
' . . . for love of my dream and of the night.'
All the gold . . . blue all around . . .

I feel it is the hour . . . all loses colour . . .
'Close me, oh Night, in your maternal breast,
while the pale earth bathes itself.

But may dawn be born from my blood
and the eternal sun from my short dream!'
My dreams . . . still to be able to dream . . .

One by one I have lost my dreams . . .
and without dreams you are no longer . . .

Sources

*Summary of the original Italian volumes
in which the poems published in this study appeared*

A. POZZI: All from *Parole*.

D. MENICANTI: 'Pavia', 'Epigramma 4' from *Città Come*; 'Agli Amici', 'Foglie per i morti' from *Un nero d'ombra*; 'Per un passante', 'L'amore (non) è eterno', 'E vedrai che' and 'Non si sa' from *Poesie per un passante*, 'Lieto fine', 'Il miracolo', 'Identità' from *Ferragosto*; 'Serpente' from *Altri amici*; 'Dicembre' from *Ultimo quarto*.

M. GUIDACCI: 'Furono ultime a staccarsi le voci' from *La sabbia e l'angelo*, 'Giorno dei Santi' from *Giorno dei Santi*, 'La morte' from *Morte del ricco*, 'Il tuo linguaggio è indecifrabile' from *Poesie*, 'Madame X', 'La madre pazza' and 'Nero con movimento' from *Neurosuite*, 'Versi per un prigioniero' from *Il vuoto e le forme*, 'Questa pausa' and 'Il girasole' from *Inno alla gioia*, 'Meteore d'inverno' and 'Giorno delfico' from *Il buio e lo splendore*; the remaining poems are from *Anelli del tempo*.

B. MARNITI: 'Sono terra che uomo ha scavato' from *Più forte è la vita*, 'Siamo altri figli' from *Città, creatura viva*, 'Mia terra', 'Roma, città sul verde fiume', and 'Demone o luce' from *Più forte è la vita*, 'Tristezza e buio', 'Dura pietra voglio rimanere' and 'Il mio ricordo è fredda luna' from *Racconto d'amore*, 'Filo spinato', 'La tregua' and 'La sindone' from *Il gomitolo di cera*; and 'La solitaria' from *La ballata del mare*.

M.L. SPAZIANI: 'Come un grumo di sangue' and 'Lettera 1951' from *Le acque del sabato*, 'La Via Crucis' from *Utilità della memoria*, 'da "Il mare"' from *L'occhio del ciclone*, 'Avatar', 'Preistoria', and 'Viaggio a Corinto' from *Transito con catene*; all the others are from *La stella del libero arbitrio*.

A. ROSSELLI: 'Contiamo infiniti cadaveri', 'Il soggiorno in inferno era di natura divina', 'Il corso del mio cammino era una delicata fiamma', and 'Tutto il mondo . . . ' from *Variazioni belliche*, 'Quanti campi che come spugna vorrebbero', 'I fiori vengono in dono e poi si dilatano', 'Per Gianfranco' from *Documento 1966–1973*, '(a Pier Paolo Pasolini)' from *Appunti sparsi e persi*, and 'Must I tire my mind out' from *Sleep – Poesi in inglese*.

A. MERINI: 'Il gobbo', 'Confessione', 'Il testamento', 'Dies Irae' and 'Povera è la mia vita' from *La presenza di Orfeo*, 'E piú facile ancora', 'Ho conosciuto in te le meraviglie' and 'Resta pur sempre a me' from *Testamento*, 'Io ero un uccello', 'Sono nata il ventuno a primavera', 'Alda Merini', 'Le piú belle poesie' and 'La Terra Santa' from *Vuoto d'amore*, 'Anima anima ricorda lui' from *Ipotenusa d'amore* and 'A Manganelli' from *La palude di Manganelli*.

J. INSANA: 'Niente dissi', 'Un'altra afasia' and 'E venga un nuovo scorticatore' from *Fendenti fonici*, 'Hai detto poeta' from *Il collettame*, 'Non c'è tempo', and 'a calda forza precipita la ripida assenza' from *La Clausura*; 'mi stringo addosso il giorno' is as yet unpublished; the remaining poems come from *Medicina carnale*.

B. FRABOTTA: The first six poems come from *Il rumore bianco*, the rest from *La Viandanza*.

V. LAMARQUE: The first seven poems come from *Teresino*; 'Il signore che partiva' and 'La signora di quarant'anni' from *Il signore d'oro*; these are followed by six poems from *Poesie dando del lei*; 'Il signore del bastimento', 'La signora della paura', 'Il signore e la signora stelle' come from *Il signore degli spaventanti*; these are followed by 'Testamento' and 'Ruanda' a from *Questa quieta polvere*.

P. VALDUGA: The first seven poems come from *Medicamenta e altri medicamenta*, 'Padre mio, benedicimi ti prego', 'Anima, perduta anima, cara', 'Oh no, non lui, Signore, prendi me' and 'Oh padre, padre, patria del perdono' from *Requiem*, 'Poi goccia a goccia misuro le ore', and 'Ammetti, non può esser che così' from *Donna di dolori*; the remaining two poems come from *Corsia degli incurabili*.

Index